Time*lines*

Time*lines*

PAUL DICKSON

✦ Addison-Wesley Publishing Company, Inc.

Reading, Massachusetts New York Menlo Park, California
Don Mills, Ontario Wokingham, England Amsterdam
Bonn Sydney Singapore Tokyo Madrid San Juan

Many of the designations used by manufacturers and sellers to distinguish their products are claimed as trademarks. Where those designations appear in this book and Addison-Wesley was aware of a trademark claim, the designations have been printed in initial capital letters (e.g., Studebaker).

Library of Congress Cataloging-in-Publication Data

Dickson, Paul.
    Timelines : day by day and trend by trend from the dawn of the Atomic Age to the close of the Cold War / Paul Dickson.
       p.   cm.
     ISBN 0-201-17277-1
     1. United States—History—1945—Chronology.
2. United States—Popular culture—History—20th century—Chronology.   I. Title.
  E741.D53   1990
  973.91'02'02—dc20   90-31597

Jacket design by Hannus Design Associates
Text design by Copenhaver Cumpston
Set in 10½-point ITC Garamond Book by NK Graphics, Keene, NH

ABCDEFGHIJ—VB—943210
First printing, August 1990

The million-year period to which the burned junk from the museums and archives related would be summed up in the history books in one sentence, according to Koradubian: Following the death of Jesus Christ there was a period of readjustment that lasted for approximately one million years.

—Kurt Vonnegut
The Sirens of Titan

INTRODUCTION
On the Importance of Crammers

One of the nicest things about high school is that you can buy crammers for just about any subject. Most crammers are slim paperback books, but they come in other forms. When I was in high school in the late 1950s my favorites were heavy plastic notebook-size sheets with three holes in them to fit into your notebook. The lettering was tiny, covered both sides of the sheet, and was laid out so that there was no wasteful white space. One of these sheets might contain all of American history before 1867 while another would outline the basics of biology, and it would all be crammed into one place.

The beauty of those crammers for me was that you could grasp the essential facts and trends without all the pictures, diagrams, fancy graphics, and endless essaying of the textbook. If nothing else, they let you hit the books again with a little self-assuredness—the notion that you had an outline of what was going on, that there was more than one cause of the Civil War.

A few years back it occurred to me that, even though I was many years out of high school, I needed a new kind of crammer. I wanted one that covered all the major events and turning points from the end of World War II to the present. I realized that events and trends to and up through World War II were easily found but that the same could not be said of the postwar world.

As a writer, I found that I was forever looking for answers to simple questions like these:

Do you know when the last person set foot on the moon?

▶ Introduction

Do you know when the Polaroid camera was introduced?

Do you know when the zip code was introduced?

☞ (For an article on the snapshot) When was the Polaroid camera introduced?

☞ (For a small essay on change) When was the last time you could send a first-class letter for three cents? When did the zip code come into being?

☞ (In trying to answer one of my children) When did the last person set foot on the moon?

The list could go on and on, but the point is made that I kept losing many important things in the shuffle of modern times. The book that I wanted to have on my desk would be a crammer that would sort it all out: the breakup of the Beatles and the breakup of AT&T . . . lines for gasoline and lines for Michael Jackson tickets . . . the first issue of *Playboy* and the first issue of *Ms.* . . . the founding of the Hell's Angels and the start of the Rand Corporation.

Another reason for the crammer was that it could become a personal document. It would be a chronology that I could annotate, literally write all over, with the things that had occurred to me and my family during those years. It would allow me to put the important dates of my life into the context of events and thus turn the crammer into a personal outline of lived history. It would be, among other things, a cultural road map begging to be marked with big things like births, deaths, and weddings, which become more vivid in the context of events, but also things like where the family vacationed in the summer of '73, when the oil embargo turned a 300-mile trip into a major odyssey.

This is how it should be. We do not live in sealed compartments. I drove from Washington to New York in April 1968 to get married on the 13th and smelled the smoke of four major cities burning in the wake of the King assassination. Our first son was born on June 27, 1973, as John Dean inflicted irrevocable damage on the Nixon presidency.

I decided to create my own crammer. It started out not as a book but rather a file in the form of two scrapbooks (which my editor, Martha Moutray, jokingly insists should be called data bases) into which I began pasting items chronologically. I was interested not only in dates and events, which I glued into one data base, but

► Introduction

also in the fads, trends, names, statistics, and slogans that defined a given year and went into the second book.

All of this immediately fell into the realm of the subjective. I listed what I felt was important and the only qualification I had for this was I had been around for all of it. I decided what was important and had lasting impact and interest. Many natural disasters, strikes, prizes, and international meetings are not here, but the birth control pill and the introduction of long-distance direct dialing are. Individual Super Bowls and Miss America winners are not listed, but the merger of the American and National Football Leagues is, as well as the first Miss America to show up naked in the pages of a skin magazine.

Needless to say, somewhere along the way this personal crammer turned into this book. I hope others find it as useful as I do and, unless it is a library book, people turn it into their own personal data base by marking it up and sticking stuff in the margins.

Four people provided great help with this project. They are Charles D. Poe of Houston, Joseph C. Goulden of Washington, D.C., and Gordon Connolly of Garrett Park, Maryland, who turned over his collection of historic newspapers. The late Rainbow Fletcher helped immeasurably as a spotter and compiler of bumper sticker messages.

Do you know when it cost three cents to send a first-class letter?

The year in which the war ▶
comes to a dramatic end ▶
and the nuclear age begins ▶ *1945*

JANUARY

20 ▶ President Franklin D. Roosevelt is inducted into office for his fourth term. As he did with his third term, FDR breaks the tradition against more than two presidential terms.

24 ▶ Russian soldiers cross the Oder River and land on German soil for the first time.

25 ▶ Grand Rapids, Michigan, becomes the first U.S. city to add fluoride to a municipal water supply for the prevention of tooth decay.

27 ▶ Auschwitz is liberated by Soviet troops.

FEBRUARY

01 ▶ A spectacular force of 1,000 U.S. bombers raids Berlin.

14 ▶ John D. Rockefeller, Jr., donates $8.5 million for the purchase of land along New York City's East River to erect the permanent headquarters of the United Nations.

19 ▶ American troops land on Iwo Jima where they fight the Japanese until March 16.

MARCH

07 ▶ The United States First Army crosses the Rhine River at Remagen, south of Cologne, Germany. All German forces are now east of the Rhine.

January 27, 1945: Auschwitz is liberated by Soviet Troops.

▶ 1

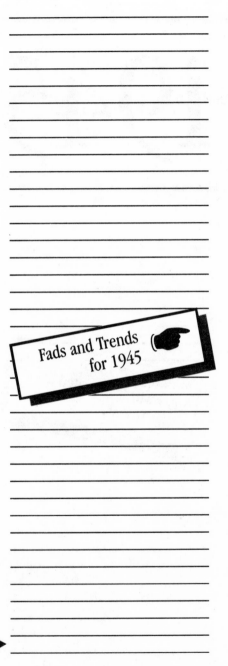

Fads and Trends for 1945

12 ► Fourteen-year-old Anne Frank dies in the Nazi concentration camp at Bergen-Belsen. Her *Diaries* are published later and her plight and optimism move many, again underscoring the Nazi madness.

► ***Also occurring today:*** Governor Thomas E. Dewey signs a bill in Albany making New York the first state to set up a permanent commission to eliminate discrimination in employment.

16 ► Iwo Jima falls to the U.S. Marines.

21 ► In one of the war's greatest coordinated air efforts, 7,000 Allied airplanes drop 12,000 tons of explosives on Germany in full daylight.

27 ► General Dwight D. Eisenhower announces that German defenses on the Western Front have been broken. The last V-2 rocket lands on London.

■ ■

☞ 1. Bop comes into fashion with the help of Dizzy Gillespie.

☞ 2. There is a profound national fascination with technical discoveries made during the war but kept secret for reasons of security.

☞ 3. BEST SELLERS FOR THE YEAR: fiction—*Forever Amber* by Kathleen Windsor; nonfiction—*Brave Men* by Ernie Pyle, who was killed in the Pacific early in the year.

☞ 4. A photograph taken on February 23 of Marines raising a flag atop Mount Suribachi on Iwo Jima becomes an icon of the American spirit.

☞ 5. A soon-to-be children's book classic is published: E. B. White's *Stuart Little.*

☞ 6. Almost immediately following the explosion of the first atomic bombs, reports are made of the vast promise of atomic energy. A syndicated article that appears in the *Rocky Mountain News* for August 9 says that if the power of the atom in simple matter is harnessed, "all other forms of energy would be antiquated, such as fuels and explosives. Dams and electrical transmissions would be as outmoded as stagecoaches." The energy in a breath of air "would operate a powerful airplane for a year continuously."

☞ 7. A major theme in consumer advertising is the promise that consumer goods will be back in production as soon as wartime demands have ended. Alcoa uses this line in its ads: "It's worth waiting a little longer for things made from Alcoa aluminum."

☞ 8. *Ebony* magazine is a hit among blacks, immediately selling out its first issue in November.

☞ 9. A number of states pass laws that require bakers to enrich bread with certain vitamins and minerals.

☞ 10. Plastics exhibits are all the rage. One staged in a Portland, Oregon, department store features "Fifteen hundred different things ranging from bomber noses and jettison fuel tanks to such everyday things as coat hangers and screw drivers."

■■■■■■■■■■■■■■■■■■■■■■■■■■■■■■■■

APRIL

01 ► The United States invades Okinawa.

12 ► Franklin Delano Roosevelt, thirty-second president of the United States, dies in Warm Springs, Georgia, at 4:35 in the afternoon. His vice president, Harry S Truman, is sworn in as the new president.

　► *Also occurring today:* American troops liberate the Nazi concentration camp at Buchenwald. They encounter a scene whose horror defies description.

26 ► Benito Mussolini is caught and shot by partisan Italians.

30 ► The leader of the Third Reich, Adolf Hitler, commits suicide in an underground bunker in Berlin. Dying with him: Eva Braun, his longtime mistress and wife of one day.

April 30, 1945: Adolf Hitler commits suicide in an underground bunker in Berlin.

► 3

► 1945

May 7, 1945:
In a school in Rheims, France, German military leaders unconditionally surrender to General Dwight D. Eisenhower.

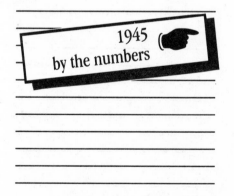

1945 by the numbers

MAY

07 ► In a school in Rheims, France, German military leaders unconditionally surrender to General Dwight D. Eisenhower. "The mission of this Allied force was fulfilled at 0241, local time, May 7, 1945," Ike announces.

08 ► Celebrations across America and Europe mark VE Day, the end of the war in Europe.

11 ► A kamikaze attack on the aircraft carrier *Bunker Hill* kills 373 and reminds Americans that the war continues.

JUNE

21 ► The struggle for Okinawa Island in the southwest Pacific comes to an end at ten o'clock in the evening as the Japanese forces there surrender to the American command.

26 ► The charter of the United Nations is signed by fifty countries in San Francisco. The charter, effective October 24, pledges "to save succeeding generations from the scourge of war, which twice in our lifetime has brought untold sorrow to mankind."

■■■■■■■■■■■■■■■■■■■■■■■■■■■■■■■

☞ 1. The U.S. Armed Forces reach a peak of 7.2 million.

☞ 2. The gross national product of the nation is $211 billion.

☞ 3. As a result of the war, some 54.8 million people have died worldwide.

☞ 4. American casualties for the war amount to 292,000 killed or missing, 613,611 wounded.

☞ 5. Shortages and rationing dictate that the per capita consumption of sugar for Americans is 62.1 pounds, down from 89 pounds in 1944.

☞ 6. Most daily newspapers cost a nickel and Sunday editions are fifteen cents. Home delivery in many cities is $1.50 per month.

☞ 7. Of 286 cities surveyed, 98.5 percent have a shortage of single-family homes. Only one, in a coal region, has an oversupply.

☛ 8. Americans take 23 billion rides on mass transit vehicles, a number that drops like a rock in the years ahead (to 8 billion in 1967).

☛ 9. Prices at the Fred Meyer Stores in Portland per the ad in the *Oregon Journal* for April 30: coffee, $.25 per pound; La India Kings Puerto Rican handmade cigars in a box of 50, $5.95; sirloin steak, $.40 a pound; and assorted baby foods in 4½-ounce cans, $.05.

☛ 10. Americans now buy 85 percent of their bread at the store, as contrasted with 1939 when a third of the bread was baked at home.

■ ■

JULY

02 ► With the war in Europe over, the lights go on in the British Isles for the first time since September 3, 1939.

03 ► The first postwar civilian passenger automobile made since February 1942 leaves the Ford Motor Company's Detroit assembly line.

► *Also occurring today:* American occupation troops, made up of the Second Armored Division, start to enter Berlin.

14 ► U.S. warships begin bombarding Japan.

16 ► The United States explodes its first experimental atomic bomb in the desert of Alamogordo, New Mexico, ushering in the nuclear age. It lights up a rattlesnake-infested stretch of New Mexico desert called the Jornada del Muerto—the Dead Man's Trail. The code name for the test is Trinity. The test vaporizes the hundred-foot steel tower on which the five-ton atomic device was mounted.

20 ► The U.S. flag is raised over Berlin as the first American troops move in to take part in the post–World War II occupation.

July 3, 1945:
The first postwar civilian passenger automobile made since February 1942 leaves the Ford Motor Company's Detroit assembly line.

> *July 28, 1945:*
> An army bomber crashes into the seventy-ninth floor of the Empire State Building in New York, killing fifteen people and setting eleven floors on fire.

23 ► Marshal Henri Pétain of France—head of the Nazi-collaborating Vichy government during the war—goes on trial. He ultimately is condemned to death but his sentence is commuted. Ironically, he dies on this date in 1951.

26 ► Winston Churchill resigns as Britain's prime minister after his Conservatives are soundly defeated in elections by the Labor Party. Clement Attlee becomes the new prime minister.

28 ► An army bomber crashes into the seventy-ninth floor of the Empire State Building in New York, killing fifteen people and setting eleven floors on fire. *EMPIRE STATE STRUCK BY BOMBER* read the immense, so-called "second coming" headline in the *New York World-Telegram.*

► *Also occurring today:* The U.S. Senate ratifies the United Nations charter, eighty-nine to two.

AUGUST

02 ► The Potsdam Conference ends, and Truman, Stalin, and Clement Attlee agree to few things except the disarming of Germany.

06 ► Harry Truman announces the dropping of the atomic bomb on Hiroshima, Japan. Weighing only 400 pounds., its destructive power exceeds that of 20,000 tons of TNT. The air detonation kills over 100,000 including the entire Second Japanese Army and levels four square miles of the city. The late edition of the *Denver Post* announces it this way: *TRUMAN REVEALS ATOMIC BOMB HAS BEEN LOOSED UPON JAPAN—NEW EXPLOSIVE 20,000 TIMES POWER OF TNT.*

09 ► An atomic bomb is dropped on the Japanese city of Nagasaki killing an additional 36,000 people. Kept secret from the world is that the U.S. supply of A-bombs is exhausted and there are no others in reserve. Meanwhile, the Russians cross into Manchuria.

12 ► Edward R. Murrow, whose wartime radio broadcasts from Europe gave many Americans their most immediate sense of World War II, speaks of the mood in Europe now that

it is over: "Seldom, if ever, has a war ended leaving the victors with such a sense of uncertainty and fear, with such a realization that the future is obscure and that survival is not assured."

14 ▶ At 7:00 P.M. Eastern time President Truman announces Japan has unconditionally surrendered, ending the hostilities of World War II.

15 ▶ VJ—for Victory in Japan—Day is celebrated.

25 ▶ Captain John M. Birch, Baptist missionary and army intelligence expert, is killed by Chinese Communists in northern Anhwei Province. The first victim of the "cold war with communism," he becomes the symbolic hero of Robert H. W. Welch, Jr., who founds the John Birch Society in his honor.

30 ▶ General Douglas MacArthur arrives in Japan and sets up headquarters in the New Grand Hotel in Yokohama. At the same time, United States Marines land in Tokyo Bay and take over the Yokosaka naval base there.

SEPTEMBER

02 ▶ Aboard the United States battleship *Missouri* in Tokyo Bay the Japanese formally sign the terms of unconditional surrender ending World War II. General Douglas MacArthur signs the documents for the United States. As the Allied Supreme Commander, MacArthur is assigned the task of occupying Japan and rehabilitating the Japanese.

▶ *Also occurring today:* Communist-led Viet Minh under Ho Chi Minh seize power in Hanoi and proclaim an independent Vietnam. At least ten Frenchmen are killed as a result of the nationalist uprisings in Hanoi.

22 ▶ French forces return to Vietnam.

■■■■■■■■■■■■■■■■■■■■■■■■■■■■■■■■■■■■

1. *All animals are created equal, but some animals are more equal than others* (from George Orwell's allegorical work *Animal Farm*)

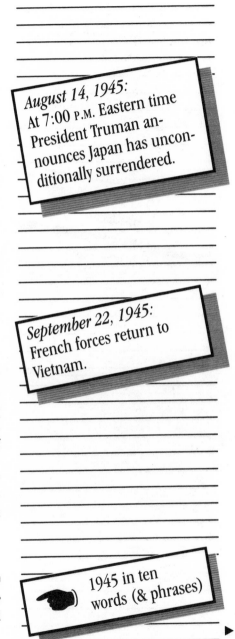

August 14, 1945: At 7:00 P.M. Eastern time President Truman announces Japan has unconditionally surrendered.

September 22, 1945: French forces return to Vietnam.

1945 in ten words (& phrases)

_____
_____
_____
_____
_____
_____
_____
_____
_____
_____

1945 in ten words (& phrases) ☞

_____
_____
_____
_____
_____
_____
_____
_____
_____
_____
_____
_____
_____
_____
_____

☞ 2. *bug* (computer error, defect, or problem. Navy pioneer Grace Hopper later reports that the term was coined in 1945 by her team working on the Mark II, the first large-scale American computer, in response to a glitch that occurred when a two-inch moth got stuck in one of the Mark II's relays.)

☞ 3. *curfew* (In the last months of the war the government decrees that all places of entertainment must close at midnight. The rule is nationwide and even the New York nightclubs cannot get exemptions.)

☞ 4. *black market* (These spring up all over Europe at the war's end as people use illegal means to get food, tobacco, liquor, and other goods.)

☞ 5. *Trinity* (code name for the first A-bomb tested. The religious meaning of the term seems overlooked.)

☞ 6. *bug bombs* (a natural name for the new spray insecticides coming on the market)

☞ 7. *CARE* (Cooperative for American Remittance to Europe. It is an organization created to bring relief to war-torn nations.)

☞ 8. *2-4-D* (the name of the weed killer that keeps many lawns free of intruders for years to come)

☞ 9. *chemotherapy* (an idea showing increasing promise in the fight against cancer. Articles about it are now in the news.)

☞ 10. *channel* (what a station will be called on television. This is the year when the Federal Communications Commission sets aside thirteen channels for commercial use.)

■ ■

OCTOBER

04 ► American occupation authorities in Japan order the imperial government to end all restrictions on freedom of speech, religion, and assembly, disband the "thought police," and release 3,000 political prisoners.

29 ▶ The first American ballpoint pens go on sale at Gimbels in New York City. They cost $12.50 each and quickly sell out.

NOVEMBER

23 ▶ The government ends the wartime rationing of all foods except sugar, which means that meat and butter are now available without restriction.

29 ▶ Yugoslavia becomes a federated republic after Marshal Tito reads a proclamation to the Constituent and National Assemblies.

DECEMBER

20 ▶ Tire rationing ends.

21 ▶ General George S. Patton, America's master of tank warfare, dies peacefully in his sleep in Heidelberg, Germany. He suffered chest wounds in a Jeep accident on December 9.

27 ▶ The Moscow Conference held by the United States, Great Britain, and the USSR makes preliminary plans for establishing atomic energy control, the unification of Korea, and the drafting of peace agreements.

As best as can be determined, one of the first, if not the very first, true bumper stickers came out of the Gill Studios of Shawnee Mission, Kansas. The firm's founder, Forest Gill, had been working with fluorescent inks and with self-sticking labels. As World War II ended, he was getting orders for cardboard bumper signs, and he began experimenting with self-sticking signs with colorful ink. The early slogans are on the level of VISIT / VOTE FOR / COME TO / and BUY.

■■■■■■■■■■■■■■■■■■■■■■■■■■■■■■

☞ 1. Dwight David Eisenhower
☞ 2. Harry S Truman
☞ 3. West Point football greats Glenn Davis and Doc Blanchard

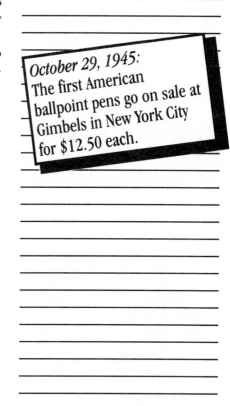

October 29, 1945: The first American ballpoint pens go on sale at Gimbels in New York City for $12.50 each.

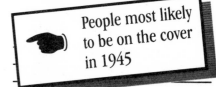

People most likely to be on the cover in 1945

▶ 1945

☛ 4. Joseph Stalin
☛ 5. Winston Churchill
☛ 6. Admiral Chester Nimitz
☛ 7. Bill Mauldin
☛ 8. Chiang Kai-shek
☛ 9. General Douglas MacArthur
☛ 10. Adolf Hitler

■ ■

The year in which housing ▶
is in short supply and the ▶
cold war gets underway ▶

1946

JANUARY

01 ▶ Kathleen Casey Wilkens of Philadelphia is born one second after midnight, making her America's first official baby boomer. According to a June 29, 1986, Gannett News Service article, "She is now a single parent raising two teenage daughters in Haddon Heights, N.J. and is studying for a new career in hotel and restaurant management."

Between Wilkens's birth and 1964, 76 million babies are born in the United States.

10 ▶ The United Nations holds its first session in London. After that meeting, it moves to Lake Success, New York, and then on to its permanent skyscraper home at East 43rd Street, New York City, in 1952.

FEBRUARY

15 ▶ The first digital computer is dedicated in Philadelphia. It is called ENIAC, an acronym standing for Electronic Numerical Integrator and Computer.

24 ▶ Juan Perón is elected president of Argentina.

28 ▶ Secretary of State James F. Byrnes, speaking before the Overseas Press Club in New York, sets the theme for the new, firm "get tough with Russia" policy.

January 1, 1946:
Kathleen Casey Wilkens of Philadelphia is born one second after midnight, making her America's first official baby boomer.

▶ 11

March 5, 1946:
In a speech at Westminster College in Fulton, Missouri, Winston Churchill says an "iron curtain" has come down across Europe.

Fads and Trends for 1946 ☞

MARCH

05 ► In a speech at Westminster College in Fulton, Missouri, Winston Churchill says an "iron curtain" has come down across Europe. He urges close cooperation between the United States and Britain in combating Communism.

11 ► One of several "nylon riots" that occur during the year takes place in Washington, D.C., where consumers break windows and take swipes at one another over a limited supply of nylon stockings. This risk of life and limb to secure a pair of stockings is seen as the symbolic dawning of the golden age of plastics and synthetics.

■ ■

☞ 1. Dr. Benjamin Spock's *Baby and Child Care* quickly establishes itself as the authority for raising the babies of the baby boom.

☞ 2. The low-slung, one-level ranch-style home is an immediate hit and remains so for years to come.

☞ 3. Irving Berlin's score for *Annie Get Your Gun* produces a cluster of hits including "There's No Business Like Show Business" and "Doin' What Comes Natur'lly."

☞ 4. Alfred Hitchcock's *Notorious* debuts, putting the world on notice that he will be a major force in postwar cinema.

☞ 5. Aviation and air power show promise for the future. Helicopters are first applied to civilian use (including rescue at sea), and for the first time a jet plane takes off from the flight deck of an aircraft carrier (the *Franklin D. Roosevelt*).

☞ 6. Tide ushers in the era of the power detergent—good for clothes and dishes.

☞ 7. New fashions arrive from Paris and create great interest and excitement.

☞ 8. The nation finds itself in the grips of a series of bitter labor disputes; they become a hallmark of the year.

☞ 9. Las Vegas goes on the map with the construction of the garish Flamingo Hotel and Casino.

☞ 10. Mickey Spillane's *I, the Jury* is, for its time, a gutsy, dirty, popular shocker.

■■■■■■■■■■■■■■■■■■■■■■■■■■■■■■■■■

APRIL

01 ► The United Mine Workers strike, part of a widespread movement by organized labor, including steelworkers, auto workers, and trainmen, to catch up on the raises and benefits that were deferred during the war years.

MAY

30 ► Canadian scientist Dr. Louis Slotin dies after exposure to radiation during a Los Alamos Laboratory accident on May 21.

JUNE

30 ► In Poland a national referendum approves a program of government nationalization, land reform, and a parliament with one house—all as proposed by the Communists.

■■■■■■■■■■■■■■■■■■■■■■■■■■■■■■■■■

☞ 1. A syndicate headed by Larry McPhail and Dan Topping, two prominent sportsmen, buys the New York Yankees baseball team for $3 million.

☞ 2. During a bad year for labor-management relations, strikes involve 4.6 million workers.

☞ 3. There are 18,000 vacuum tubes in ENIAC, the first computer.

☞ 4. The death toll in America's worst air crash to date—on October 3—is thirty-nine.

☞ 5. Meat and poultry prices soar to the point where chicken costs as much as a dollar per pound. In some cities consumers turn to horse meat, which ranges in price from fifteen to twenty-two cents a pound.

☞ *1946 by the numbers*

6. *A GOOD MEAL IN 1946:* The fixed price of an entire dinner—including a smorgasbord appetizer—is $3.50 at the swank Kungsholm Restaurant in Chicago.

7. The price of a new Crosley four-passenger convertible sedan is $250.

8. Timex watches hit the market and can be had for as little as $6.95.

9. The heavily advertised new radio, the Philco Palladium, also plays records. You put a record in the slot, close the door, and it plays. Yours for a mere $83.75.

10. Twenty quarts of ice cream are produced for every man, woman, and child in America, making this the all-time banner year for the frozen dessert.

JULY

01 ► Atomic bomb tests are held at Bikini Atoll in the South Pacific.

04 ► President Truman uses American Independence Day to proclaim the Philippines a republic.

05 ► The bikini, designed by Louis Reard, makes its debut at a fashion show in Paris. It is named after the nuclear explosion on Bikini Atoll in the Pacific four days earlier.

07 ► Italian-born Mother Frances Zavier Cabrini is canonized as the first American saint.

AUGUST

01 ► The United States Atomic Energy Commission is established as part of the McMahon Act for the control of atomic energy. According to the legislation signed by President Truman on July 26, the development and use of atomic energy is vested in a five-member civilian commission appointed by the president and confirmed by the Senate.

02 ► Congress passes the Legislative Reorganization Act, which

July 5, 1946:
The bikini, designed by Louis Reard, makes its debut at a fashion show in Paris. It is named after the nuclear explosion on Bikini Atoll in the Pacific four days earlier.

requires the registration of lobbyists and a recording of the money spent lobbying.

SEPTEMBER

20 ► President Harry S Truman asks Secretary of Commerce Henry A. Wallace for his resignation following a speech made by the secretary on September 12 criticizing the current United States policy toward Russia.

■ ■

1946 in ten words (& phrases)

☛ 1. *automation* (term coined by Ford engineer D. S. Harder for a system he invents to manufacture car engines)

☛ 2. *the Roosevelt dime* (New this year, it is found in the pockets and purses of Americans for decades to come.)

☛ 3. *hard line* (increasingly common term used to describe the relationship between the United States and the Soviet Union)

☛ 4. *electric blanket* (The one with a thermostatic switch is invented this year.)

☛ 5. *Cannes Film Festival* (gets underway for the first time, giving the world a new source of cinematic gossip and excess)

☛ 6. *Nuremberg* (As the site of the tribunal that convicts and executes Nazi leaders, this name becomes symbolic of the responsibility that leaders must face for war and atrocity.)

☛ 7. *the best years of our lives* (title of a William Wyler movie about returning vets and their problems, which becomes a slogan for the hopes of Americans)

☛ 8. *the hucksters* (title of a book by Frederic Wakeman that gives the language a new name for the people who work on Madison Avenue)

☛ 9. *the snake pit* (title of a book by Mary Jane Ward that depicts life in a mental hospital and becomes a metaphor for bad psychiatric care)

October 25, 1946:
Facing demands for housing from returning veterans and others who waited during the war, President Truman declares a state of emergency in housing and lifts import restrictions on lumber, but the shortage eases only when builders develop new ways to produce inexpensive tract housing on a large scale.

People most likely to be on the cover in 1946

10. *ranch style* (new style in housing, furnishings, and food)

■■■■■■■■■■■■■■■■■■■■■■■■■■■■■■■■■

OCTOBER

16 ▶ Ten top German Nazi war criminals are hanged in Nuremberg.

25 ▶ Facing demands for housing from returning veterans and others who waited during the war, President Harry Truman declares a state of emergency in housing and lifts import restrictions on lumber, but the shortage eases only when builders develop new ways to produce inexpensive tract housing on a large scale.

NOVEMBER

12 ▶ The Exchange National Bank of Chicago offers a new service, called Autobank. Motorists drive directly to one of ten windows, where tellers sit behind bullet-proof glass and use drawers to handle transactions.

DECEMBER

19 ▶ The Viet Minh initiate an eight-year Indochina war against the French.

■■■■■■■■■■■■■■■■■■■■■■■■■■■■■■■■■

1. Trygve Lie
2. Joe Lewis
3. Henry Wallace
4. John L. Lewis
5. Marian Anderson
6. Albert Einstein

▶ 1946

- 7. Frank Leahy
- 8. Henry Ford II
- 9. Cardinal Spellman
- 10. George C. Marshall

■■■■■■■■■■■■■■■■■■■■■■■■■■■■■■

December 19, 1946:
The Viet Minh initiate an
eight-year Indochina war
against the French.

JANUARY

29 ▶ The United States announces that it will no longer attempt to mediate between the Nationalist and Communist factions in China as civil war becomes more dangerous. Most of the 12,000 American troops stationed there leave immediately.

FEBRUARY

10 ▶ In Paris peace treaties for Italy, Finland, Rumania, Hungary, and Bulgaria are signed.

MARCH

12 ▶ President Truman asks Congress for $597 million to be used for military and economic aid to Greece and Turkey. The president says that American aid is necessary to help those nations who are trying to withstand the inroads of Communism. The principle at work here is known as the Truman doctrine and comes from his proclamation that it will be the policy of the United States "to support free peoples who are resisting subjugation by armed minorities or by outside pressures." The money is later granted by Congress.

1947 bumper sticker: Forward with President Truman — No Retreat.

▶ 19

_____
_____
_____
_____
_____
_____
_____
_____
_____
_____
_____
_____
_____
_____

Fads and Trends for 1947 ☞

_____
_____
_____
_____
_____
_____
_____
_____
_____
_____
_____
_____
_____
_____
_____

14 ► Military and naval bases in the Philippine Islands are leased by the United States government for ninety-nine years.

22 ► President Truman issues Executive Order 9835, calling for loyalty investigations of all federal employees.

■■■■■■■■■■■■■■■■■■■■■■■■■■■■■■■■■■■

☞ 1. Great controversy in the United States attends the showing of women's wear featuring the New Look, which amounts to full dresses falling close to the ankles.

☞ 2. Marcel Marceau uses the character of a white-faced clown to bring the art of mime into the mainstream.

☞ 3. The startlingly new and sleek Studebaker Champion debuts as the first true postwar car. It sells well.

☞ 4. The move to the suburbs creates a tremendous demand for power lawn mowers; 380,000 are sold this year.

☞ 5. Inflation is a matter of great concern as the cost of food, clothing, and rent seems out of control.

☞ 6. There is genuine fascination with the exploits of Norwegian explorer Thor Heyerdahl and his raft _Kon Tiki_. He uses the drifting raft to advance his theory that the people of Polynesia were originally South American Indians who sailed there on rafts like his.

☞ 7. The issue of public schooling comes to the forefront. Most agree that teachers' salaries are too low and there is a shortage of classroom space for the number of children about to enter the system.

☞ 8. Book buyers show a renewed interest in American history.

☞ 9. Novelty songs like _The Too Fat Polka_ and _The Woody Woodpecker Song_ are selling a lot of 78 RPM records.

☞ 10. Foreign films become so popular that Hollywood studios report a 25 percent decline in American movie production.

■■■■■■■■■■■■■■■■■■■■■■■■■■■■■■■■■■■

► 1947

APRIL

11 ► For the first time in baseball history, a black man plays with a major league team. Jackie Robinson joins with the Brooklyn Dodgers today in an exhibition game with the New York Yankees.

16 ► A ship explodes in Texas City, Texas, and sets off a terrible fire that kills 500 and destroys the city.

MAY

07 ► William Levitt Sons rents its first Levittown homes to veterans for $65 a month, with option to buy, contingent on winning Hempstead town approval of a building code change. Full purchase price is $6,990. Approval is granted and on October 1, 1947, the first families move into the development, Levittown, Long Island, New York.

31 ► The Communists take over in Hungary while the nation's anti-Communist premier is out of the country. This act is interpreted as a direct Soviet challenge to the Truman doctrine of containment.

JUNE

05 ► Secretary of State Lieutenant General George C. Marshall delivers a speech at Harvard University that lasts less than ten minutes. In it, he calls for massive help to Europe based on a policy "directed not against any country or doctrine but against hunger, poverty, desperation and chaos." It leads to the establishment of the European Recovery Program or Marshall Plan in 1948. Over the next four years, more than $13 billion in free grants are pumped into the ailing economies of Europe. By any measure, the Marshall Plan is a resounding success.

11 ► Sugar rationing ends in the United States.

23 ► The Taft-Hartley Act is passed despite the veto of President Truman. It overturns a number of the victories that were

June 11, 1947: Sugar rationing ends in the United States.

► 21

gained by organized labor during the Depression. The unconditional closed shop is taken away from labor, for instance, and unions now have to publish their financial statements. It also allows employers to sue unions for broken contracts and strike damages and creates the role of federal mediator.

25 ► Kenneth Arnold of Boise, Idaho, reports seeing flying saucers over Mount Rainier, Washington. It is the first of many such reports of "shining saucerlike objects."

27 ► Automobile workers receive the first pension provision in automotive history as the Ford Motor Company in Detroit agrees to contribute $200 million to start and $15 million a year thereafter to the plan.

■ ■

☞ 1. There are now thirty-eight magazines in America with circulations in excess of a million.

☞ 2. A new ground speed record is established: 394.196 MPH.

☞ 3. Enrollment of veterans at American colleges, aided and spurred by the provisions of the GI bill of rights (or the Serviceman's Readjustment Act of 1944), hits a peak with more than a million former servicemen in the nation's colleges and universities.

☞ 4. *A GOOD MEAL IN 1947:* Luncheon at Le Petit Cafe at the Palmer House, Chicago, is a flat $1 and includes soup, an entree, a vegetable, rolls and butter, dessert, and beverage.

☞ 5. Two million federal workers are investigated for possible Communist connections. As a result 526 resign their jobs and another 98 are fired.

☞ 6. For the first time, U.S. agricultural chemical production reaches close to 2 billion pounds.

☞ 7. A telephone strike sees 350,000 people walk off the job; of these, 230,000 workers are women. The strike is not the largest ever but involves the largest number of women ever to walk out on strike.

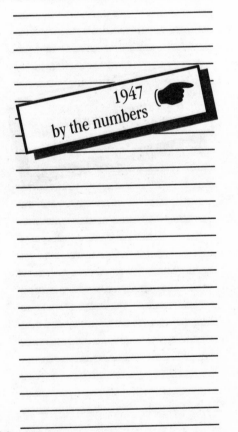

1947 by the numbers ☞

☞ 8. Pan Am offers a ticket for a flight around the world for $1,700.

☞ 9. At the moment of independence the population of India is 400 million.

☞ 10. A Hershey bar costs a nickel and contains 1⅛ ounces of chocolate.

■ ■

JULY

04 ▶ A United Airlines crew reports being passed by nine flying discs over the state of Idaho. They are described as flat, round, and larger than an aircraft.

05 ▶ Larry Doby signs a contract with the Cleveland Indians, becoming the first black player in baseball's American League.

06 ▶ Army aircraft are dispatched to search the skies over the West Coast after widely reported flying disc sightings have been made.

08 ▶ Demolition work begins in New York City to make way for the new permanent headquarters of the United Nations.

26 ▶ President Harry S Truman signs the National Security Act, creating the Department of Defense, the National Security Council, the Central Intelligence Agency, and the Joint Chiefs of Staff. It amounts to a major overhaul and restructuring that remains in force for decades to come.

July 4, 1947:
A United Airlines crew reports being passed by nine flying discs over the state of Idaho. They are described as flat, round, and larger than an aircraft.

AUGUST

15 ▶ Great Britain ends its 200-year-old rule over India, and two new sovereign states come into existence, India and Pakistan.

28 ▶ The death by goring of bullfighter Manolete plunges Spain into mourning.

29 ▶ Because of its shaky economic condition and a shortage of foodstuffs, England cuts its meat ration to the equivalent

of twenty cents a person a week and orders an end to nonessential automobile driving after October 1.

SEPTEMBER

17 ► As a result of the newly organized United States Department of Defense (merging into one administrative agency all of the branches of the armed services) James V. Forrestal is sworn in as the nation's first Secretary of Defense.

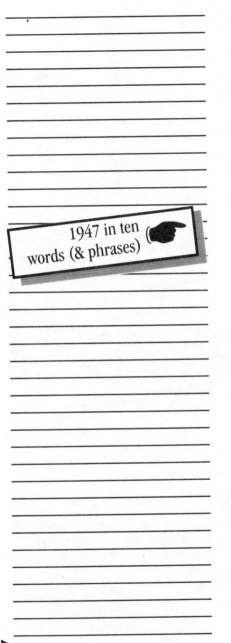

1947 in ten words (& phrases)

■ ■

☞ 1. *flying saucers* (numerous sightings and widespread publicity—"Mildred, get out here and look at this!")

☞ 2. *Truman doctrine* (policy of Soviet containment)

☞ 3. *loyalty oath* (an increasingly common requirement of public employment seen as a means of combating Communism at home)

☞ 4. *Benelux* (Belgium, the Netherlands, and Luxembourg as an economic and cultural unit)

☞ 5. *cold war* (debate exists as to who coined the term but this year it enters the national vocabulary)

☞ 6. *gamesmanship* (writer Steven Potter's coinage for approaching life as if it were a game)

☞ 7. *msg* (Monosodium glutamate is introduced under the brand name Accent.)

☞ 8. *color bar* (what Jackie Robinson broke when he joined the Brooklyn Dodgers)

☞ 9. *Hollywood blacklist* (name for a list created by studio executives of alleged Communist sympathizers in the film industry)

☞ 10. *Spruce Goose* (a creation of Howard Hughes, the wooden plane is the largest airplane ever built)

■ ■

► 1947

OCTOBER

05 ► During the course of the first televised presidential address, Americans are asked to give up eating meat on Tuesdays and poultry on Thursdays in order to help alleviate food shortages and starvation in Europe.

14 ► Air force captain Charles Yeager, flying the Bell X-1, exceeds the speed of sound to become the world's first supersonic flier. The sound barrier has been broken.

20 ► The House Un-American Activities Committee opens public hearings into Communist influence in Hollywood, laying the groundwork for a blacklist of suspected subversives in the movie industry.

29 ► Conducting experiments on the control of weather, the General Electric Company uses dry ice to seed cumulus clouds at Concord, New Hampshire. It produces rain.

NOVEMBER

11 ► Soviet Foreign Minister Molotov makes a public statement claiming that the secrets of the atomic bomb are no longer secret. There is little question in the West that the USSR will have the A-bomb in a few years.

29 ► The United Nations authorizes the creation of the state of Israel through a proposal sponsored by the United States and the Soviet Union. The new nation will be proclaimed on May 14, 1948.

DECEMBER

23 ► A team of Bell Laboratories physicists under William Shockley invents the transistor as a replacement for vacuum tubes.

26 ► The blizzard of 1947 hits, dropping 25.8 inches on New York City within twenty hours. About eighty people die in

October 14, 1947:
Air force captain Charles Yeager, flying the Bell X-1, exceeds the speed of sound to become the world's first supersonic flier.

December 23, 1947:
A team of Bell Laboratories physicists under William Shockley invents the transistor as a replacement for vacuum tubes.

the Northeast in the heaviest snowstorm to hit Gotham since 1888.

30 ▶ The Communists in Rumania demand and get the abdication of King Michael. The end of the last monarchy in the growing Soviet world underscores the success of Communism in Europe.

■■■■■■■■■■■■■■■■■■■■■■■■■■■■■■■■

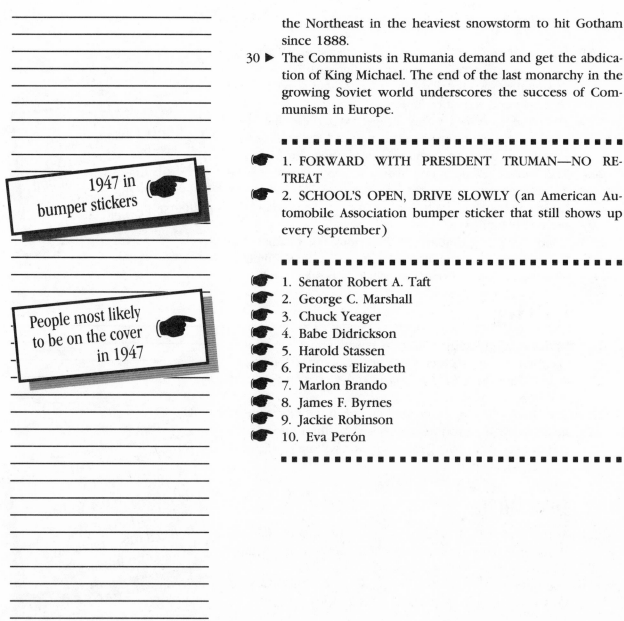

1947 in bumper stickers ☞

☞ 1. FORWARD WITH PRESIDENT TRUMAN—NO RETREAT

☞ 2. SCHOOL'S OPEN, DRIVE SLOWLY (an American Automobile Association bumper sticker that still shows up every September)

■■■■■■■■■■■■■■■■■■■■■■■■■■■■■■■■

People most likely to be on the cover in 1947 ☞

☞ 1. Senator Robert A. Taft
☞ 2. George C. Marshall
☞ 3. Chuck Yeager
☞ 4. Babe Didrickson
☞ 5. Harold Stassen
☞ 6. Princess Elizabeth
☞ 7. Marlon Brando
☞ 8. James F. Byrnes
☞ 9. Jackie Robinson
☞ 10. Eva Perón

■■■■■■■■■■■■■■■■■■■■■■■■■■■■■■■■

The year of ▶
the Berlin blockade ▶ **1948**
and Allied airlift ▶

JANUARY

04 ▶ Burma becomes an independent nation.

12 ▶ The U.S. Supreme Court, in a unanimous ruling, orders the state of Oklahoma to provide Ada Lois Fisher, a black woman, with the same education in law that it offers white students. Miss Fisher, thus far, has been barred from entering the University of Oklahoma Law School. Five days later, the Supreme Court of Oklahoma rules that the state must establish a separate but equal law school for Miss Fisher.

28 ▶ The first Emmy Awards for television excellence are presented.

30 ▶ Mohandas K. Gandhi is assassinated by a Hindu extremist, Ram Naturam, in the gardens of Birla House, New Delhi, where Gandhi was leading a thousand followers into a summer house for evening devotions.

FEBRUARY

02 ▶ President Truman sends his civil rights package to Congress. It asks for an end to employment discrimination and segregated schools. Strong opposition is immediate.

25 ▶ Communists take control of Czechoslovakia in a bloodless coup.

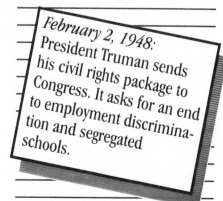

February 2, 1948: President Truman sends his civil rights package to Congress. It asks for an end to employment discrimination and segregated schools.

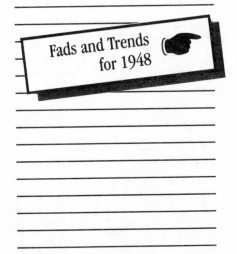

March 17, 1948:
The Hell's Angels are formed as two smaller gangs join to form a larger gang with twenty-five members.

Fads and Trends for 1948

MARCH

08 ► The U.S. Supreme Court abolishes the practice of religion in the public schoolroom, declaring that such practices violate the first amendment to the U.S. Constitution.

17 ► The Hell's Angels are formed as two smaller gangs join to form a larger gang with twenty-five members. The name comes from a 1931 Jean Harlow movie and a World War II bomber that toured the United States in a war bond sales campaign.

■ ■

☞ 1. The demand for a coiled-wire stair-descending toy known as the Slinky is insatiable.

☞ 2. Crude air conditioning systems show up—with great hoopla—in top-of-the-line Detroit cars.

☞ 3. Milton Berle—"Uncle Miltie"—becomes Mr. Television in part because people actually buy their first television sets to see him in action.

☞ 4. General Mills and Pillsbury introduce prepared cake mixes, signaling a new era of convenience foods.

☞ 5. The television western rides into view with *The Lone Ranger* and *Hopalong Cassidy* in the saddle. The era of the horse opera is a long one.

☞ 6. The cool jazz era begins with Miles Davis and his combo.

☞ 7. The landmark *Sexual Behavior in the Human Male* is released by social scientist Alfred Kinsey.

☞ 8. Two blockbuster novels about World War II appear: Noman Mailer's *Naked and the Dead* and Irwin Shaw's *Young Lions.*

☞ 9. Movement on the food frontier: the McDonald brothers begin to franchise their name for hamburger stands, and Baskin-Robbins comes into being with the merger of two smaller chains.

1948

10. An Oklahoma faith healer named Oral Roberts starts to appear on radio and television to gain converts and givers to his Healing Waters Inc. ministry.

■■■■■■■■■■■■■■■■■■■■■■■■■■■■■■■■■■■■■

APRIL

01 ▶ A Soviet land blockade is erected that cuts West Berlin off from the rest of West Germany. (See June 21.)

19 ▶ In Italy's first postwar elections, the Communist party is narrowly defeated.

20 ▶ Walter P. Reuther, president of the United Automobile Workers Union, is seriously wounded as an unidentified assailant fires a shotgun at him through the window of the Reuther home in Detroit.

26 ▶ The charter creating the Organization of American States is adopted in Bogotá.

MAY

03 ▶ The Supreme Court forbids the states to enforce property "restrictive covenants"—those agreements that bind owners not to sell property to racial and religious minorities.

10 ▶ All railroads in the nation are seized by the United States government in order to forestall a national strike.

14 ▶ Israel declares independence. David Ben-Gurion is the prime minister of the new state. The United States gives Israel de facto recognition. With this, Great Britain ends its thirty-one-year rule in Palestine. The boundaries of the new state conform in general to those defined by the United Nations in 1947 for the partition of Palestine into sovereign Jewish and Arab states. Five Arab states invade Israel, marking the start of the first Arab-Israeli war.

25 ▶ General Motors and the United Automobile Workers agree to the first automatic cost-of-living wage increases. It will affect 265,000 hourly GM workers.

Trend of 1948: Movement on the food frontier: the McDonald brothers begin to franchise their name for hamburger stands, and Baskin-Robbins comes into being with the merger of two smaller chains.

June 21, 1948:
In response to the Soviet blockade of West Berlin, the United States and its allies begin a massive airlift of food, fuel, and other supplies.

JUNE

18 ► The United Nations Commission on Human Rights adopts its International Declaration of Human Rights.

19 ► Congress enacts the Displaced Persons Act, providing for the admission of 205,000 refugees and homeless Europeans during the next two years.

21 ► In response to the Soviet blockade of West Berlin, the United States and its allies begin a massive airlift of food, fuel, and other supplies.

► *Also occurring today:* Dr. Peter Goldmark of CBS/Columbia Records introduces his 33⅓ RPM long-playing record at the Waldorf-Astoria Hotel in New York. Each side plays for twenty-three minutes, compared to four minutes for the standard 78 RPM record.

24 ► Communist forces cut off all land and water routes between West Germany and West Berlin.

26 ► In response to the Soviet blockade of West Berlin, the United States announces it will increase its daily cargo flights to the western sector of the isolated German city. The operation is dubbed the Berlin airlift.

28 ► The Red monolith looks a little less strong today when Joseph Stalin breaks with Marshal Josip Broz Tito of Yugoslavia.

30 ► Bell Laboratories announces the development of the transistor as a tiny, inexpensive substitute for the radio vacuum tube. Both devices amplify and oscillate electric impulses, but the transistor is cheaper, operates with greater efficiency and power, and has no heated cathode—it operates instantaneously and cold. The transistor enters commercial use in 1953.

1948 by the numbers ☞

1. The nickel subway fare in New York City disappears as all of the city's lines boost their fares to a dime.

2. Eddie Arcaro becomes the first jockey to win the Kentucky Derby four times.

☞ 3. The budget for the first Ed Sullivan television show, *The Toast of the Town,* which debuts on June 20, is $1,375, with $375 of that total reserved for talent.

☞ 4. Cost for the first fifteen months of the Marshall Plan is pegged at a cool $16.8 billion.

☞ 5. Tuition for one year at Harvard costs $455.

☞ 6. A family-size Chevrolet sells for $1,255 and the gas to fuel it costs 25.9 cents per gallon.

☞ 7. A new speed record is established at the Indianapolis 500: 119.813 miles per hour.

☞ 8. President Truman logs in 10,000 miles on his "whistle stop" tour of America. Some say it accounts for his win.

☞ 9. The largest-known single-piece meteor falls in Kansas. It weighs 2,360 pounds.

■■■■■■■■■■■■■■■■■■■■■■■■■■■■■■■■

JULY

05 ▶ Britain's National Health Service Act, which provides free government-financed medical and dental care, goes into effect to the tune of $2 billion a year.

07 ▶ Six reservists become the first women sworn into the regular U.S. Navy.

17 ▶ Southern Democrats from thirteen states meet in Birmingham, Alabama, and organize a States' Rights Party to oppose the Truman-Barkley ticket adopted by the regular Democratic Convention in Philadelphia on July 15. Six thousand delegates nominate Governor J. Strom Thurmond of South Carolina for president and Governor Fielding L. Wright of Mississippi for vice president. The new party is immediately called the Dixiecrats.

22 ▶ Breakaway left-leaning Democrats form the Progressive Party and select former vice president Henry Wallace to run against Harry Truman.

26 ▶ Segregation is barred in the armed forces per an executive order from President Truman.

July 7, 1948:
Six reservists become the first women sworn into the regular U.S. Navy.

▶ 1948

August 16, 1948:
Baseball player Babe Ruth dies in New York of cancer at age fifty-three.

1948 in ten words (& phrases)

30 ▶ The British Citizenship Act goes into effect giving all citizens of Commonwealth countries British citizenship. This act attracts many from Africa, Asia, and the Caribbean to the British Isles.

31 ▶ As 900 airplanes fly overhead, President Harry S Truman dedicates the New York International Airport at Idlewild Field in New York City.

AUGUST

03 ▶ Whittaker Chambers, a senior editor of *Time* magazine and an admitted ex-Communist, names Alger Hiss, former United States Department of State official, as a onetime key member of the Communist underground operating in Washington.

15 ▶ The Republic of South Korea is created with Syngman Rhee as its leader.

16 ▶ Baseball player Babe Ruth dies in New York of cancer at age fifty-three.

SEPTEMBER

09 ▶ The Korean People's Democratic Republic is declared by Kim Il Sung. Although immediately regarded as the republic of the north, it claims authority over all Korea.

■ ■

1. *cybernetics* (coined this year by mathematician Norbert Weiner of M.I.T.)
2. *aureomycin* (another miracle drug whose name Americans are learning to say)
3. *Porsche* (a new sportscar from Germany)
4. *Honda* (a new motorcycle being made in Japan)
5. *Land Rover* (the Brits build a Jeep for civilians)
6. *dramamine* (name for a new drug that relieves the effects of motion sickness)

► 1948

☞ 7. *latex paint* (Dow Chemical and Glidden work together to free the do-it-yourselfer from messy oil-based paints.)

☞ 8. *tail fin* (Small ones first show up on the 1948 Cadillac. The '59 Caddy has fins that rise a full foot over the car's rear fender.)

☞ 9. *living* (an old term used to sell new books: *A Guide to Confident Living* by Norman Vincent Peale and *How to Stop Worrying and Start Living* by Dale Carnegie)

☞ 10. *discount store* (This concept is born with the opening of the E. J. Korvette Department Store in New York. The public does not have to be convinced.)

■ ■

OCTOBER

14 ► New York City begins a fluoridation program by coating the teeth of 50,000 schoolchildren with sodium fluoride.

22 ► Inventor Chester Carlson puts on the first public demonstration of xerography in New York City.

NOVEMBER

03 ► Harry S Truman pulls a stunning upset in his election race against heavily favored Thomas E. Dewey of New York. The Democrats take control of both houses.

The Chicago *Tribune* appears with the banner headline *DEWEY DEFEATS TRUMAN*. Truman poses with the headline and the gaff becomes such a milestone that by late 1985 a copy of the paper fetches $950 at an auction of Americana.

04 ► The air force announces the creation of the nonprofit Rand Corporation. It is the first of the government-supported think tanks that have a major impact on postwar military policy.

29 ► The practice of "untouchability" is officially abolished in India.

October 22, 1948: Inventor Chester Carlson puts on the first public demonstration of xerography in New York City.

December 24, 1948: A solar heating system designed by Dr. Maria Telkes is installed in a house in Dover, Massachusetts

► 1948

DECEMBER

15 ► Former State Department official Alger Hiss is indicted for perjury after denying that he passed on secret government documents to journalist Whittaker Chambers, then a Communist agent.

23 ► Wartime premier Tojo and six other leaders are hung in Japan as war criminals.

24 ► A solar heating system designed by Dr. Maria Telkes is installed in a house in Dover, Massachusetts.

■■■■■■■■■■■■■■■■■■■■■■■■■■■■■■■■

☛ 1. GIVE 'EM HELL, HARRY
☛ 2. START PACKING HARRY—THE DEWEYS ARE COMING
☛ 3. PHOOEY ON DEWEY
☛ 4. ME FOR TRUMAN-BARKLEY FOR ME
☛ 5. THINK! PREVENT WALLACITIS
☛ 6. WIN WITH WALLACE—'48

■■■■■■■■■■■■■■■■■■■■■■■■■■■■■■■■

☛ 1. Arturo Toscanini
☛ 2. Joe DiMaggio
☛ 3. Henry Wallace
☛ 4. Betty Grable
☛ 5. Thomas E. Dewey
☛ 6. Satchel Paige
☛ 7. Gregory Peck
☛ 8. Barbara Ann Scott
☛ 9. Strom Thurmond
☛ 10. David Ben-Gurion

■■■■■■■■■■■■■■■■■■■■■■■■■■■■■■■■

1948 in buttons & bumper stickers ☛

People most likely to be on the cover in 1948 ☛

The year in which Russia ▶
gets the bomb and the ▶
United States is offered ▶
the Fair Deal ▶

1949

JANUARY

05 ▶ President Harry S Truman labels his administration the Fair Deal in the course of delivering his state of the union message to Congress.

07 ▶ A cease-fire is imposed in Palestine.

19 ▶ A new congressional act increases the salaries of the president and vice president of the United States and the speaker of the House of Representatives. As of this date, the president's salary is increased from $75,000 to $100,000, with a tax-free expense allowance of $50,000 annually. Both the vice president's and speaker's salaries are increased from $20,000 to $30,000, with each official to receive an annual $10,000 tax-free expense allowance.

21 ▶ Generalissimo Chiang Kai-shek retires from office as the Chinese Communists battle Nanking, the government's capital. Li Tsung-jen takes over as acting president and starts a series of unsuccessful negotiations with the rebels.

28 ▶ A bill introduced in the Senate by Senator Richard Russell of Georgia would redistribute the nation's black population throughout the nation "equitably." It proposes creating a racial relocation bureau within the government with a $4.5 billion budget.

29 ▶ President Truman creates the policy of granting U.S. aid to underdeveloped countries as he proposes the Four Point Program.

January 29, 1949: President Truman creates the policy of granting U.S. aid to underdeveloped countries as he proposes the Four Point Program.

FEBRUARY

10 ▶ *Death of a Salesman,* written by Arthur Miller and starring Lee J. Cobb, Arthur Kennedy, and Mildred Dunnock, opens at the Morosco Theatre in New York.

MARCH

02 ▶ The *Lucky Lady II,* an air force B-50 Superfortress, completes the first nonstop round-the-world flight at Fort Worth, Texas. (The bomber covers 23,452 miles in ninety-four hours, one minute.)

31 ▶ Newfoundland becomes Canada's tenth province, following a plebiscite held on July 22, 1948.

■■■■■■■■■■■■■■■■■■■■■■■■■■■■■■■■

Fads and Trends for 1949

☞ 1. Chic Young's *Blondie* is determined to be the most popular comic strip in the world.

☞ 2. LPs (from CBS) and 45s (from RCA) go head to head in the record stores. The old standard 78 suddenly looks old-fashioned.

☞ 3. General Mills and Pillsbury come out with their own versions of the prepared cake mix.

☞ 4. Roller Derby makes a brash entrance as wrestling on wheels.

☞ 5. Family comedies warm up television with debuts for *The Goldbergs, One Man's Family, Mama,* and *The Life of Riley.*

☞ 6. The Latin samba is the hot new ballroom dance.

☞ 7. George Orwell's *1984* creates a horrific, totalitarian image of the future.

☞ 8. Paris decrees "daring décolletage" for women's evening wear, and 1949 becomes known as the year of the "plunging neckline."

☞ 9. Rogers and Hammerstein's *South Pacific* is the big Broadway smash hit.

☞ 10. Arthur Miller's play *Death of a Salesman* provides

strong theater and a dark, new metaphor for the American dream.

■■■■■■■■■■■■■■■■■■■■■■■■■■■■■■■

APRIL

04 ▶ The United States signs the North Atlantic Treaty Organization—or NATO—pact. It pledges to join Canada and ten West European countries in mutual resistance of armed attack on any member nation. At the signing in Washington, D.C., President Truman tells the delegates, "What we are about to do here is a neighborly act. We are like a group of householders, living in the same locality, who decide to express their community of interests by entering into a formal association for their mutual self-protection."

18 ▶ The Republic of Ireland comes into being after 780 years of British rule.

20 ▶ The discovery of cortisone is announced. Its most immediate use: for relief of rheumatoid arthritis.

MAY

11 ▶ The first Polaroid Land camera goes on sale in New York City for $89.75. It produces a finished photograph in sixty seconds.

12 ▶ After 328 days the Soviet occupation authorities in Berlin announce the end of the land blockade of the German capital.

JUNE

13 ▶ George Orwell's *1984* is published in New York.

14 ▶ Philadelphia Phillies first baseman Eddie Waitkus is shot and seriously wounded by Ruth Steinhagen, who claims she loves him.

29 ▶ The South African government enacts a ban against racially

April 4, 1949:
The United States signs the North Atlantic Treaty Organization—or NATO—pact.

April 20, 1949:
The discovery of cortisone is announced.

June 29, 1949:
The South African government enacts a ban against racially mixed marriages and suspends the automatic granting of citizenship to immigrants. Apartheid is now the law of the land.

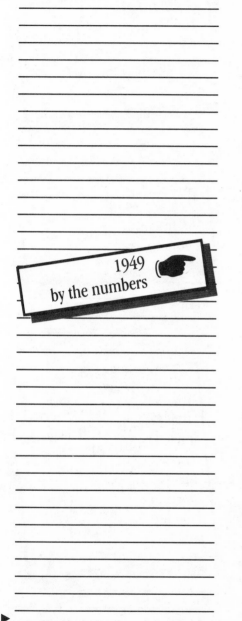

1949
by the numbers

mixed marriages and suspends the automatic granting of citizenship to immigrants. Apartheid is now the law of the land.

31 ▶ The current interest in uranium prospecting prompts a New York sporting-goods store to advertise "a large stock of Geiger Counters at $54.50 each. Operates on flashlight batteries and fits in a coat pocket. Carry it with you to detect uranium deposits."

1. The national debt reaches a record $250 billion.

2. Americans are buying television sets at the stunning rate of 60,000 a week.

3. There are now a million television sets in the nation.

4. Golf's top male and female money-makers for the year are Sam Snead with $31,593.83 and Babe Didrikson Zaharias at $4,650.

5. The German Volkswagen is introduced in the United States and two cars are sold.

6. The total number of flights that comprise the Berlin airlift: 277,264.

7. The NCAA college basketball championship is won by Kentucky, which beats Oklahoma by a score of forty-six to thirty-six.

8. The Department of Commerce determines that there are 90,067 movie theaters in 116 nations around the world with a combined seating capacity of 48,750,147.

9. Here is what you can purchase with a dollar and still get back change: a gallon of gas (twenty-five cents), a pack of cigarettes (twenty-one cents), a loaf of bread (fifteen cents), a Coke (five cents), and a quart of milk (twenty-one cents).

10. Unemployment during the year averages 1.5 million.

# ▶ 1949

JULY

13 ▶ The Vatican today announces that it henceforth will feel free to excommunicate Catholics who defend and spread Communism.

20 ▶ War between Israel and the Arab League ends with an armistice.

AUGUST

06 ▶ New secretary of state Dean Acheson (who replaced Marshall on January 21) presents a white paper in which he blames Chiang Kai-shek's "reactionary clique" for the fact that the nationalists are losing the Chinese civil war. He bars any further aid to the nationalists.

26 ▶ A federal court restores American citizenship to three Japanese-American women who renounced it under pressure as inmates in a World War II camp for Japanese-Americans. The decision affects 4,394 other Nisei (or Japanese-Americans).

SEPTEMBER

05 ▶ In a period of twelve minutes in Camden, New Jersey, thirteen people are gunned down and killed by a man named Howard Unruh. After being taken into custody, he is quoted as saying, "I'd have killed a thousand if I'd had enough bullets."

18 ▶ Sir Stafford Cripps, chancellor of the exchequer, announces in a radio broadcast from London that the British pound is being devalued from $4.03 to $2.80 because of an acute shortage of American dollars needed in international trade.

21 ▶ The German Federal Republic (West Germany) comes into formal existence when the Allied High Commission transfers to it the administration of the American, British, and French zones of occupation.

September 21, 1949: The German Federal Republic (West Germany) comes into formal existence.

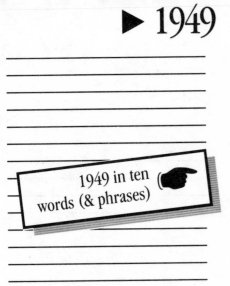

1949 in ten words (& phrases)

September 23, 1949: President Truman issues a grave announcement: Russia has the bomb.

23 ► President Truman issues a grave announcement: Russia has the bomb.

30 ► The Berlin airlift, which began in June of 1948, comes to an end as the land blockade of the city is lifted.

1. *Big Brother* (via George Orwell's *1984,* along with . . .)
2. *newspeak* and . . .
3. *doublethink*
4. *push-button warfare* (term increasingly used for war as it will be fought in the future)
5. *Thailand* (new name for Siam as of May 11, 1949)
6. *Pillsbury Bake-Off* (a new way to promote the use of flour)
7. *canasta* (an Argentinian card game that sweeps America)
8. *Willy Loman* (the central character in Arthur Miller's *Death of a Salesman,* whose name becomes symbolic for the failed dream of respect and prosperity)
9. *45* (funny little records with a big hole in the middle)
10. *UNICEF Christmas card* (debuts in 1949)

OCTOBER

01 ► Mao Tse-tung officially proclaims China to be a Communist state.

06 ► President Harry Truman signs the Mutual Defense Assistance Act, which will give $1.3 billion to our NATO allies.

14 ► Eleven top Communist leaders are convicted of conspiring to advocate the overthrow of the U.S. government. On October 21 all are fined $10,000 and given jail sentences of three to five years.

26 ► The president signs a bill that raises the minimum wage from forty to seventy-four cents an hour.

▶ 1949

NOVEMBER

29 ▶ It is determined that today's explosion of an American Airlines plane in Dallas and the loss of twenty-eight establish this as the most dangerous month to this point in the history of aviation. The Dallas deaths bring the total to 149.

DECEMBER

07 ▶ The Chinese Nationalist government moves its headquarters from the mainland to Taipei, Formosa. The Chinese civil war is over with a clear victory going to the Communists.

■■■■■■■■■■■■■■■■■■■■■■■■■■■■■■■

☞ 1. Konrad Adenauer
☞ 2. Ingrid Bergman
☞ 3. Milton Berle
☞ 4. Mao Tse-tung
☞ 5. Stan Musial
☞ 6. Harry S Truman
☞ 7. Frank Sinatra
☞ 8. Perle Mesta
☞ 9. Albert Schweitzer
☞ 10. Katharine Hepburn and Spencer Tracy

■■■■■■■■■■■■■■■■■■■■■■■■■■■■■■■

December 7, 1949: The Chinese Nationalist government moves its headquarters from the mainland to Taipei, Formosa. The Chinese civil war is over with a clear victory going to the Communists.

☞ People most likely to be on the cover in 1949

▶ 41

The United States ▶
is drawn into ▶
the war in Korea ▶ **1950**

JANUARY

17 ▶ Nine robbers, wearing Halloween masks, hold up Brink's, Incorporated, a Boston armed car service, and escape with $1 million in cash and $500,000 in checks, the largest cash robbery in the nation's history.

18 ▶ The United States Senate repeals the federal tax on oleo-margarine despite pressure from American dairy interests.

21 ▶ Alger Hiss, former official in the State Department, is found guilty of perjury by a federal jury in New York City. The jury deliberates twenty-three hours and forty minutes. Hiss is later sentenced to five years' imprisonment.

31 ▶ President Truman announces he has ordered the development of the hydrogen bomb, saying, "I have directed the Atomic Energy Commission to continue its work on all forms of atomic weapons, including the so-called hydrogen or super-bomb."

FEBRUARY

07 ▶ The United States recognizes the southern state of Vietnam as opposed to Ho Chi Minh's northern Democratic Republic of Vietnam.

09 ▶ The era of McCarthyism can be said to begin today. A charge that the State Department is infested with Communists is made by Senator Joseph R. McCarthy (R., Wis.)

January 31, 1950: President Truman announces he has ordered the development of the hydrogen bomb, saying, "I have directed the Atomic Energy Commission to continue its work on all forms of atomic weapons, including the so-called hydrogen or super-bomb."

during a speech delivered before the Republican Women's Club of Ohio County in Wheeling, West Virginia: "I have in my hand fifty-seven cases of individuals who would appear to be either card-carrying members or certainly loyal to the Communist Party." He goes on to charge that as many as 205 Communists have infiltrated the State Department.

15 ► In Moscow, China and the Soviet Union sign a thirty-year friendship and mutual defense pact.

MARCH

14 ► After a prolonged drought, the City of New York, fearful for its scant water supply, hires Dr. Wallace E. Howell, director of the Mount Washington Observatory, as its official rainmaker. Dr. Howell receives $100 a day for his efforts to create rainfall.

■■■■■■■■■■■■■■■■■■■■■■■■■■■■■■■■■

Fads and Trends for 1950

☞ 1. Mass movement to suburbia is in full swing, spurring growth in other institutions, including...

☞ 2. shopping malls (usually anchored by one or more major department stores)...

☞ 3. drive-in movie theaters (called "passion pits" for good reason) and...

☞ 4. chain supermarkets (which eat mom 'n' pop grocery stores for snacks).

☞ 5. Antihistamines are the new medical miracle.

☞ 6. Jackson Pollock popularizes the drip painting, and art, for some, becomes a matter of action.

☞ 7. The television trend is to quiz and panel shows—*What's My Line?, Beat the Clock,* and *You Bet Your Life.*

☞ 8. Diner's Club markets the first credit card. It is the brainchild of Alfred S. Bloomingdale (1916–1982).

☞ 9. Charles Schulz introduces his *Peanuts* comic strip.

☞ 10. Hopalong Cassidy is the first great cowboy hero of the television era, and by 1950 his name and face are on everything from pajamas to lunch boxes.

☛ 11. Bowling booms, and kids and their parents flock to the alleys.

☛ 12. Wheat germ sales soar following claims for its health benefits.

■■■■■■■■■■■■■■■■■■■■■■■■■■■■■■■■

APRIL

03 ► Today is the day on which American workers theoretically get to keep all of their earnings. Called tax freedom day, it assumes that all money made before this date goes to paying federal, state, and local taxes. This day fell on February 13 in 1930 and March 8 in 1940.

MAY

09 ► The United States announces that it will provide military and economic aid to the French in Indochina beginning with an immediate grant of $10 million. This moment begins a debilitating involvement with Vietnam that does not end until 1975, when the last of the American troops leave.

10 ► Vice President Alben Barkley appoints a Senate subcommittee to investigate interstate crime. Senator Estes Kefauver (D., Tenn.) chairs the crime hearings, which, in the months ahead, put organized crime in the headlines and on television.

JUNE

25 ► Five years after World War II ends, war breaks out once more in Asia as Communist forces invade South Korea. Although war is never officially declared, 3 million soldiers and civilians are reported killed or wounded by the time peace talks conclude in 1953.

May 9, 1950:
The United States announces that it will provide military and economic aid to the French in Indochina beginning with an immediate grant of $10 million.

▶ 1950

June 25, 1950:
Five years after World War II ends, war breaks out once more in Asia as Communist forces invade South Korea. Although war is never officially declared, 3 million soldiers and civilians are reported killed or wounded by the time peace talks conclude in 1954.

1950
by the numbers

27 ▶ President Truman orders the air force and navy into the Korean conflict following a call from the UN Security Council for member nations to help South Korea repel an invasion by North Korea.

Little-noticed at the time is that Truman also sends a thirty-five-member military mission to Vietnam to act in an advisory capacity.

28 ▶ North Korean forces capture Seoul, South Korea.

▪▪▪▪▪▪▪▪▪▪▪▪▪▪▪▪▪▪▪▪▪▪▪▪▪▪▪▪▪▪▪▪▪

☛ 1. The U.S. population is 150,697,361 according to the 1950 Census. The population center of the nation is now northwest of Olney in Richland County, Illinois.

☛ 2. Sixty-four percent of all Americans now live in cities.

☛ 3. There are now 10 million television sets in the nation— an astonishing jump from a million in 1949.

☛ 4. Sixty percent of all medical patients are being prescribed penicillin, the miracle drug first introduced in 1945.

☛ 5. The United Nations reports that 480 million of the world's 800 million children are undernourished.

☛ 6. There is now one automobile for every 3.75 Americans, up from 1930's 5.5.

☛ 7. The nation can now boast 1.68 million miles of paved roads.

☛ 8. There are nineteen approved synthetic food colors in the American diet.

☛ 9. The population of the world hits 2.52 billion.

☛ 10. The average American farmer raises food for 15.5 people, double the production at the turn of the century.

▪▪▪▪▪▪▪▪▪▪▪▪▪▪▪▪▪▪▪▪▪▪▪▪▪▪▪▪▪▪▪▪▪

▶ 1950

JULY

01 ▶ The first U.S. ground forces arrive in Korea.

03 ▶ American and North Korean forces clash for the first time in the Korean War.

08 ▶ General Douglas MacArthur is named commander-in-chief of United Nations forces in Korea.

AUGUST

25 ▶ In order to avoid a strike, President Truman orders the army to seize control of the nation's railways.

SEPTEMBER

23 ▶ The Internal Security Act is adopted by Congress over President Harry Truman's veto. The act provides for the registration of Communists and their internment in times of emergency.

26 ▶ U.S. troops recapture Seoul.

29 ▶ Bell Laboratories and Western Electric create the first telephone answering machine.

■■■■■■■■■■■■■■■■■■■■■■■■■■■■■■■■■

☞ 1. *police action* (Americans are having to learn that the Korean War is one of these, not a war. Even after more than 33,000 Americans die there, this remains the official term for the conflict.)

☞ 2. *californium* and . . .

☞ 3. *berkelium* (new elements announced by the University of California)

☞ 4. *Doomsday* (This biblical term comes back in the growing debate over the possibility that the world could be destroyed by nuclear weapons.)

☞ 5. *thermonuclear* or *nuclear blackmail* (a dreadful new idea in which a desperate aggressor holds the earth hostage)

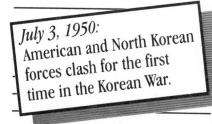

July 3, 1950:
American and North Korean forces clash for the first time in the Korean War.

September 29, 1950:
Bell Laboratories and Western Electric create the first telephone answering machine.

☞ 1950 in ten words (& phrases)

☛ 6. *instant* (This is suddenly a new name for coffee—as in, instant or regular?—as Maxwell House introduces the first modern instant coffee.)

☛ 7. *witch hunt* (old term brought back to describe the pursuit of Communists in government, a pursuit led by Senator Joseph McCarthy)

☛ 8. *the ten most wanted criminals* (a very successful publicity idea from the FBI)

☛ 9. *other-directed* (the new American personality—working to get along with and adjusting to others—explored in the best-selling book *The Lonely Crowd*)

☛ 10. *Sucaryl* (one name for the new artificial sweeteners that come on the market)

■■■■■■■■■■■■■■■■■■■■■■■■■■■■■■■

OCTOBER

07 ▶ U.S. forces invade North Korea.

11 ▶ The Columbia Broadcasting System receives government authorization to broadcast programs in color.

NOVEMBER

01 ▶ Two Puerto Rican nationalists try to force their entrance into Blair House, in Washington, to assassinate President Harry S Truman. One guard is killed, two are seriously injured, but Truman is unharmed.

20 ▶ U.S. troops reach the Yalu River on the border of Manchuria.

29 ▶ A sudden reversal takes place in Korea as American forces retreat under heavy attack from Chinese units.

DECEMBER

16 ▶ The situation in Korea is such that President Truman declares a national emergency.

October 7, 1950:
U. S. forces invade North Korea.

► 1950

23 ► The United States signs a Mutual Defense Assistance Agreement with the state of Vietnam.

■■■■■■■■■■■■■■■■■■■■■■■■■■■■■■■■■

☞ 1. Althea Gibson
☞ 2. Sugar Ray Robinson
☞ 3. Jimmy Stewart
☞ 4. Mary Martin
☞ 5. Al Capp
☞ 6. Pablo Picasso
☞ 7. Arthur Godfrey
☞ 8. Hopalong Cassidy
☞ 9. Winston Churchill (*Time* declares him Man of the Half Century)
☞ 10. Ted Williams

■■■■■■■■■■■■■■■■■■■■■■■■■■■■■■■■■

People most likely to be on the cover in 1950

► 49

1951

JANUARY

01 ▶ Chinese troops in Korea take the area surrounding Seoul. The city falls to the Communists three days later.

FEBRUARY

01 ▶ The United Nations General Assembly condemns Communist China as an aggressor in Korea.

26 ▶ James Jones's novel *From Here to Eternity,* destined to become one of the best-selling books of all time, is published in New York.

▶ ***Also occurring today:*** The twenty-second amendment to the Constitution is adopted. It stipulates that no person can be elected to the presidency for more than two terms and would have prevented Franklin D. Roosevelt from serving a third term if enacted earlier.

MARCH

14 ▶ UN forces recapture Seoul.

29 ▶ Julius and Ethel Rosenberg are found guilty of conspiracy to commit wartime espionage.

March 29, 1951: Julius and Ethel Rosenberg are found guilty of conspiracy to commit wartime espionage.

■ ■

☞ 1. BEST SELLERS FOR THE YEAR: fiction—*From Here to Eternity* by James Jones; nonfiction—*Look Younger, Live Longer* by Gayelord Hauser.

☞ 2. Crew cuts are the manly rage. Hell, even Bogart has one.

☞ 3. Meanwhile, many women have adopted the two-tone do.

☞ 4. General MacArthur's farewell speech, which recalls the line "Old soldiers never die, they just fade away," inspires a series of gags that play on the line. Sample: "Old fishermen never die, they just smell that way."

☞ 5. Paperback books have a boom year and more and more publishers start "softback" lines.

☞ 6. Mickey Mantle, age nineteen, joins the New York Yankees; Willie Mays, twenty, joins the New York Giants, and baseball has its new stars.

☞ 7. A college basketball scandal in New York shocks the sports world when it is discovered that payoffs were accepted to throw games.

☞ 8. The *Dennis the Menace* comic strip debuts and is immediately picked up by 750 newspapers.

☞ 9. J. D. Salinger's *Catcher in the Rye* is published.

☞ 10. The Kefauver hearings on organized crime are televised and capture the attention of the nation.

■ ■

APRIL

04 ► A debate that has been raging in Congress since January 5 is resolved with approval of the president's power to defend Europe with ground forces.

05 ► Julius and Ethel Rosenberg are sentenced to die in the electric chair for the crime of stealing atomic-bomb secrets.

11 ► President Truman relieves General Douglas MacArthur of his commands in the Far East. A statement issued by the president from the White House states, "I have concluded

April 11, 1951:
President Truman relieves General Douglas MacArthur of his commands in the Far East.

that General of the Army Douglas MacArthur is unable to give his wholehearted support to the policies of the United States government and of the United Nations in matters pertaining to official duties." Behind all of this is the general's desire to attack military positions in China, which the president feels would be tantamount to declaring war on China and Russia and risking World War III.

Lieutenant General Matthew B. Ridgway is appointed to succeed MacArthur.

19 ▶ General Douglas MacArthur, recalled from Korea by President Truman, closes his military career by addressing a joint session of Congress: "The world has turned over many times since I took the oath on the plain at West Point . . . but I still remember the refrain of one of the most popular barracks ballads of that day which proclaimed most proudly that old soldiers never die; they just fade away. And like the old soldier of that ballad, I now close my military career and just fade away."

MAY

27 ▶ China announces the "liberation" of Tibet. The smaller nation agrees to stop resisting the Chinese and agrees to become a Chinese province.

JUNE

14 ▶ Univac I, the first commercially built computer, goes into operation at the Census Bureau in Philadelphia.

25 ▶ The first commercial color telecast takes place as CBS broadcasts a one-hour special from New York to four other cities. The show features such television personalities as Arthur Godfrey, Faye Emerson, Sam Levinson, and Ed Sullivan.

May 27, 1951:
China announces the "liberation" of Tibet.

June 14, 1951:
Univac I, the first commercially built computer, goes into operation at the Census Bureau in Philadelphia,

▶ 1951

1951 by the numbers ☞

July 10, 1951:
Armistice talks aimed at ending the Korean conflict begin at Kaesong.

☞ 1. America produces 100 million tons of steel a year.

☞ 2. Some 400,000 pounds of penicillin are produced in America.

☞ 3. Three hundred million stars are in the Milky Way, according to the National Geographic Society.

☞ 4. The American Telephone and Telegraph Company is able to report that it is the first corporation to have more than 1 million stockholders.

☞ 5. There are 8.2 million trucks in the United States.

☞ 6. An 8.3-cubic-foot General Electric refrigerator costs $330.

☞ 7. Citation becomes the first race horse to earn more than a million dollars.

☞ 8. There are now 12,000 trade associations in the United States.

☞ 9. At the end of the year there are 164,896 adults in prison, down 900 since 1950.

☞ 10. Eleven thousand new books are published in the United States.

JULY

04 ▶ A reporter for the *Madison* (Wisconsin) *Capital-Times* is rebuffed by 99 out of 100 people he asks to sign a petition made up of quotations from the Declaration of Independence and Bill of Rights. Many call the petition subversive.

10 ▶ Armistice talks aimed at ending the Korean conflict begin at Kaesong.

18 ▶ A deal is struck between the United States and Spain by which Spain will get American military and economic aid in exchange for the right to put U.S. air and naval bases in Spain.

▶ 1951

AUGUST

03 ▶ A scandal rocks the United States Military Academy at West Point, New York, as authorities there dismiss ninety cadets, including most of the members of the football team, for cheating on examinations.

SEPTEMBER

08 ▶ A peace treaty between Japan and forty-nine nations is signed in San Francisco.

■■■■■■■■■■■■■■■■■■■■■■■■■■■■■■■■■■■■

1951 in ten words (& phrases)

☞ 1. *rock 'n' roll* (Leo Mintz, owner of a large record store, tells a disc jockey named Alan Freed that rhythm and blues songs are becoming more and more popular among white youngsters. Freed, of WJW, starts featuring this kind of music on his show and in an effort to "avoid the racial stigma of the old classification" chooses to call it rock 'n' roll.)

☞ 2. *phoney* (given new importance when uttered by Holden Caulfield in J. D. Salinger's *Catcher in the Rye,* a book that finds a large, young audience)

☞ 3. *jet ace* (James Jabara, a World War II flying ace, repeats the feat in Korea in a jet fighter.)

☞ 4. *World War III* (The situation in Korea—especially the entry of the Chinese into the fray—has people talking in terms of WWIII.)

☞ 5. *Search for Tomorrow* (a new television soap opera that has a long, long tomorrow)

☞ 6. *old soldiers never die, they just fade away* (refrain from an old barracks ballad, which General Douglas MacArthur uses to great effect in his farewell speech)

☞ 7. *chemise Lacoste* (words you must learn to say if you want a high-status tennis shirt with a tiny alligator on the breast)

8. *power steering* (installed in 10,000 new Chrysler Crown Imperials)

9. *Heartbreak Ridge* (Korean objective that falls to United Nations forces after thirty-seven days of combat)

10. *Stella!* (Marlon Brando stars in the movie version of *A Streetcar Named Desire* and every kid in the country is bellowing the name in brutish Brandoese.)

■■■■■■■■■■■■■■■■■■■■■■■■■■■■■■■■■

OCTOBER

03 ► The most exciting moment in baseball history takes place when Bobby Thompson hits a home run in the ninth inning of a playoff game, thereby giving the pennant to the New York Giants over the Brooklyn Dodgers. The Giants had forced the playoff after coming from 13½ games behind to tie the Dodgers.

NOVEMBER

05 ► The first section—fifty-one miles long—of the New Jersey turnpike opens.

24 ► President Truman officially declares that a state of war no longer exists between the United States and Germany.

DECEMBER

17 ► A delegation of blacks, led by Paul Robeson and William L. Patterson, presents a petition to the United Nations that charges the U.S. government with a policy of genocide against its citizens of color.

■■■■■■■■■■■■■■■■■■■■■■■■■■■■■■■■■

1. General Douglas MacArthur
2. Ava Gardner
3. Bobby Thompson

November 5, 1951:
The first section – fifty-one miles long – of the New Jersey turnpike opens.

People most likely to be on the cover in 1951

▶ 1951

☞ 4. Matthew B. Ridgway
☞ 5. GI Joe (*Time*'s Man of the Year)
☞ 6. Harry S Truman
☞ 7. Mario Lanza
☞ 8. Margaret Truman
☞ 9. Dwight D. Eisenhower
☞ 10. Estes Kefauver

■■■■■■■■■■■■■■■■■■■■■■■■■■■■■■

The year in which Ike is ▶
elected president on ▶
the promise that ▶
he will go to Korea ▶

1952

JANUARY

16 ▶ Soviet Russia orders all foreign diplomats in Moscow to limit their movements to within twenty-five miles of the city. Twenty-two cities in Russia and Siberia are declared out-of-bounds for all foreigners, including members of diplomatic missions.

▶ ***Also occurring today:*** *The Today Show* with Dave Garroway opens new territory for television.

26 ▶ Egyptian mobs in Cairo burn and destroy property belonging to American, British, and French citizens. The embassies of all three governments are stoned. (These "antiforeigner" riots are associated with native demands for Great Britain to withdraw from the Suez area.)

31 ▶ Angered over Senator Joseph R. McCarthy's repeated attacks on federal employees as well as his charges that Communists have infiltrated the government, President Truman denounces the Republican senator as pathological, untruthful, and a character assassin who apparently requires no information for his accusations.

FEBRUARY

06 ▶ George VI dies of lung cancer in London.

11 ▶ For the third time in two months, a major air disaster takes

January 16, 1952:
The Today Show with Dave
Garroway opens new
territory for television.

place in Elizabeth, New Jersey, resulting in the deaths of thirty-three persons. (The first accident took place on December 16, 1951, when an airliner crashed in the city, killing fifty-six persons. The second occurred on January 22, 1952, and resulted in twenty-nine deaths).

MARCH

02 ▶ The Supreme Court affirms the right of public school systems to fire teachers considered to be subversive.

08 ▶ China and the Soviet Union allege that the United States has employed germ warfare in Korea. The charges are later dropped by the United Nations when an offer to investigate the situation by the International Red Cross is rejected by the Soviets.

■■■■■■■■■■■■■■■■■■■■■■■■■■■■■■■■■■

☛ 1. Panty raids are staged at colleges across the country as college boys demand—and usually get—girls' undergarments. What does it all mean? Dr. Kinsey replies calmly, "All animals play around."

☛ 2. The Mohawk hairstyle leaves many boys with a band of hair from forehead to the back of the neck.

☛ 3. *American Bandstand* comes on the ABC network with a twenty-two-year old host who keeps the show going for the next twenty-five years.

☛ 4. The low-key cop show, *Dragnet,* is the hottest new show in a year of hot new TV shows (*Jackie Gleason, Omnibus, Mr. Peepers, My Friend Irma,* and *Ozzie and Harriet*).

☛ 5. The hottest-selling book of this year and the next is the revised standard version of the Bible.

☛ 6. Twelve million would-be artists go out and buy "paint by numbers" kits so they can work on a color-coded canvas.

☛ 7. The most publicized movie star of the year is Marilyn Monroe. She—along with a few top movies like *High Noon* and *The Greatest Show on Earth*—help lure Americans away from their TV sets and back to the movie theaters.

March 2, 1952:
The Supreme Court affirms the right of public school systems to fire teachers considered to be subversive.

Fads and Trends for 1952 ☛

☞ 8. The UFO phenomenon mushrooms, and reports of flying saucers seem to come in from every crossroad in the nation.

☞ 9. A cadaverous young man named Johnny Ray wails his way into the limelight with songs like "Cry" and "The Little White Cloud That Cried."

☞ 10. The nation is in the throes of an atomic infatuation, and the magazines and newspapers are filled with articles on atomic fuel for the house, atomic aircraft, and atomic cars that can go from coast to coast on a trace amount of radioactive fuel.

☞ 11. The first pocket-size transistor radios are introduced— they are Japanese.

☞ 12. *Mad* magazine makes its debut and, as if to give it an easy target, so does the *National Enquirer*.

■■■■■■■■■■■■■■■■■■■■■■■■■■■■■■■■■■■■

APRIL

08 ► President Truman seizes the steel industry to forestall a general strike.

MAY

02 ► The first regular jet passenger service is established by British Overseas Airways between London and Johannesburg.

22 ► Playwright Lillian Hellman defies the House Un-American Activities Committee by refusing to say whether or not she was "a Red" three or four years earlier because her answer could hurt innocent people.

May 2, 1952: The first regular jet passenger service is established by British Overseas Airways between London and Johannesburg.

JUNE

14 ► At Groton, Connecticut, the president lays the keel of the first nuclear submarine, the *Nautilus*.

1952
by the numbers ☞

■■■■■■■■■■■■■■■■■■■■■■■■■■■■■■■

☞ 1. During the month of August some 16,000 people escape from East to West Berlin.

☞ 2. During '52, 2,000 new, local television stations come into being.

☞ 3. Hot dogs are big—the average American eats forty-two this year.

☞ 4. The polio toll for the year—50,000 stricken, 3,300 dead, and many crippled.

☞ 5. A new cereal from Kellogg's, Sugar Frosted Flakes, contains 29 percent sugar.

☞ 6. By opening its 351st restaurant, Howard Johnson becomes the world's largest food chain.

☞ 7. At year's end the Office of Education estimates that the nation needs 325,000 more classrooms now—at a cost of $10.7 billion—and 600,000 in all by 1960.

☞ 8. College graduates are in short supply and can command as much as $4,500 a year on graduation.

☞ 9. At the time of his death, Joseph Stalin can be said to have 800 million people under his influence.

☞ 10. The nation collects a record $69.6 billion in income tax receipts.

■■■■■■■■■■■■■■■■■■■■■■■■■■■■■■■

JULY

03 ► King Farouk of Egypt is deposed in a military coup ending that nation's hereditary monarchy. His appetite for food and sex established in power continues in exile.

16 ► The president signs a GI bill of rights that gives the veterans returning from the Korean War the same kind of benefits that accrued to those who fought in World War II.

25 ► Puerto Rico becomes a self-governing U.S. commonwealth.

July 25, 1952:
Puerto Rico becomes a self-governing U.S. commonwealth.

▶ 1952

AUGUST

11 ▶ Prince Hussein of Jordan becomes king as his mentally ill father is declared unfit to rule.

SEPTEMBER

23 ▶ With his political career in jeopardy because of a secret campaign slush fund, Senator Richard M. Nixon addresses the nation on television, insisting he never benefited personally from the fund and is guilty only of accepting a pet dog, Checkers, which he will not give back. A million letters and telegrams are sent in support of the vice president. For the rest of Nixon's political career the Checkers speech stands out as a moment of triumph.

■■■■■■■■■■■■■■■■■■■■■■■■■■■■■■■■

☛ 1. *bathtub ring* (This suddenly becomes a matter for national attention as Procter & Gamble brings out a new product, Zest, that will get rid of it.)

☛ 2. *Reserpine* (the first successfully marketed prescription tranquilizer)

☛ 3. *Mau-Mau* (Kenyan radicals driving colonists from their land with terror; the term carries a certain terror of its own.)

☛ 4. *DNA* (the stuff of genetics)

☛ 5. *invisible man* (The title of Ralph Ellison's novel of black life in America becomes a telling metaphor for the position of most blacks in white society.)

☛ 6. *no-cal* (first applied to ginger ale—Kirsch's No-Cal Ginger Ale—with no sugar and no salt)

☛ 7. *megaton* (We needed a name for the equivalent of 1 million tons of TNT.)

☛ 8. *megabuck* (We also needed a name for a million dollars. Both this term and the aforementioned *megaton* come from the Atomic Energy Commission.)

☛ 9. *buyer's market* (For the first time since 1939 the sellers

1952 in ten words (& phrases)

▶ 1952

October 20, 1952:
The Mau-Mau insurrection against Kenya's white settlers begins, and London immediately sends troops.

November 1, 1952:
The thermonuclear era arrives. The hydrogen or H-bomb is exploded by the Atomic Energy Commission at Eniwetok in the South Pacific.

don't control the supply of consumer goods, and this term comes back into play.)

☛ 10. *open-heart surgery* (a term that comes along with the first such operation)

■ ■

OCTOBER

03 ▶ Great Britain successfully detonates an atomic bomb.

20 ▶ The Mau-Mau insurrection against Kenya's white settlers begins and London immediately sends troops.

24 ▶ Presidential candidate General Dwight D. Eisenhower promises that if elected he will immediately go to Korea to seek an early end to the war there.

NOVEMBER

01 ▶ The thermonuclear era arrives. The hydrogen or H-bomb is exploded by the Atomic Energy Commission at Eniwetok in the South Pacific. It is the first full-scale thermonuclear explosion in history. Years later William Greider would write in the *Washington Post* that "it raised a permanent cloud which floats over all the globe together. Is the mother's milk in Lapland conditioned in some way by experiments in the Nevada desert?"

04 ▶ Dwight D. Eisenhower is elected president; Richard M. Nixon is elected vice president.

29 ▶ The president-elect flies to Korea to view the situation there firsthand. His three-day tour is kept secret until after he is out of the area. The popular move fulfills his promise to visit the war zone after he is elected to begin the search for peace.

▶ 1952

DECEMBER

02 ▶ The first known nuclear power accident occurs. An employee at an experimental nuclear power reactor at Chalk River, Canada, mistakenly lifts four of the system's twelve rods out of the fuel core, igniting a chain reaction that melts part of the uranium.

15 ▶ Christine Jorgenson returns from Denmark where she had been the subject of the first publicly announced sex-change operation in history.

30 ▶ The Tuskegee Institute reports that 1952 was the first year in seventy-one years that there were no lynchings in the United States.

■ ■

☛ 1. I LIKE IKE
☛ 2. MADLY FOR ADLAI
☛ 3. THE MAN OF THE HOUR—EISENHOWER
☛ 4. DEM-IKE-CRATS FOR EISENHOWER

■ ■

☛ 1. Adlai Stevenson
☛ 2. Eleanor Roosevelt
☛ 3. Bob Mathias
☛ 4. Rocky Marciano
☛ 5. Grace Kelly
☛ 6. Christine Jorgenson
☛ 7. Richard M. Nixon
☛ 8. Lucille Ball
☛ 9. Captain Curt Carlsen
☛ 10. King Farouk

■ ■

December 2, 1952:
The first known nuclear power accident occurs.

☛ 1952 in buttons & bumper stickers

☛ People most likely to be on the cover in 1952

The year in which the Korean ▶
armistice is signed ▶
and the Soviets lose Stalin ▶
and gain the H-bomb ▶

1953

JANUARY

03 ▶ Playwright George S. Kaufman, the center of a national controversy for the past ten days, is reinstated as a panel member of the television program, *This Is Show Business*. Mr. Kaufman was dropped from the show shortly before Christmas when he criticized the excessive playing and singing of the carol "Silent Night" over radio and television programs.

07 ▶ In his state-of-the-union address to Congress, President Truman announces that the United States has developed a hydrogen bomb. Says the president, "From now on, man moves into a new era of destructive power, capable of creating explosions of a new order of magnitude, dwarfing the mushroom clouds of Hiroshima and Nagasaki."

15 ▶ Many senators predict that the Senate will refuse to confirm Charles Erwin Wilson as President-elect Eisenhower's secretary of defense, since Wilson is unwilling to sell $2.5 million worth of General Motors' stock. When he finally agrees to dispose of the shares, his name is submitted to the Senate on January 22 and confirmed January 26.

20 ▶ For the first time in twenty years the nation inaugurates a Republican president, as General Dwight D. Eisenhower takes the oath of office as the thirty-fourth president of the United States.

January 20, 1953:
For the first time in twenty years the nation inaugurates a Republican president.

▶ 67

_____
_____
_____
_____
_____
_____

> *March 3, 1953:*
> The first crash of a commercial jet takes place.

_____
_____
_____
_____
_____
_____
_____
_____
_____
_____
_____
_____
_____
_____
_____
_____
_____
_____

FEBRUARY

12 ► Soviet Russia breaks off diplomatic relations with Israel after terrorists bomb the Russian legation in Tel Aviv.

MARCH

03 ► The first crash of a commercial jet takes place.

05 ► Premier Joseph Stalin of Russia, age seventy-three, dies in his apartment in the Kremlin in Moscow after being stricken with a cerebral hemorrhage on March 1. The body of the dictator is interred beside Lenin's in the Lenin mausoleum of Red Square on March 9 after the most spectacular funeral in Soviet history.

17 ► The last price controls set up during World War II in the United States are discarded when the Office of Price Stabilization ends controls on steel, machine tools, sulphur, metal cans, and scarce metal alloys.

18 ► The Boston Braves baseball club moves to Milwaukee where they will be known as the Milwaukee Braves. It is the first shift of a baseball franchise in fifty years and serves as a harbinger of other moves to come. On September 29 of this year the American League approves the transfer of the St. Louis Browns to Baltimore, where they will be known as the Orioles, and on November 8 the league allows the Philadelphia Athletics to move to Kansas City.

26 ► Dr. Jonas Salk announces the discovery and initial testing of a new vaccine that gives lasting protection against poliomyelitis. Within the year, Salk begins mass inoculations with his newly developed polio vaccine. The epidemic peaked in the United States from 1942 to 1953, forcing mass closings of swimming pools and movie theaters—wherever children congregated in large numbers. In 1950 there were more than 33,000 U.S. cases.

► 1953

■■■■■■■■■■■■■■■■■■■■■■■■■■■

☞ 1. Sales of *Scrabble*, a word game introduced in 1952, skyrocket, and it is on its way to becoming one of the best-selling board games of all time.

☞ 2. Bermuda shorts stroll into fashion; some advocate them for men to wear to work.

☞ 3. Low-cost aerosol cans become an element of workaday life and are used to propel everything from dessert toppings to oil-based paint.

☞ 4. Ian Fleming publishes the first of thirteen James Bond novels, *Casino Royale*. Agent 007 is airborne.

☞ 5. *Bwana Devil*, the first feature-length 3-D film, is released.

☞ 6. Alfred Charles Kinsey publishes the academic but no less titillating work *Sexual Behavior in the Human Female*.

☞ 7. Cinemascope, an immense wide-screen process for making and showing movies, comes on wide and bold. The first such movie is *The Robe*.

☞ 8. Fear of things with a red or pink tinge becomes an increasing reality of American life. The State Department, for instance, removes hundreds of books from its overseas libraries because their authors are suspect.

☞ 9. Americans fall in love with a fiberglass and plastic sports car known as the Corvette.

☞ 10. A few new items are added to the male fashion wardrobe—the Homberg hat (the kind Ike wore for his inauguration instead of the standard tall silk hat), loafers for the feet, and suits with two pairs of trousers.

■■■■■■■■■■■■■■■■■■■■■■■■■■■■■■■■

APRIL

01 ► Congress creates the omnibus Department of Health, Education, and Welfare.

03 ► The first issue of *TV Guide* is published. It is an immediate success.

☞ Fads and Trends for 1953

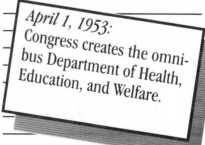

April 1, 1953: Congress creates the omnibus Department of Health, Education, and Welfare.

04 ► The first chapter of the scholastic fraternity Phi Beta Kappa to be established in a black college is activated at Fisk University, Nashville, Tennessee.

07 ► Dag Hammarskjöld of Sweden is elected secretary-general of the United Nations for a five-year term beginning April 10. (He succeeds Trygve Lie, the first secretary-general of the United Nations.)

11 ► Oveta Culp Hobby is sworn in as the nation's first secretary of the Department of Health, Education, and Welfare. The department achieves Cabinet status on this date. Hobby is the second woman in history to become a member of a president's Cabinet. The first was Frances Perkins, named as secretary of labor in 1933 by President Franklin D. Roosevelt.

MAY

22 ► President Eisenhower signs a bill surrendering federal ownership of $80 billion of offshore oil and gas reserves to the oil corporations. The Supreme Court had earlier ruled that this oil is the property of the whole nation. A former U.S. solicitor general calls the episode "the largest wholesale looting of national assets in history."

29 ► Edmund P. Hillary, thirty-four, a New Zealand beekeeper, and Tensing Norkay, forty-two, a tribesman of Nepal, are the first persons in history to reach the top of Mount Everest, the world's highest mountain, more than 29,000 feet above sea level.

JUNE

02 ► Queen Elizabeth II, twenty-seven years old, is crowned in Westminster Abbey, London, by the archbishop of Canterbury. More than a million people from all over the world jam the streets of the city to catch a glimpse of the queen in the coronation procession.

08 ► Reversing a previous ruling of the United States Court of Appeals on January 22, the United States Supreme Court

May 29, 1953:
Edmund P. Hillary, thirty-four, a New Zealand beekeeper, and Tensing Norkay, forty-two, a tribesman of Nepal, are the first persons in history to reach the top of Mount Everest, the world's highest mountain.

rules, eight to zero, that restaurants in the District of Columbia may not legally refuse to serve "well-behaved and respectable" black patrons.

09 ▶ Convicted spies Julius and Ethel Rosenberg become the only American civilians ever to be executed for espionage. They die at Sing Sing Prison in Ossining, New York.

17 ▶ East Berliners momentarily revolt but are quickly stopped by Soviet forces.

18 ▶ An air force C-124 transport crashes near Tokyo. Altogether 129 crew and troops are killed, making it the first aircraft accident to claim more than 100 victims.

26 ▶ Fidel Castro leads an attack on the Moncada barracks in Cuba in an attempt to overthrow the Batista dictatorship. Castro is jailed.

27 ▶ Following the longest truce negotiations in the history of warfare (2 years, 17 days, and some 575 meetings between the belligerents), the war in Korea is over. An armistice is signed at Panmunjom.

■ ■

☞ 1. The Tuskegee Institute reports that 1953 is the second year in a row in which there have been no lynchings.

☞ 2. The city of Los Angeles announces that it has surpassed Philadelphia as the nation's third-largest city. L.A. now has a population of 2,104,663 while Philly stands at 2,071,605.

☞ 3. In the last two years the nation's farm population has dwindled by 239,000. The farm population of the United States is now 24,819,000.

☞ 4. The U.S. obligates itself to $226 million in aid to Spain in return for the right to keep existing military bases in the country.

☞ 5. Television sets now are in 60 percent of all American households.

☞ 6. As unemployment falls to its lowest level since World War II, 63.4 million Americans have jobs.

☞ 7. At the end of its first year, the circulation of *TV Guide* is a stunning 1.5 million.

June 9, 1953: Convicted spies Julius and Ethel Rosenberg become the only American civilians ever to be executed for espionage.

1953 by the numbers

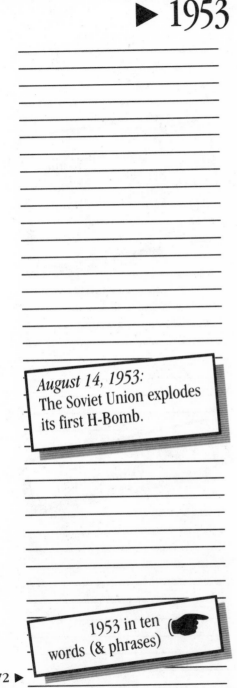

August 14, 1953:
The Soviet Union explodes its first H-Bomb.

1953 in ten words (& phrases)

☞ 8. Kellogg's Sugar Smacks comes on the market with sugar as its prime ingredient—56 percent to be exact.

☞ 9. There are now 15,000 pizzerias in America and over 100,000 stores where the prefab version can be bought from the refrigerator case.

☞ 10. The new magazine *Playboy* is started with $10,000 and a nude photo of Marilyn Monroe.

■■■■■■■■■■■■■■■■■■■■■■■■■■■■■■■■■

JULY

10 ► The first deputy premier of the Soviet Union, Lavrenti Beria, is discharged as an "enemy of the people," signaling a major post-Stalin purge in the Soviet Union. He is executed on December 23.

AUGUST

01 ► The United States Information Agency (USIA) is established to coordinate U.S. propaganda overseas.

14 ► The Soviet Union explodes its first H-Bomb.

SEPTEMBER

02 ► U.S. Waves are assigned to ships for the first time. They will sail with the Military Sea Transportation Service.

30 ► President Dwight D. Eisenhower names Governor Earl Warren of California chief justice of the United States Supreme Court.

► *Also on this day:* The U.S. promises an additional $385 million to the French military effort in Indochina.

■■■■■■■■■■■■■■■■■■■■■■■■■■■■■■■■■

☞ 1. *DMZ* (for demilitarized zone, as one is established between North and South Korea)

2. *House of Wax* (there is now a name for the 3-D schlock movie.)

3. *dynasty* (term that is routinely applied to the New York Yankees before and after they win their fifth World Series in a row)

4. *momism* (American malady attacked in Philip Wylie's *Generation of Vipers*)

5. *IBM 701* (Big Blue's first computer)

6. *Irish coffee* (a term and a drink that originate at San Francisco's Buena Vista Cafe)

7. *Scientology* (church founded by writer L. Ron Hubbard in Washington, D.C.)

8. *abominable snowman* (in the news as a British team travels to the Himalayas to look for it)

9. *Piltdown man* (shown to be a hoax. The bones were "planted" at the site in 1908.)

10. *double helix* (description of the structure of DNA that is first described in 1953)

OCTOBER

22 ▶ Representatives of France and the Indochinese state of Laos sign a treaty in Paris making Laos "fully independent and sovereign."

NOVEMBER

01 ▶ The first issue of *Playboy* is published in Chicago by Hugh Hefner, age twenty-seven, who turns it into what he later deems "an empire."

09 ▶ Confirming a decision handed down in 1922, the Supreme Court rules that big-league baseball does not come "within the scope of the Federal anti-trust laws." It declares that it is a sport rather than a business or trade monopoly.

November 1, 1953:
The first issue of *Playboy* is published in Chicago by Hugh Hefner, age twenty-seven, who turns it into what he later deems "an empire."

► 1953

People most likely to be on the cover in 1953

1. Mamie Eisenhower
2. Roy Campanella
3. Queen Elizabeth II
4. Edmund Hillary
5. Dag Hammarskjöld
6. Chief Justice Earl Warren
7. Mickey Mantle
8. Audrey Hepburn
9. Grandma Moses
10. Charles E. Wilson

The year in which the Army- ▶
McCarthy hearings dominate ▶
the news and the H-bomb ▶
generates the jitters ▶

1954

JANUARY

07 ▶ In his state-of-the-union message, President Eisenhower asks that persons convicted of conspiracy against the government lose their citizenship.

21 ▶ The first atomic-powered submarine, the *Nautilus,* is launched at Groton, Connecticut. It is christened by the first lady.

26 ▶ Citizens of Norwalk, Connecticut, engage in a bitter local controversy when they discover that the Norwalk post of the Veterans of Foreign Wars has formed a secret committee to turn over to the Federal Bureau of Investigation the names of all local residents suspected of Communist sympathies.

28 ▶ Twenty-one American, one British, and 325 South Korean prisoners of the Korean War are returned to North Korea because they have chosen to live in a Communist state. The case of the American turncoats has an immediate and disturbing effect on the United States. (There was little consolation in the fact that 14,000 Chinese POWs refused repatriation.)

FEBRUARY

03 ▶ In India, 340 pilgrims are killed in a stampede as they try to bathe in the Ganges River.

January 21, 1954:
The first atomic-powered submarine, the *Nautilus,* is launched at Groton, Connecticut.

▶ 75

▶ 1954

February 4, 1954:
Senator Joseph R. McCarthy begins a schedule of "Lincoln Week" speech-making across the country, his theme being the Democratic Party's "twenty years of treason."

March 1, 1954:
Five congressmen are shot on the floor of the House of Representatives by Puerto Rican nationalists seeking the independence of their country.

04 ▶ Senator Joseph R. McCarthy (R., Wis.) begins a schedule of "Lincoln Week" speech making across the country, his theme being the Democratic Party's "twenty years of treason."

23 ▶ The first mass inoculation against polio is given to students in Pittsburgh.

24 ▶ Secretary of the Army Robert T. Stevens yields to Senator Joseph R. McCarthy's demand and agrees to permit army officers to testify in the investigation of Dr. Irving Peress, a former member of the Army Dental Corps and currently under fire by McCarthy as an alleged subversive.

MARCH

01 ▶ Five congressmen are shot on the floor of the House of Representatives by Puerto Rican nationalists seeking the independence of their country.

▶ *Also on this day:* The United States sets off its second H-bomb in the Marshall Islands. It turns out to be much more violent and powerful than expected by the scientists who planned the test. This monster is later determined to be 600 to 700 times as powerful as the bomb that destroyed Hiroshima.

18 ▶ RKO Pictures Corporation stockholders approve the sale of the company to Howard Hughes. After Hughes writes out a check for $23,489,478, he becomes the first individual ever to be sole owner of a major motion picture company.

20 ▶ After editorial writers for the *Washington Post and Times Herald* advocate the construction of a highway along the route of the old Chesapeake & Ohio Canal from Cumberland, Maryland, to Washington, D.C., Associate Justice William O. Douglas of the United States Supreme Court leads a 189-mile hike along the route to prove that the highway would spoil the scenic beauty of the area. (Douglas and

eight of the fifty-five persons who start out on the hike complete it on March 27, amid general agreement that the road should be built elsewhere.)

■ ■

☞ 1. *I Love Lucy* starring Lucille Ball as a daffy but resourceful housewife is the most popular TV show in the nation.

☞ 2. TV dinners are introduced to a market that gobbles them up.

☞ 3. The Newport Jazz Festival has its first season.

☞ 4. *Lord of the Flies* and *Lord of the Rings* are published and two postwar classics are born.

☞ 5. All twenty-six comic book publishers agree to a code banning vulgar and obscene material. The great age of comic horror is brought to an abrupt halt. Boo!

☞ 6. The popularity of television is now such that large numbers of radio stations switch from drama and the spoken word to musical programming. This move helps set the stage for rock 'n' roll's quick takeover of pop music in the months ahead.

☞ 7. The Army-McCarthy hearings bring a new form of daytime drama to the nation.

☞ 8. Largely because of stunning advances in H-bomb technology the nation and the world develop, in the words of *The World Book Annual,* "as bad a case of bomb jitters as the world has ever known." The chairman of the Atomic Energy Commission, Lewis L. Strauss, declares that one H-bomb can take out a city. When asked what size city he was talking about, he replies, "Any city."

☞ 9. The Cuban mambo is a boon to the ballrooms and dance studios of America. Songs like *Papa Loves Mambo, They Were Doing the Mambo,* and *The St. Louis Blues Mambo* are hits.

☞ 10. During the eighth inning of the first game of the World Series, Willie Mays makes a catch on the dead run of a 450-foot blast off the bat of Vic Wertz that is so remarkable that

Fads and Trends for 1954

April 6, 1954:
Senator Joseph R. McCarthy charges in a nationwide telecast that the well-known news commentator and analyst Edward R. Murrow "engaged in propaganda for Communist causes" as far back as twenty years ago."

April 6, 1954:
Rock'n'roll's first true smash hit, Bill Haley's *Shake, Rattle and Roll*, is recorded today on the Decca label.

thirty-five years later it will still be known as *the catch.*
☞ 11. The cha-cha arrives from Cuba.

APRIL

05 ► The Supreme Court rules that radio and television quiz and giveaway shows are legal and do not violate antilottery and gambling laws.

06 ► Senator Joseph R. McCarthy (R., Wis.) charges in a nationwide telecast that the well-known news commentator and analyst Edward R. Murrow "engaged in propaganda for Communist causes" as far back as twenty years ago. (The McCarthy speech answers an attack made by Murrow on March 9, at which time he accused the senator of stepping over "the line between investigating and persecuting.")

08 ► President Eisenhower expounds on the domino theory, which holds that when one country falls to Communism, it causes others to topple.

► *Also today:* Rock 'n' roll's first true smash hit, Bill Haley's *Shake, Rattle and Roll,* is recorded today on the Decca label.

13 ► Dr. J. Robert Oppenheimer, world-famous scientist and often referred to as the "father of the atomic bomb," is suspended by the Atomic Energy Commission as a possible security risk. On June 1 he is barred from future employment as a government consultant.

22 ► The Army-McCarthy hearings are first carried on live television. By the end of their five-week run, Joseph McCarthy, the red-baiting Republican senator from Wisconsin, is publicly disgraced.

MAY

06 ► Roger Bannister breaks the four-minute mile with a run of 3 minutes and 59.4 seconds.

▶ 1954

07 ▶ The forces of Ho Chi Minh defeat the French at Dienbien-phu, ending French power in Indochina and setting up the division of the nation into North and South Vietnam. Some 16,000 men are killed, wounded, or captured during the siege, which began eight weeks earlier.

17 ▶ The Supreme Court rules unanimously in *Brown v. Board of Education of Topeka* that segregated education is illegal and that systems must move at "all deliberate speed" to desegregate schools.

JUNE

02 ▶ The District of Columbia moves to end segregation in its schools.

21 ▶ The American Cancer Society reports that "heavy" ciga-rette smokers, age fifty to seventy, have a death rate up to 75 percent higher than nonsmokers.

▶ *Also occurring today:* In Geneva a conference ends on the resolution of the Indochina War. The central decision is the division of Vietnam into two zones separated along the seventeenth parallel. Laos and Cambodia are made in-dependent.

29 ▶ The Atomic Energy Commission votes against reinstating Dr. J. Robert Oppenheimer's access to classified informa-tion.

■■■■■■■■■■■■■■■■■■■■■■■■■■■■■■■

☛ 1. The U.S. birthrate is at about 4 million a year and remains at that rate for the next ten years.

☛ 2. Due to a rise in prices from Brazil, the cost of a cup of coffee in most restaurants jumps from a dime to fifteen cents. In grocery stores the cost of a pound of coffee is as high as $1.35.

☛ 3. Chain supermarkets now account for two-fifths of the food sold at the retail level.

☛ 4. General Motors turns out its 50 millionth automobile on November 23.

May 6, 1954:
Roger Bannister breaks the four-minute mile with a run of 3 minutes and 59.4 seconds.

June 21, 1954:
The American Cancer Society reports that "heavy" cigarette smokers, age fifty to seventy, have a death rate up to 75 percent higher than nonsmokers.

1954
by the numbers

5. On August 3 the largest-known divorce settlement in history is awarded to Mrs. Barbara (Bobo) Rockefeller as her marriage to Winthrop Rockefeller is terminated. Mrs. Rockefeller is awarded a $5.5 million settlement—about $2 million short of the sum the United States paid Russia for the purchase of Alaska.

6. One hundred fifty-four Americans make $1 million or more a year, down from 513 at the time of the 1929 stock market crash.

7. A pound of round steak is edging toward a dollar a pound—ninety-two cents in an October survey.

8. Lake Erie produces 75 million pounds of fish sold commercially. Pollution is still relatively light.

9. Northland, the world's largest shopping center, opens in Detroit with 100 stores. It cost $30 million to build.

10. There are 94 million telephones in the world, of which 52 million are in the United States.

JULY

06 ▶ Elvis Presley, a self-taught nineteen-year-old singer, makes his first record, a combination of country music on one side and rhythm and blues on the other that portends a revolution in popular music.

20 ▶ Geneva accords affirm the division of Vietnam into north and south, with capitals in Hanoi and Saigon.

27 ▶ Great Britain and Egypt agree on terms ending the seventy-two-year British occupation of the Suez Canal Zone.

AUGUST

02 ▶ The United States Senate votes, seventy-five to twelve, to form a select committee to weigh a motion of censure against Senator Joseph R. McCarthy (R., Wis.).

10 ▶ Work begins on the St. Lawrence Seaway as a joint U.S.-

July 6, 1954:
Elvis Presley, a self-taught nineteen-year-old singer, makes his first record, a combination of country music on one side and rhythm and blues on the other that portends a revolution in popular music.

▶ 1954

Canadian effort. Envisioned for more than a century, it will provide the means by which ocean-going vessels will be able to service the heart of North America by way of the Great Lakes.

11 ▶ A formal announcement ends the seven-year war in Indochina between France and forces of the Communist Viet Minh.

12 ▶ The first issue of *Sports Illustrated* is published. Circulation reaches 600,000 by the end of the year, but it loses $26 million before turning its first profit in 1964.

16 ▶ Eisenhower signs a national tax code, which grants tax relief to many Americans and moves the individual income tax deadline from March 15 to April 15.

24 ▶ President Eisenhower signs the Communist Control Act of 1954, outlawing the Communist Party in the United States.

SEPTEMBER

06 ▶ Groundbreaking is held in Shippingport, Pennsylvania, for the world's first nuclear power plant.

23 ▶ Aikichi Kuboyama, a Japanese fisherman, dies today, becoming the world's first H-bomb fatality. He was dusted with radioactive debris during the explosion of an H-bomb by the U.S. on March 1.

27 ▶ *The Tonight Show* makes its NBC network debut with Steve Allen as host.

30 ▶ A festive ceremony is held in Asbestos, Quebec, to dedicate the world's largest asbestos mill, which is operated by the Johns-Manville Company.

■ ■

☞ 1. *the new look* (Ike's term for a smaller but better-equipped armed forces)

☞ 2. *thermonuclear* (Americans learned that this adjective describes H-bomb war as opposed to A-bomb war, which is atomic.)

August 24, 1954: Eisenhower signs the Communist Control Act of 1954, outlawing the Communist Party in the United States.

September 27, 1954: The Tonight Show makes its NBC network debut with Steve Allen as host.

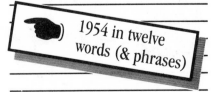
☞ 1954 in twelve words (& phrases)

3. *fallout* (The term is given currency as trace amounts of radioactive strontium 90 show up in food.)

4. *strontium 90* (a new and unwanted food additive)

5. *desegregate* (This idea is novel enough to make it to *The World Book Annual* list of new words and phrases for 1954.)

6. *rumble* (teenage gang talk for a fight)

7. *antifluoridationist* (part of a growing legion of people who oppose the adding of sodium fluoride to water supplies as a means of controlling tooth decay)

8. *black power* (a term introduced as the title of a report on Africa's Gold Coast by expatriate black writer Richard Wright)

9. *TV dinner* (The term, the concept, and the dinner itself—turkey with trimmings—comes onto the marketplace with a suggested retail price of ninety-nine cents. This ushers in the day of, ta-da—the...)

10. *TV table* (on which to place the aforementioned dinner)

11. *Miltown* (new tranquilizer. Another one is...)

12. *Equanil*

■■■■■■■■■■■■■■■■■■■■■■■■■■■■■■■■■

November 12, l954: Ellis Island closes as a processing center for immigrants. In its sixty-two years in operation it has processed 20 million immigrants.

OCTOBER

07 ▶ Marian Anderson becomes the first black singer hired by the Metropolitan Opera Company in New York.

23 ▶ West Germany is granted sovereignty and admitted to NATO.

24 ▶ President Eisenhower advises Premier Diem of South Vietnam that the United States will provide assistance directly to that country rather than channeling it through France.

27 ▶ *Disneyland* (later to become *The Wonderful World of Disney*) premieres on TV as a means of promoting the new Disneyland amusement park in Anaheim, California, scheduled to open in the summer of 1955.

31 ▶ A revolt against the French breaks out in Algeria.

NOVEMBER

12 ► Ellis Island closes as a processing center for immigrants. In its sixty-two years in operation it has processed 20 million immigrants.

24 ► An inmate named William W. Remington is beaten to death by three other inmates at the Lewisburg Federal Penitentiary in Pennsylvania. The man was a former government economist serving a three-year sentence for having denied that he was once a Communist.

DECEMBER

02 ► The United States Senate condemns—but does not censure—Senator Joseph McCarthy. The short-lived but what will be long-remembered McCarthy era is over.

20 ► One of the largest talent contracts ever executed by an entertainer is drawn up between television comedian Jackie Gleason and the Buick Motor Company. Under the terms of the contract, Gleason agrees to produce and star in seventy-eight half-hour television programs for Buick during the next two years. His fee: $6,142,500.

24 ► Rhythm and blues singer Johnny Ace accidentally kills himself during a Christmas Eve Russian roulette game. His record *Pledging My Love* later becomes a hit. This strange death helps put the world on notice that rock 'n' roll has a somewhat forbidden element lacking in mainstream popular music.

1. Gina Lollobrigida
2. Joe DiMaggio and Marilyn Monroe
3. Willie Mays
4. Gamal Abdel Nassar
5. Dr. Jonas Salk
6. Senator Joseph McCarthy

December 24, 1954: Rhythm and blues singer Johnny Ace accidentally kills himself during a Christmas Eve Russian roulette game.

People most likely to be on the cover in 1954

▶ 1954

☞ 7. Jack Webb
☞ 8. Billy Graham
☞ 9. Roger Bannister
☞ 10. Edward R. Murrow

■ ■

The year in which the ▶
president has a heart attack ▶
and the Salk polio vaccine ▶
tests successfully ▶

1955

JANUARY

03 ▶ In retaliation for long-standing Soviet restrictions, the United States closes parts of thirty-nine states to Soviet citizens for reasons of security.

07 ▶ Marian Anderson, playing Ulrica in Verdi's *A Masked Ball,* becomes the first black singer to perform at the Metropolitan Opera in New York.

10 ▶ Egypt announces that oil has been discovered on the Sinai Peninsula.

19 ▶ President Eisenhower holds the first presidential TV news conference. It is also the first to which motion picture cameras are allowed. Aides to the president say that newsreel and TV cameras will be allowed into future conferences on the same basis as other accredited reporters.

28 ▶ After a bitter debate, the Senate follows the lead of the House and passes a resolution permitting President Eisenhower to use armed forces abroad to defend Formosa and the Pescadores Islands and "related positions and territories" against possible attacks by the Chinese Communists.

FEBRUARY

08 ▶ In a shift in power in the Kremlin, Nikita S. Khrushchev emerges as the top leader in the USSR.

January 19, 1955: President Eisenhower holds the first presidential TV news conference.

▶ 85

Fads and Trends for 1955 ☞

MARCH

23 ► President Eisenhower pledges that the nation will not use atomic weapons in a police action.

■■■■■■■■■■■■■■■■■■■■■■■■■■■■■■■

☞ 1. The Ford Thunderbird is an immediate hit as a two-seat sports car.

☞ 2. Easy payment schemes lure many into debt, and installment buying becomes a major fact of life for most families.

☞ 3. Three one-hour _Disneyland_ installments on Davy Crockett capture the imagination of America's kids. There is a run on coonskin caps that imperils the raccoon population.

☞ 4. Big-buck TV quiz shows debut with the _$64,000 Question._

☞ 5. The modern TV western is born with _The Life and Times of Wyatt Earp_ and _Gunsmoke._ Because their appeal goes beyond children, they are called adult westerns.

☞ 6. The color pink invades men's fashion and is often paired with a dark gray called charcoal.

☞ 7. The merengue is the dance craze of '55.

☞ 8. Rock 'n' roll has its first big year and Chuck Berry puts the world on its ear with real rock 'n' roll hits like _Maybellene, Roll Over Beethoven,_ and _Rock 'n' Roll Music._

☞ 9. Meanwhile, Lawrence Welk begins a musical television show that attests to the popularity of cornball music.

☞ 10. New periodicals come into being—_National Review_ and _The Village Voice_ for starters—that attract readers with special interests as the big weekly magazines die off.

■■■■■■■■■■■■■■■■■■■■■■■■■■■■■■■

APRIL

05 ► Prime Minister Winston Churchill, eighty-one years old, goes to Buckingham Palace and again submits his resignation to Queen Elizabeth II, after serving as prime minister

eight years, seven months, twenty-five days. He offers the queen as his recommendation for a successor the name of Sir Anthony Eden.

12 ▶ A survey is released showing the Salk vaccine to be successful; 1.8 million were given the vaccine in 1954 and it was shown to be 80 to 90 percent effective.

18 ▶ Delegates of twenty-nine nations meet in Bandung, Indonesia to open the Asian-African Conference. One of the first pieces of business is a resolution rejecting all forms of colonialism.

MAY

05 ▶ West Germany is given its independence by France, Great Britain, and the United States.

12 ▶ The face of New York City is changing as the last riders—they call themselves "mourners"—ride the Third Avenue Elevated Railway in preparation for its demolition.

14 ▶ In Warsaw a treaty—hereafter the Warsaw Pact—calling for the mutual defense of Albania, Bulgaria, Czechoslovakia, Hungary, Poland, Rumania, East Germany, and the Soviet Union is signed.

23 ▶ The Presbyterian General Assembly accepts women ministers, and in October the Reverend Margaret Towner is ordained.

May 23, 1955:
The Presbyterian General Assembly accepts women ministers, and in October the Reverend Margaret Towner is ordained.

JUNE

06 ▶ Pope Pius XII excommunicates Argentine President Juan Domingo Perón. The ban is lifted eight years later.

▶ ***Also on this date:*** Organized labor's first guaranteed annual wage agreement is reached by the United Automobile Workers with Ford. The contract calls for a $55 million unemployment benefit fund for laid-off workers.

12 ▶ A race car hurtles into the crowd at Le Mans, France, and eighty-two spectators are killed.

15 ▶ The United States stages its first nationwide civil defense

1955
by the numbers ☞

exercise. Called *Operation Alert,* it assumes sixty cities are under nuclear attack.

29 ► Pan American Airlines makes its fifty thousandth Atlantic crossing since pioneering the route in 1939.

■■■■■■■■■■■■■■■■■■■■■■■■■■■■■■■■■■

☞ 1. At a dime a throw, it is now estimated that a billion comic books are sold a year in the United States.

☞ 2. For the first time ever, U.S. employment reaches 64 million.

☞ 3. The salaries of senators and members of the House of Representatives rise from $15,000 to $22,500. Supreme Court justices get a boost from $25,000 to $35,000.

☞ 4. General Motors becomes the first company—at any time, at any place, anywhere—to make $1 billion in a single year.

☞ 5. Automobile deaths over the Christmas weekend total 609—a record.

☞ 6. An inventory published by the Department of Defense reveals that the military wealth of the United States amounts to about $124 billion in property and equipment.

☞ 7. On May 27 the census clock at the Commerce Department in Washington tells us that there are now 165 million Americans. The clock tells us that a baby is born every eight seconds and a death occurs every 22 seconds.

☞ 8. The American automobile industry has its biggest year to date producing 9,188,000 cars, trucks, and buses—a million more than the previous record year of 1950. Cars alone account for 7,169,108 units, of which a mere 5,200 are imports.

☞ 9. Organized labor is 15 million strong.

☞ 10. The nation can now boast of 1,800 shopping centers and 30,000 motels.

■■■■■■■■■■■■■■■■■■■■■■■■■■■■■■■■■■

▶ 1955

JULY

11 ▶ The new U.S. Air Force Academy is dedicated at Lowry Air Base in Colorado.

▶ *Today is also the day on which:* President Eisenhower signs a bill into law that requires the inscription *In God We Trust* on all U.S. currency.

17 ▶ Arco, Idaho, a town of 1,350 people, becomes the first community in the world to receive all its light and power from atomic energy. The demonstration lasts for an hour. The source of the energy is an experimental plant twenty miles away.

18 ▶ The first modern summit conference is held in Geneva. No agreement comes out of it, but it sets an important precedent. Leaders of the United States, USSR, France, and Great Britain meet for this one.

▶ *This is also the day on which:* Disneyland, a vast theme park celebration of nostalgia and fantasy, opens in Anaheim, California.

29 ▶ President Eisenhower announces that the U.S. will launch an artificial earth-circling satellite into space in 1957 or 1958.

AUGUST

01 ▶ The Georgia Board of Education orders all teachers in the state holding membership in the National Association for the Advancement of Colored People to resign from that organization by September 15 or have their teaching licenses revoked for life.

04 ▶ After more than two and a half years spent as prisoners of Chinese Communists, eleven United States Air Force fliers are released and reach Hong Kong. (The airmen had been captured during the Korean War on January 12, 1953, and charged with espionage.)

12 ▶ The minimum wage jumps from $.75 to $1.00 an hour as the president signs the Minimum Wage Act.

July 17, 1955: Arco, Idaho, a town of 1,350 people, becomes the first community in the world to receive all its light and power from atomic energy.

July 29, 1955: President Eisenhower announces that the U. S. will launch an artificial earth-circling satellite into space in 1957 or 1958.

► 1955

August 28, 1955:
Emmett Louis Till is murdered in Money, Mississippi. He is black and is killed for speaking to a white woman.

17 ► A Code of Conduct for American Prisoners of War is approved by the president. It has been created to prevent collaboration with the enemy and brainwashing of POWs.

18 ► Floods from Hurricane Diane hit the northeastern United States, killing 200 people.

28 ► Emmett Louis Till is murdered in Money, Mississippi. He is black and is killed for speaking to a white woman.

SEPTEMBER

16 ► A soft, flexible glop called Play-Doh is brought on the market. It becomes a childhood staple, and by the time of its thirtieth anniversary in 1985 some 800 million cans have been sold.

19 ► President Juan Perón of Argentina is ousted from office following the army and navy revolts of the past three days. (Two days later Perón is permitted to seek asylum aboard a gunboat owned by the government of Paraguay.)

20 ► East Germany is granted sovereignty by the USSR.

24 ► President Eisenhower suffers a heart attack in his sleep while vacationing in Colorado.

26 ► As a result of the news of President Dwight D. Eisenhower's heart attack, the New York Stock Exchange suffers its worst price break since 1929. During the day—immediately dubbed Black Monday—7,720,000 shares are traded on the floor of the exchange. (By September 28, 58 percent of the loss has been recovered.)

30 ► James Dean is killed as his Porsche 550 Spyder crashes in an accident near Paso Robles, Texas.

■ ■

1. *why Johnny can't read* (The title of a book by Rudolph Flesch becomes a broader issue. Flesch says Johnny's problem stems from the fact that the schools are not teaching phonics.)

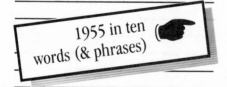

1955 in ten words (& phrases)

▶ 1955

2. *television special* (new name for what was first called a spectacular)

3. *bugging* (snooping with a hidden microphone or other electronic device)

4. *exurbanite* (term for those living beyond the established suburbs, from a book of the same title by A. C. Spectorsky)

5. *fantasyland* (A realm in the new Disneyland, it quickly becomes a term for any place where reality does not prevail.)

6. *play by ear* (old musical term now applied to any form of improvisation)

7. *M-I-C-K-E-Y M-O-U-S-E* (refrain from the march from the *Mickey Mouse Club*, which debuts in October)

8. *nymphet* (word that is given a new meaning and popularity because of the Vladimir Nabokov novel *Lolita*)

9. *Coke* (For the first time the Coca-Cola Company uses this term to describe its product—giving official recognition to the fact that this is what people have been calling it all along.)

10. *Dacron* (a new miracle fabric that is introduced this year)

■■■■■■■■■■■■■■■■■■■■■■■■■■■■■■■■

September 30, 1955:
James Dean is killed as his Porsche 550 Spyder crashes in an accident near Paso Robles, Texas.

OCTOBER

03 ▶ *Captain Kangaroo* and *The Mickey Mouse Club* premier on CBS and ABC, respectively.

23 ▶ In the first election ever to take place in South Vietnam, Indochina, the people oust Bao Dai as chief of state and replace him with Ngo Dinh Diem, who immediately declares that elections scheduled for July 1956 are cancelled. The election also establishes the Republic of South Vietnam.

> *October 24, 1955:*
> An eighteen-day siege of smog in Los Angeles ends when strong winds clear the air.

24 ▶ An eighteen-day siege of smog in Los Angeles ends when strong winds clear the air.

25 ▶ The air force releases the conclusion of its top secret Project Saucer, which is that many reports of flying saucers were illusions or explainable as misinterpretations of "conventional phenomena."

NOVEMBER

01 ▶ A United Air Lines plane explodes in midair after leaving Denver. Later John G. Graham is charged with putting the bomb in the plane in order to collect his mother's life insurance.

11 ▶ President Eisenhower is released from the hospital.

DECEMBER

01 ▶ Rosa Parks, a black seamstress, refuses to give up her seat on a Montgomery, Alabama, bus to a white man. A boycott is coordinated by a then-unknown Baptist minister named Martin Luther King, Jr.

05 ▶ The American Federation of Labor and the Congress of Industrial Organizations merge, with George Meany presiding as president.

12 ▶ The Ford Foundation announces a gift of a half billion dollars to the nation's private hospitals, colleges, and medical schools, the largest single philanthropic act in world history.

■ ■

☞ 1. Walter Reuther
☞ 2. Marshal Tito
☞ 3. Fess Parker (as Davy Crockett)
☞ 4. Walt Disney
☞ 5. James Dean
☞ 6. Herman Wouk

People most likely to be on the cover in 1955

▶ 1955

7. John Foster Dulles
8. Dag Hammarskjöld
9. Julie Harris
10. Marshal Nikolai A. Bulganin and Nikita S. Khrushchev

■■■■■■■■■■■■■■■■■■■■■■■■■■■■■

December 1, 1955:
Rosa Parks, a black seamstress, refuses to give up her seat on a Montgomery, Alabama, bus to a white man.

JANUARY

28 ▶ Elvis Presley makes his television debut with the Dorsey Brothers' CBS *Stage Show.*

FEBRUARY

01 ▶ Autherine Lucy, a twenty-six-year-old student, is admitted to the University of Alabama on orders issued by a federal court. She is the first black to be admitted to the university. Segregationists riot and throw eggs at Lucy.

24 ▶ At the twentieth congress of the Soviet Communist Party, Nikita Khrushchev denounces the methods of Joseph Stalin.

29 ▶ Ike announces that he will run for a second term.

MARCH

12 ▶ The Dow Jones Industrial Average reaches a milestone of 500.24 points.

▶ *Also today:* The Southern pledge is made as Southern members of both houses of Congress declare that they will use all means at their disposal to reverse the May 17, 1954, Supreme Court decision ordering school desegregation.

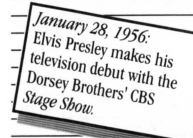

January 28, 1956: Elvis Presley makes his television debut with the Dorsey Brothers' CBS *Stage Show.*

March 12, 1956: The Dow Jones Industrial Average reaches a milestone of 500.24 points.

■ ■

☞ 1. Movies and movie stars start appearing on television in numbers for the first time as Hollywood's unwritten ban on television guest shots falls away.

☞ 2. Cars are highly styled, finned, and have loooooow rooflines. You can now buy a Chevy with something called fuel injection.

☞ 3. On the head: bouffant hair for the ladies and flat sports-car caps for the gents.

☞ 4. *My Fair Lady,* the Lerner and Lowe musical, captures Broadway. Its songs are everywhere and it emits a whiff of the Edwardian.

☞ 5. Elvis Aron Presley draws mobs and sells records with names like *Hound Dog, Heartbreak Hotel,* and *Love Me Tender.*

☞ 6. Harry Belafonte's *Calypso* is released, setting the album, the artist, and that form of music on several years of stardom.

☞ 7. Grace Metalious's lurid novel *Peyton Place,* about small-town sex and intrigue, is a hot best seller.

☞ 8. The scaled-down go-cart race vehicle hits the dirt tracks of America.

☞ 9. The beat period gives off its earliest beats with Allen Ginsberg's book of hip poems, *Howl.* Sample line: "I have seen the best minds of my generation destroyed by madness."

☞ 10. For the first time, the business of nuclear testing becomes a mainstream public issue.

■ ■

APRIL

08 ▶ Six Marine recruits die during a night training march off Parris Island, South Carolina.

13 ▶ The last eyewitness to the death of Abraham Lincoln dies in Arlington, Virginia, ninety-one years after the event. The man is Samuel J. Seymour.

April 13, 1956:
The last eyewitness to the death of Abraham Lincoln dies in Arlington, Virginia, ninety-one years after the event.

► 1956

19 ► With more than 1,500 press, radio, television, and newsreel reporters covering the event, film actress Grace Kelly of Philadelphia is married to Prince Rainier III, sovereign of Monaco, in the cathedral of St. Nicholas in Monte Carlo. (Kelly, the first American to marry a reigning sovereign, married the prince a day earlier in a civil ceremony.)

23 ► The Supreme Court upholds a lower court ban on segregation on interstate buses.

MAY

21 ► The United States drops its first H-bomb from an airplane in the Pacific.

22 ► At the Ohio State Penitentiary, ninety-six volunteer for live cancer injections.

JUNE

08 ► Eisenhower is stricken with ileitis, an intestinal disease. He is operated on the following day.

29 ► President Eisenhower signs the law creating the highway trust fund, which will pay for 90 percent of the interstate highway system; the states will pay the rest. Although the 42,500-mile system (97 percent complete in 1989) constitutes only 1 percent of our highways, it carries 50 percent of the traffic. It is a public works project of remarkable cost and impact on American commerce, transportation, and society and literally and figuratively changes the face of the nation.

30 ► A midair collision over the Grand Canyon claims 128—the worst disaster in commercial aviation to this date.

■ ■

☞ 1. Highway accidents claim 6.28 lives for every 100 million miles traveled.

☞ 2. After taxes the income of the average American is $1,700, up about $63 from 1955.

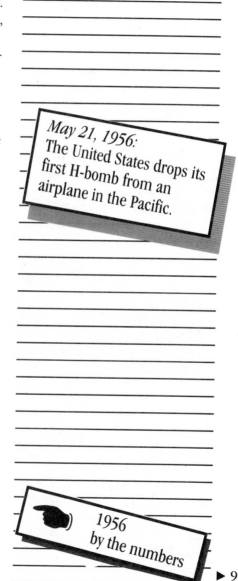

May 21, 1956: The United States drops its first H-bomb from an airplane in the Pacific.

☞ 1956 by the numbers

☞ 3. The average weekly take-home rate for a worker with three dependents rises to $74.04 in September.

☞ 4. The new minimum wage is $1.00 an hour, which effectively raises the pay of 2 million Americans.

☞ 5. The gross national product rises to $408 billion.

☞ 6. Americans export 700 million cases of canned goods.

☞ 7. Baseball draws 16,533,625, with the Milwaukee Braves outdrawing all other teams with 2,046,331.

☞ 8. A dollar buys only as much food in 1956 as forty-one cents brought in 1939.

☞ 9. The nation's 132,000 model railroad buffs spend $15 million on their hobby this year.

☞ 10. Twenty-seven billion dollars in bills and coins is in circulation among the people of the United States. Banks hold an additional $3 billion.

■■■■■■■■■■■■■■■■■■■■■■■■■■■■■■■■■■■

JULY

16 ► Ringling Brothers & Barnum and Bailey Circus folds up its last canvas circus tent in Pittsburgh. It reopens in 1957 in air-conditioned arenas.

25 ► Fifty-one lives are lost when the Italian liner *Andrea Doria* sinks after it collides with the Swedish ship *Stockholm* south of Nantucket Island off the New England coast.

26 ► Egypt announces the seizure of the Suez Canal.

AUGUST

02 ► Albert Woolson, the last Union soldier of the Civil War, dies at the age of 109. (Also see December 19, 1959.)

06 ► A new kidnapping law goes into effect that allows the FBI to enter a case twenty-four hours after an abduction.

SEPTEMBER

06 ► The National Guard is sent into Sturgis, Kentucky, by Governor A. B. Chandler after mobs demonstrate against

July 26, 1956:
Egypt announces the seizure of the Suez Canal.

the enrollment of black students in the local high school.

■■■■■■■■■■■■■■■■■■■■■■■■■■■■■■■■

☞ 1. *brainstorming* (using a group of bright people to create new ideas and plans)

☞ 2. *angry young man* (a dark literary movement from England that gets its start with John Osborn's *Look Back in Anger*)

☞ 3. *de-Stalinization* (term for debunking the myth of Joseph Stalin in the process of creating a less harsh, less repressive Soviet Union)

☞ 4. *tranquilizer* (term for a drug whose prime purpose is the relief of anxiety)

☞ 5. *soil bank* (name for a federal plan by which farmers are paid to take land out of production)

☞ 6. *clean* (describing a nuclear device with low radiation levels, as opposed to . . .)

☞ 7. *dirty* (for radioactive)

☞ 8. *freedom fighters* (term for those who stand up to Communism in Hungary and other eastern bloc countries)

☞ 9. *We will bury you!* (Nikita Khrushchev's line about the West, which he delivers to a group of diplomats on November 17. The full quote: "History is on our side. We will bury you!")

☞ 10. *the organizational man* (title of a book by William Whyte, Jr., that refers to the bureaucratization of the individual within organizations. The term is used widely by people who have never read the book.)

■■■■■■■■■■■■■■■■■■■■■■■■■■■■■■■■

1956 in ten words (& phrases)

OCTOBER

06 ► A new live-virus polio vaccine is announced by Professor Albert B. Sabin of the University of Cincinnati.

October 8, 1956:
The first World Series perfect game is pitched by Don Larsen of the New York Yankees

1956 in buttons & bumper stickers ☞

People most likely to be on the cover in 1956 ☞

08 ▶ The first World Series perfect game is pitched by Don Larsen of the New York Yankees.

23 ▶ A popular revolt begins in Budapest, Hungary, and spreads throughout the country.

NOVEMBER

04 ▶ The Soviet Union launches a heavy attack against Hungary.

06 ▶ Eisenhower and Nixon are reelected in a forty-one state landslide victory.

13 ▶ The Supreme Court, reviewing a Montgomery, Alabama, law, rules that segregation on interstate buses is unconstitutional (furthering its April 23, 1956 decision).

25 ▶ The air force sends eight B-52s from California and Maine to the North Pole to demonstrate that nuclear weapons can be delivered to any point on the globe nonstop.

27 ▶ South Africa is stripped of most of its representation at the United Nations because of its racial policies.

DECEMBER

21 ▶ Racial segregation ends on the Montgomery, Alabama, bus system. Blacks can ride the buses for the first time since their boycott began on December 5, 1955.

■■■■■■■■■■■■■■■■■■■■■■■■■■■■■■

☞ 1. I STILL LIKE IKE
☞ 2. PEACE, PROSPERITY, PROGRESS (Republican campaign slogan)

■■■■■■■■■■■■■■■■■■■■■■■■■■■■■■

☞ 1. Admiral Arleigh Burke
☞ 2. Eisenhower and Nixon
☞ 3. Estes Kefauver
☞ 4. Rock Hudson
☞ 5. Julie Andrews
☞ 6. Robin Roberts

▶ 1956

☛ 7. Sherman Adams
☛ 8. Princess Grace Kelly
☛ 9. Elvis Presley
☛ 10. William Holden

November 27, 1956: South Africa is stripped of most of its representation at the United Nations because of its racial policies.

The year of Sputnik *and* ▶ *the start of the space age* ▶ *and the intercontinental* ▶ *ballistic missile* ▶ 1957

JANUARY

05 ▶ The Eisenhower doctrine for the Middle East is presented to Congress. It allows the president to commit American troops to the prevention of Communist aggression in the area.

16 ▶ A U.S. B-52 Superfortress makes the first nonstop round the globe flight in forty-five hours and nineteen minutes.

MARCH

06 ▶ The new nation of Ghana is created in Africa.

13 ▶ In Cuba, forty-six die in an unsuccessful attempt to overthrow the regime of Fulgencio Batista.

■ ■

☞ 1. Elvis Presley becomes the king of rock 'n' roll. His monster hits are *Hound Dog* and *Don't Be Cruel.*

☞ 2. Ducktail or DA (for "duck's ass") haircuts are cause for suspension in some high schools.

☞ 3. The Edsel is unleashed by Ford as the $250 million car. The new Ford Skyliner comes with an optional retractable roof.

☞ 4. Jack Kerouac's *On the Road* is the immediate centerpiece for the new, hip, cool, and against-the-grain beat movement in literature.

January 16, 1957: A U.S. B-52 Superfortress makes the first nonstop round-the-globe flight in forty-five hours and nineteen minutes.

☞ Fads and Trends for 1957

☞ 5. *Droodles*—doodles with a punch line—are on everybody's note pad. They are the creation of comedian Roger Price.

☞ 6. The shapeless, unfitted sack dress comes into vogue for women.

☞ 7. For men, the Ivy League look—characterized by button-down shirt collars, three-button single-breasted suits, and pleatless pants—spreads and becomes the dominant influence.

☞ 8. For men and women both, the three-quarter-length car coat becomes part of the uniform of suburbia.

☞ 9. An article on the subject of wife swapping in *Mr.* magazine touches off widespread interest in this formerly taboo topic.

☞ 10. Small cars from overseas are extremely popular as the number of imports doubles from 1956. The hot imports include the German Volkswagen, the Swedish Volvo, the French Renault, the English Austin, and the Italian Fiat.

■ ■

APRIL

22 ▶ The Defense Department announces that some of America's larger cities will soon be guarded with the new Nike Hercules atomic missiles.

MAY

11 ▶ On a tour of the United States President Diem of South Vietnam makes a joint statement with President Eisenhower declaring Communism a threat to the free nations of Asia.

▶ 1957

JUNE

06 ▶ The directors of the Automobile Manufacturers' Association decide that they will no longer emphasize speed and horsepower in automobile advertising. The American car makers also decide that they will no longer formally support auto racing.

■ ■

☞ 1. Ford invests $250 million in a new line of Edsels to compete with General Motors' Oldsmobile.

☞ 2. A thousand computers are built, bought, and shipped this year.

☞ 3. In the greatest year yet for foreign travel Americans on vacation drop $1.8 billion in other countries.

☞ 4. Chairman Mao's Great Leap Forward puts half a billion Chinese into communes.

☞ 5. American consumption of margarine overtakes that of butter for the first time. In 1957 the average margarine intake is 8.6 pounds while butter settles down to 8.3 pounds.

☞ 6. Plastic products now account for a $2 billion slice of the economy.

☞ 7. There are now seventy-one cities in the world with populations in excess of 1 million.

☞ 8. President Eisenhower presents a record peacetime budget totaling $71.807 billion.

☞ 9. Work begins on a new State Department building in Washington, D.C. It will cost an estimated $57.4 million.

☞ 10. The world's first nuclear submarine, *Nautilus*, travels 60,000 miles on 8.3 pounds of fuel.

■ ■

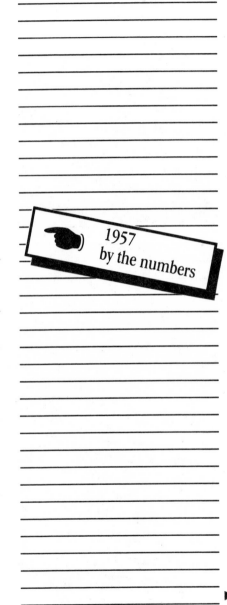

1957
by the numbers

► 1957

JULY

05 ► Tennis star Althea Gibson of the United States becomes the first black to win the women's singles title at Wimbledon.

AUGUST

26 ► Moscow announces that it has successfully tested its first intercontinental ballistic missile. Although this attracts less attention than the first *Sputnik* launch of October, it creates far greater alarm in Congress and elsewhere in official Washington. The United States is still months from its first ICBM. (See December 17, 1957.)

30 ► Senator Strom Thurmond sets a new filibuster record in the Congress speaking twenty-four hours, twenty-seven minutes, against civil rights legislation.

SEPTEMBER

01 ► Evangelist Billy Graham's New York crusade comes to a close. Over sixteen weeks he draws more than 2 million people.

04 ► Arkansas Governor Orval Faubus calls out the National Guard to prevent nine students of African descent from entering Central High in Little Rock.

09 ► President Eisenhower signs into law the first civil rights legislation since Reconstruction.

19 ► The United States sets off the first underground nuclear test in a mountain tunnel near Las Vegas.

24 ► Dwight Eisenhower orders troops to Little Rock, Arkansas, to enforce court-ordered desegregation of public schools.

► *Also today:* The last game is played at Ebbets Field in Brooklyn as the Dodgers plan their move to Los Angeles. This date and that of February 23, 1960—the day the structure is torn down—will live in infamy among ardent fans of the team.

August 26, 1957:
Moscow announces that it has successfully tested its first intercontinental ballistic missile.

September 24, 1957:
Dwight Eisenhower orders troops to Little Rock, Arkansas, to enforce court-ordered desegregation of public schools.

▶ 1957

■ ■

☞ 1. *brinkmanship* (John Foster Dulles's term for the diplomacy conducted on the edge—brink—of nuclear war)

☞ 2. *beat*...

☞ 3. *beatnik*...

☞ 4. and *beat generation* (a set of terms created and popularized by beats Jack Kerouac, Gregory Corso, and Allen Ginsberg)

☞ 5. *-nik* (suffix attached to all sorts of things in the wake of *Sputnik*)

☞ 6. *Asian flu* (a new flu virus that originates in Asia)

☞ 7. *subliminal perception* (technique of influencing people with material that is not seen with the naked eye but that registers on the subconscious)

☞ 8. *Common Market* (organization uniting Europe into a single trade and tariff entity)

☞ 9. *SANE* (The National Committee for a Sane Nuclear Policy is founded this year by a group whose members include Erich Fromm, author of *The Sane Society.*)

☞ 10. *Darvon* (The new painkiller seen as a nonaddictive alternative to codeine is manufactured by Eli Lilly.)

■ ■

OCTOBER

04 ▶ The space age begins with the launching of the *Sputnik* spacecraft by the Soviet Union.

▶ *Also on this day:* The family comedy *Leave It to Beaver* debuts on CBS.

07 ▶ A fire in the Windscale plutonium production reactor north of Liverpool, England, spreads radioactive iodine throughout the countryside. In 1983 the British government said thirty-nine people probably died of cancer because of the accident. It is also discovered that at about this same time a chemical explosion in the Soviet Union's Ural Mountains spreads radioactive material. It is believed at least thirty

October 4, 1957:
The space age begins with the launching of the Sputnik spacecraft by the Soviet Union.

villages were abandoned, their names subsequently deleted from maps.

NOVEMBER

03 ► Two months after *Sputnik,* the USSR chalks up another stunning space first by putting the first living thing from earth into space. *Sputnik 2* carries a female dog named Laika.

30 ► The *National Geographic* announces that the resting place of Captain Bligh's *Bounty,* scuttled after a 1790 mutiny, has been found.

DECEMBER

06 ► The Teamsters Union is expelled from the AFL-CIO for corrupt leadership.

17 ► The United States fires its first Atlas intercontinental ballistic missile (ICBM) from Cape Canaveral; 1957 is the first year of the space age as well as the start of the missile age.

18 ► At Shippensport, Pennsylvania, the first large-scale American nuclear power plant goes into operation and begins supplying electricity to the Pittsburgh area.

■ ■

☞ 1. Martin Luther King, Jr.
☞ 2. Senator John F. Kennedy
☞ 3. Mickey Mantle
☞ 4. Hank Aaron
☞ 5. Leonard Bernstein
☞ 6. Lyndon B. Johnson
☞ 7. Kim Novak
☞ 8. Billy Graham
☞ 9. Yul Brynner
☞ 10. Pat Boone

■ ■

December 6, 1957:
The Teamsters Union is expelled from the AFL-CIO for corrupt leadership.

People most likely
to be on the cover ☞
in 1957

The year in which ▶ the space and missile ▶ race heats up ▶ 1958

JANUARY

31 ▶ The first American satellite—*Explorer 1*—is launched by an army Jupiter-C rocket from Cape Canaveral and goes into orbit. It is followed in short order by the second, *Vanguard 1,* on March 17 and third, *Explorer 3,* on March 26.

FEBRUARY

01 ▶ The United Arab Republic is created by the merger of Egypt and Syria.

MARCH

27 ▶ Nikita Khrushchev becomes Soviet premier in addition to first secretary of the Communist party.

■■■■■■■■■■■■■■■■■■■■■■■■■■■■■■■■

☛ 1. The hula hoop creates a craze of historic magnitude. For six months, between 100 to 200 million of these thirty-inch hoops are sold, and then the fad dies as quickly as it started.

☛ 2. Stereophonic long-playing records come into wide-spread use.

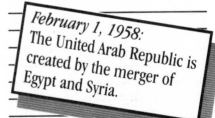

February 1, 1958: The United Arab Republic is created by the merger of Egypt and Syria.

Fads and Trends for 1958

—————————————————
—————————————————
—————————————————
—————————————————
—————————————————
—————————————————
—————————————————
—————————————————
—————————————————
—————————————————
—————————————————
—————————————————
—————————————————
—————————————————
—————————————————
—————————————————
—————————————————
—————————————————
—————————————————
—————————————————
—————————————————
—————————————————
—————————————————
—————————————————

☛ 3. Interest in beat literature widens, and it is called a movement.

☛ 4. It is a great year for rock 'n' roll with big hits by Elvis, the Coasters, Chuck Berry, Little Richard, Eddie Cochran, and Little Anthony.

☛ 5. Permanent-press woolen clothing is new and everyone wants to try it.

☛ 6. For the first time, computers appear to be making inroads into science, business, and industry.

☛ 7. Donation of the Hope Diamond to the Smithsonian spurs fascination with it and other big rocks.

☛ 8. The '59 model cars from Detroit are the longest and lowest yet and they carry the biggest fins ever. Lotsa' chrome 'n' lotsa' glass.

☛ 9. There is a boom in worldwide credit cards, which become widely available this year.

☛ 10. Brussels hosts the first world's fair since 1939 and attracts 45 million. Domes and spheres are its dominant look.

■ ■

APRIL

14 ▶ American pianist Van Cliburn wins the International Tchaikovsky Piano Competition in Moscow. He becomes a media sensation in both countries.

15 ▶ Major league baseball becomes a national phenomenon as it opens on the West Coast as the San Francisco Giants and Los Angeles Dodgers play at Seals Stadium in San Francisco.

MAY

01 ▶ The first U.S. Law Day is celebrated. It is intended as a counter to the Communist May Day.

▶ *Also today is the day on which:* The National Academy of Sciences announces that American satellites have detected a radiation barrier or belt 600 miles in space.

May 1, 1958:
American satellites have detected a radiation barrier or belt 600 miles in space.

► 1958

■■■■■■■■■■■■■■■■■■■■■■■■■■■■■■■

☛ 1. Unemployment reaches nearly 8 percent in this year of recession.

☛ 2. The cost of mailing a first-class letter rises from three to four cents. The three-cent rate had been in effect since 1932.

☛ 3. This is the peak year for the American drive-in movie, with 4,063 outdoor screens nationwide.

☛ 4. The suggested retail price of a pair of Levi's jeans, $3.75.

☛ 5. At the end of the year there are 64,750,000 telephones on line in the United States.

☛ 6. A year's tuition at Harvard now costs $1,250, triple its cost in 1948.

☛ 7. New economy fares are introduced on transatlantic runs. One-way from New York to London now can be had for as little as $232.

☛ 8. With Senate approval of the addition of Alaska, the United States will soon officially jump to the position of fourth-largest nation in the world in land mass. Only the USSR, China, and Canada are larger.

☛ 9. Unemployment reaches a postwar high of 5.5 million.

☛ 10. The top 1 percent of the population enjoys 9 percent of the nation's total disposable income, down from 19 percent in 1929.

■■■■■■■■■■■■■■■■■■■■■■■■■■■■■■■

☛) *1958
by the numbers*

JULY

15 ► In the face of a perceived threat by Moslem rebels, President Eisenhower orders American marines into Lebanon at the request of the Christian regime in power.

17 ► British troops land in Jordon at the request of King Hussein I.

28 ► President Eisenhower signs the National Aeronautics and Space Act of 1958. Among other things, it creates the space

agency or National Aeronautics and Space Administration (NASA).

AUGUST

01 ▶ The United States explodes an atomic bomb in a missile in the South Pacific as a demonstration of ICBM technology.

03 ▶ The American nuclear submarine *Nautilus* crosses under the North Pole. The feat is announced on August 8 by President Eisenhower.

SEPTEMBER

22 ▶ Sherman Adams, an assistant to President Eisenhower, resigns because he has accepted a freezer from Boston industrialist Bernard Goldfine.

■■■■■■■■■■■■■■■■■■■■■■■■■■■■■■■■

☛ 1. *bottom out* (a verb describing the end of a recession. 1958 was a recession year in which recovery began.)

☛ 2. *stereo* (what you play your new stereophonic records on—no longer a record player or hi-fi)

☛ 3. *bionics* (term for things artificial that behave as if they were organic)

☛ 4. *charge it* (This is the year that the international plastic credit card comes into its own.)

☛ 5. *the affluent society* (a John Kenneth Galbraith title that argues for an ever-expanding economy but becomes a term to describe the American way of life)

☛ 6. *moonshot* (proper name for a rocket to the moon)

☛ 7. *megacorpse* (gruesome term from the realm of nuclear planning for a million dead people)

☛ 8. *cartnapping* (the crime of taking supermarket shopping carts and not returning them)

☛ 9. *slumlord* (name for one who rents lousy housing for outrageous prices)

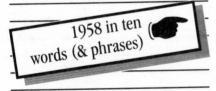

August 3, 1958:
The American nuclear submarine *Nautilus* crosses under the North Pole.

1958 in ten words (& phrases)

▶ 1958

☞ 10. *T* (firing time, as in "T minus ten" for ten minutes before firing time)

■■■■■■■■■■■■■■■■■■■■■■■■■■■■■■■

OCTOBER

04 ▶ The first transatlantic passenger jet service goes into operation between London and New York. The carrier is British Overseas Airways Corporation (BOAC).

21 ▶ The first women are admitted to the British House of Lords.

NOVEMBER

03 ▶ For the first time in the United States, a commercial jet is used to move the mail.

DECEMBER

30 ▶ Batista's sons arrive in New York and warn that Cuba is about to fall to Fidel Castro.

■■■■■■■■■■■■■■■■■■■■■■■■■■■■■■■

☞ 1. Charles de Gaulle
☞ 2. Orval Faubus
☞ 3. Fidel Castro
☞ 4. Nelson Rockefeller
☞ 5. Van Cliburn
☞ 6. Private Elvis Presley
☞ 7. Bob Hope
☞ 8. Jack Benny
☞ 9. Eleanor Roosevelt
☞ 10. Pope John XXIII
☞ 11. Sir Alec Guinness
☞ 12. Jack Paar

■■■■■■■■■■■■■■■■■■■■■■■■■■■■■■■

October 4, 1958: The first transatlantic passenger jet service goes into operation between London and New York.

☞ People most likely to be on the cover in 1958

▶ 113

The year in which ▶
Fidel Castro takes over Cuba ▶
and Alaska and Hawaii ▶
achieve statehood ▶

1959

JANUARY

01 ▶ Fidel Castro leads his guerrilla army into Havana. His revolution has succeeded and the Batista regime is ousted.

03 ▶ Alaska becomes the forty-ninth state.

FEBRUARY

03 ▶ Buddy Holly, the Big Bopper, and Richie Valens are killed in an aircraft accident near Mason City, Iowa. The moment is sadly immortalized in Don McLean's 1971 hit, *American Pie*, as "the day the music died"—only the music didn't die.

06 ▶ Fidel Castro becomes premier of Cuba.

13 ▶ The original Barbie doll is introduced by Mattel, Inc. It quickly establishes itself as the most popular doll of all time. At the time of Barbie's thirtieth anniversary in 1989, Mattel boasts that some 500 million Barbies (and friends) have been sold along with over 1 billion sets of clothes.

MARCH

13 ▶ A revolt breaks out in Tibet against the Chinese, who now hold it as a province. Before the month is out, the revolt is crushed and the Dalai Lama flees to India.

January 3, 1959:
Alaska becomes the forty-ninth state.

February 6, 1959:
Fidel Castro becomes premier of Cuba.

▬▬▬▬▬▬▬▬▬▬▬▬▬▬▬▬▬▬▬▬▬▬▬▬▬▬▬▬▬

☞ 1. Urban renewal begins on a pilot basis in New Haven. Congress appropriates $650 million in a billion-dollar housing bill for slum clearance. Is this the salvation of the cities?

☞ 2. With an eye on the import statistics, Detroit turns to the compact car, and Americans hear a lot of new names like Falcon, Lark, Rambler, Valiant, and Corvair. They are finless or just have a suggestion of fins.

☞ 3. *Ben Hur* is the must-see movie.

☞ 4. Independent filmmakers are on the rise, and the old studios encourage the trend. Increasingly, the studios are becoming releasers of independent films.

☞ 5. Folk singing is very popular, and some folk songs make it to the hit parade—two of the biggest being *Tom Dooley* and *He's Got the Whole World in His Hands.*

☞ 6. Jazz festivals are cropping up everywhere and a number of TV shows have snappy jazz themes.

☞ 7. Quiz show scandals shock the nation and kill off the big giveaway shows.

☞ 8. White lipstick comes into its own.

☞ 9. Collegiate telephone booth stuffing becomes a national phenomenon with as many as thirty-four students shoehorning themselves into a booth (thirty-four was the apparent record set at Modesto Junior College).

☞ 10. Motown Records is founded by Berry Gordy, Jr., making the Motown and soul sounds of the next decade a possibility.

☞ 11. With the advent of good bookcase speakers (AR and KLH), component hi-fi has arrived.

▬▬▬▬▬▬▬▬▬▬▬▬▬▬▬▬▬▬▬▬▬▬▬▬▬▬▬▬▬

Fads and Trends for 1959 ☞

▶ 1959

APRIL

09 ▶ The first seven astronauts are selected.

15 ▶ Fidel Castro, Cuba's new ruler, begins an unofficial eleven-day goodwill tour of the United States and Canada.

MAY

22 ▶ Benjamin O. Davis, Jr., of the U.S. Air Force becomes America's first black major general. His father was the first black general in the U.S. Army.

JUNE

11 ▶ The U.S. Postmaster General bans D. H. Lawrence's *Lady Chatterley's Lover* from the mails. (See July 21, 1959.)

■ ■

☞ 1. The total number of Americans who have died in automotive accidents in this century reaches 1.25 million, which is more than have died in American wars to date.

☞ 2. In the United States 14,876 new books are published, and Americans spend $1.2 billion on books.

☞ 3. There are 2,340,000 arrests in the nation, of which 60 percent are made on individuals under twenty-five years of age.

☞ 4. A rebounding construction industry accounts for $55 billion.

☞ 5. A University of Michigan survey reveals that 10 percent of all American families live at the poverty line while an additional 20 percent live below it.

☞ 6. Volkswagen sells 120,000 cars in the U.S. this year, four times the number sold in 1955.

☞ 7. A congressional study determines that a nuclear war will result in the death of 50 million Americans. An additional 20 million will be wounded.

☞ 8. The United Nations determines that the world's popu-

April 9, 1959:
The first seven astronauts are selected.

☞ 1959
by the numbers

▶ 117

lation is growing at a rate of 45 million a year, or eighty-five people a minute.

☞ 9. This year 3,750 new long-playing records are released.

☞ 10. There are 32,000 supermarkets in the United States. They sell 69 percent of all food but constitute only 11 percent of all retail food stores.

■■■■■■■■■■■■■■■■■■■■■■■■■■■■■■

JULY

04 ► America's forty-nine-star flag, honoring Alaskan statehood, is officially unfurled.

08 ► During a Communist attack at Bien Hoa, Major Dale R. Buis of Imperial Beach, California, and Master Sergeant Chester M. Ovnand of Copperas Cove, California, become the first American soldiers to be killed during the Vietnam War.

21 ► Judge Frederick van Pelt Bryan rules that *Lady Chatterley's Lover* can be legally sent through the mails, overruling the postmaster general, who had banned it in June.

24 ► During a visit to the Soviet Union, Vice President Richard M. Nixon enters into an impromptu debate with Soviet leader Nikita Khrushchev on the merits of American capitalism versus Soviet communism. The confrontation becomes known as the kitchen debate because it takes place in a model kitchen at a U.S. exhibition. It is regarded as a feather in Nixon's political cap.

AUGUST

07 ► The U.S. satellite *Explorer VI* sends back the first photograph of Earth taken from space. Many later claim that this is the first image to underscore the finiteness of the earth and its position as, in the words of Buckminster Fuller, "Spaceship Earth."

21 ► Hawaii becomes the fiftieth state.

August 7, 1959:
The U.S. satellite *Explorer VI* sends back the first photograph of Earth taken from space.

1959

SEPTEMBER

13 ▶ The first manmade object reaches the moon as a Soviet *Lunik II* spacecraft unceremoniously crashes on the lunar surface. It is a stunning accomplishment that redoubles the American fear that the Soviet Union will be the first to put a man on the moon.

15 ▶ Premier Khrushchev arrives in the United States and visits with President Eisenhower, inviting him to the Soviet Union. He remains in the U.S. until September 27.

16 ▶ France offers Algeria a plan for self-determination in order to end the fighting between Algerian nationalists and French troops. The offer: Algeria can determine its own future four years after peace is established.

■■■■■■■■■■■■■■■■■■■■■■■■■■■■■■■■

☛ 1. *the fabulous fifties* (At the end of the decade this is the most popular name for it.)

☛ 2. *Velcro* (a new product that takes its name from *vel*vet and *cro*chet)

☛ 3. *Metrecal* (What else can you call a mixture of soybean flour, vitamins, minerals, and a little flavoring?)

☛ 4. *P-bomb* (term for the threat of overpopulation. The *P* is for population.)

☛ 5 *liftoff* (the initial rise of a rocket; one of a number of words and phrases from the launch pad).

☛ 6. *impact area* (where missiles are targeted)

☛ 7. *record club* (a hot idea for 1959: buy some records by mail and receive periodic bonus records)

☛ 8. *Sony* (With the introduction of the first transistorized television set, this brand name is on its way to becoming a household name.)

☛ 9. *lo-fi* (what you describe your old equipment as in this age of hi-fi)

> 1959 in ten words (& phrases)

10. *exotic fuel* (substance that delivers extraordinary power for its weight and volume)

■■■■■■■■■■■■■■■■■■■■■■■■■■■■■■■

OCTOBER

27 ► The Soviet Union releases the first pictures ever taken of the dark side of the moon. They are transmitted back to Earth from the unmanned *Lunik III.*

NOVEMBER

09 ► Dr. Arthur S. Flemming, Secretary of Health, Education, and Welfare, calls a press conference to announce that a number of cranberries apparently have been contaminated with the residue of a weed-killing chemical called aminotriazole. The chemical, Flemming says, was found in laboratory tests to cause thyroid cancer in rats. With those words, Flemming instantly wrecks the cranberry market for 1959 and cripples the industry for years to come.

DECEMBER

01 ► In Washington twelve nations sign an agreement to keep Antarctica free of political and military strife and reserve the area for scientific research.

19 ► Confederate soldier Walter Williams of Houston is the last veteran of the Civil War to die. He claims to be 117.

■■■■■■■■■■■■■■■■■■■■■■■■■■■■■■■

☞ 1. President Dwight D. Eisenhower (*Time*'s Man of the Year and the most "admired man in the world" for the seventh year in a row, according to a Gallup poll. Eleanor Roosevelt has been the most admired woman for thirteen years in a row according to Gallup.)

☞ 2. James R. Hoffa

☞ 3. Harold Macmillan

December 1, 1959:
In Washington twelve nations sign an agreement to keep Antarctica free of political and military strife and reserve the area for scientific research.

People most likely to be on the cover in 1959 ☞

▶ 1959

- 4. Shirley MacLaine
- 5. Charles Van Doren
- 6. Ernie Banks
- 7. Ingemar Johansson
- 8. Fidel Castro
- 9. Thomas Dooley
- 10. Harry Belafonte

■■■■■■■■■■■■■■■■■■■■■■■■■■■■■

The year in which Africa ▶
asserts its independence ▶
and John F. Kennedy ▶
is elected president ▶

1960

JANUARY

31 ▶ Senator John F. Kennedy announces that he is running for the presidency.

FEBRUARY

01 ▶ Black students sit down at the Charlotte, North Carolina, Woolworth's lunch counter in protest to the local custom of serving blacks only if they stand. In response, eight lunch counters in Charlotte close. There is also a sit-in at Greensboro, North Carolina. This begins the sit-in movement, which spreads to fifteen cities in five Southern states by the end of the month.

13 ▶ France explodes its first atomic bomb in the North African Sahara.

March 22, 1960: Arthur L. Schawlow and Charles H. Townes patent the laser.

MARCH

21 ▶ In Sharpeville, South Africa, seventy African blacks are killed by police in riots started over the issue of pass cards—internal passports for nonwhites. It is soon termed the Sharpeville massacre, and this and other incidents begin to focus worldwide attention on that nation's policies of racial separation.

22 ▶ Arthur L. Schawlow and Charles H. Townes patent the laser.

▶ 123

■■■■■■■■■■■■■■■■■■■■■■■■■■■■■■■■

☞ 1. The radio and pop music industries are rocked with scandal. Congressional investigators determine that 207 disc jockeys in 42 cities have accepted over $260,000 to plug records. The name given to this illegal payment is *payola.*

☞ 2. *Everybody* is talking about the Pill.

☞ 3. Detroit's new small cars are . . . bigger.

☞ 4. Trampolines are big, especially the big gymnasium-size versions.

☞ 5. Pentel's felt-tip marker, the first, is a hit.

☞ 6. The twist is a big dance and hit song by Chubby Checker. Its popularity peaks in 1962.

☞ 7. An intense African nationalism—characterized by the independence of seventeen nations—creates a new interest in the continent and things African.

☞ 8. *Psycho,* Alfred Hitchcock's gothic nightmare, sets a new and gruesome tone for scary movies.

☞ 9. Teflon-coated cookware hits the market and moves like hotcakes. (One problem with the early versions is that the Teflon comes off the pan almost as easily as a hotcake comes off the Teflon.)

☞ 10. A big year for convention centers: completions include Detroit's Cobo Hall, Pittsburgh's Gateway Center, and Chicago's McCormick Place.

■■■■■■■■■■■■■■■■■■■■■■■■■■■■■■■■

Fads and Trends for 1960 ☞

APRIL

17 ► Today is tax freedom day 1960—the day on which American working people theoretically get to start keeping all of their earnings assuming that all the money earned before this date went for federal, state, and local taxes. In 1950 tax freedom day arrived two weeks earlier, on April 3.

21 ► Brazil dedicates its new capital at Brasília.

▶ 1960

MAY

01 ▶ A U.S. U-2 reconnaissance plane is shot down over central USSR and its pilot, Gary Powers, is held by the Soviet Union. It is announced by Premier Khrushchev on the 5th. The incident leads to the collapse of the May 16 Eisenhower-Khrushchev Paris summit when the United States does not apologize, though Eisenhower does announce discontinuance of such flights.

09 ▶ The Federal Drug Administration approves the first public sale of contraceptive pills, Enovid, at $10 to $11 for a month's supply.

10 ▶ The U.S. atomic submarine *Triton* surfaces after completing the first underwater circumnavigation of the globe: 30,708 miles in 84 days.

11 ▶ Israeli secret service agents find Nazi war criminal Adolf Eichmann in a suburb of Buenos Aires, living under an assumed name, and smuggle him back to Israel. His trial, which takes place in Jerusalem from April 11 to August 14, 1961, attracts worldwide attention. The capture, however, is not announced by the Israelis until May 23.

16 ▶ The East-West summit collapses before it begins in Paris as Soviet Premier Khrushchev demands that Eisenhower apologize for the May 1 U-2 incident. The Soviet leader also cancels the president's visit to Moscow. The calm and cordial relationship between the two leaders evident in 1959 has turned to anger and invective.

24 ▶ The United States launches the *Midas II* satellite, ironically the first of a series that replaces the U-2 in military reconnaissance.

JUNE

02 ▶ Broadway goes dark as twenty-two theaters are hit by the first strike against the legitimate theater since 1919.

May 1, 1960:
A U.S. U-2 reconnaissance plane is shot down over central USSR. Its pilot, Gary Powers, is held by the Soviet Union.

May 11, 1960:
Israeli secret service agents find Nazi war criminal Adolf Eichmann in a suburb of Buenos Aires.

1960 by the numbers ☛

July 4, 1960: America's fifty-star flag is officially unfurled.

☛ 1. According to the 1960 Census 179,323,175 people live in the United States.

☛ 2. There are 27,997,377 more people in the U.S. on April 1, 1960, than there were on April 1, 1950. It is the largest population increase in American history to date.

☛ 3. For the first time, there are more than 60 million television sets in the country.

☛ 4. In the last ten years, 2,515,000 immigrants entered the United States. The number of European immigrants drops to near 50 percent as the numbers of Mexican-Americans and Asian-Americans increase.

☛ 5. The X-15 rocket plane sets a new altitude record of 136,500 feet.

☛ 6. *A GOOD MEAL IN 1960:* At McDonnell's Sea Grill in Bethesda, Maryland, one can obtain a baked whole Maine lobster stuffed with fresh deviled crabmeat, melted butter, garden peas, and French fries for $3.95. The price includes appetizer, rum buns, rolls, green salad, dessert, and beverage; however, one must pay an additional $.35 for the fresh shrimp cocktail.

☛ 7. In 1960 the world's population hits 3 billion for the first time. It reached 2 billion in 1930.

☛ 8. One out of every ten Americans lives on a farm.

☛ 9. Forty-eight percent of all Americans of African descent now live outside the eleven states in the old Confederacy—an increase of 18 percent from 1940.

☛ 10. This is the most productive year in American history to this point—the gross national product equals $503 billion.

JULY

01 ► The USSR shoots down an air force RB-47 over the Arctic, a fact announced by the Soviet premier on the 11th. On the 12th the United States angrily insists that the plane was attacked over international waters.

► 1960

04 ► America's fifty-star flag, honoring Hawaiian statehood, is officially unfurled.

09 ► Rodger Woodward, age seven, falls out of a capsized boat and becomes the first person to survive a plunge over Niagara Falls. He suffers only minor injuries.

11 ► The Bell System announces that because of communications satellite technology a true worldwide telephone and television communications system is now in operation.

   ► ***Also occurring today:*** France grants independence to eight African republics. During the year seventeen African nations emerge from colonial to independent status.

13 ► Massachusetts Senator John F. Kennedy is the Democratic presidential nominee at his party's convention in Los Angeles. Lyndon B. Johnson is his vice presidential candidate.

20 ► The nature of nuclear war changes today as a ballistic missile is fired for the first time from a submerged submarine. Off Cape Canaveral a two-stage Polaris missile is fired 1,150 miles.

21 ► Although the American public will not hear about it until November 1975, when it is revealed by the Senate Intelligence Committee, today is the day on which the CIA's Havana station arranges for an accident to kill Fidel Castro's brother Raul. The plan falls through when the assassin cannot get to Raul, and CIA headquarters halts the plan the following day. This is one of a number of venal and hairbrained schemes concocted by the CIA during the years 1959 through 1972. (See also August 14.)

27 ► Vice President Richard M. Nixon is nominated for president at the Republican convention in Chicago. Henry Cabot Lodge is his vice presidential candidate.

AUGUST

14 ► Today is the day that the CIA obtains a box of Fidel Castro's favorite cigars and has them treated with botulinum toxin. The plot to poison the Cuban leader does not go through,

but it represents the many desperate and odd plots hatched by the United States to kill Castro. In 1975 the Senate Intelligence Committee unearths eight plots to kill Castro and many more to make him look foolish, with a large number coming in 1960. One scheme called for a powder to be placed on Castro's boots that would cause his beard to fall out and another was to have an American visitor give Castro diving equipment contaminated with poison.

19 ▶ U-2 pilot Gary Powers is sentenced by the USSR to ten years in prison. He is released in exchange for a Soviet spy in 1961.

SEPTEMBER

12 ▶ Today Democratic presidential candidate John F. Kennedy confronts the issue of his religion by telling a Protestant group in Houston, "I do not speak for my church on public matters, and the church does not speak for me."

18 ▶ Premiers Castro of Cuba and Khrushchev of the Soviet Union arrive in Manhattan (to which they are restricted for security reasons) to address the United Nations.

24 ▶ At Newport News, Virginia, the USS *Enterprise* is launched; it is the world's first nuclear-powered aircraft carrier.

26 ▶ Cuban premier Fidel Castro addresses the United Nation's General Assembly and uses the occasion for a four-and-a-half-hour tirade against the United States. It follows a two-hour-and-twenty-minute tirade by Khrushchev on the 23rd.

■■■■■■■■■■■■■■■■■■■■■■■■■■■■■■■

☛ 1. *the pill* (Not the same as "a pill," this term enters the language with full force as the FDA approves the first birth control pills.)

☛ 2. *payola* (money paid to disc jockeys to play recordings)

☛ 3. *sit-in* (a peaceful protest against segregation, such as taking a seat at a lunch counter)

☛ 4. *docudrama* (documentary drama—television version)

September 12, 1960: Today Democratic presidential candidate John F. Kennedy confronts the issue of his religion by telling a Protestant group in Houston, "I do not speak for my church on public matters, and the church does not speak for me."

1960 in ten words (& phrases)

► 1960

☞ 5. *born free* (The title of Joy Adamson's bestseller and a popular song sticks as a description of the natural human and animal condition.)

☞ 6. *red dye number 2* (food dye given provisional acceptance by the Food and Drug Administration. It later is banned.)

☞ 7. *Xerox* (the name of a company and a process, but also a verb, as in, "Can you Xerox this for me?" The Xerox 914—so-called because it can handle paper as large as nine by fourteen inches—begins the copy revolution.)

☞ 8. *military industrial complex* (what President Eisenhower warns us to be wary of)

☞ 9. *thalidomide* (a name that is first heard by most when the FDA denies approval for its sale in the U.S.)

☞ 10. *Librium* (the hottest in anti-anxiety medication from Roche Laboratories)

■■■■■■■■■■■■■■■■■■■■■■■■■■■■■■■

OCTOBER

01 ► The Federation of Nigeria proclaims its independence. It was Britain's largest remaining colony.

05 ► White voters in the Union of South Africa decide to end their allegiance to the British crown and become an independent republic. Only whites are allowed to vote.

NOVEMBER

08 ► Senator John F. Kennedy is elected president. He is the first Roman Catholic and, at forty-three, the youngest president ever to be elected.

DECEMBER

05 ► The Supreme Court outlaws segregation in bus terminals.

13 ► An air force jet bomber sets a nonstop record of 10,000

November 8, 1960: Senator John F. Kennedy is elected president. He is the first Roman Catholic and, at forty-three, the youngest president ever to be elected.

miles without refueling. The mission of the B-52 was not merely to set a record but to underscore the range of manned bombers in the era of intercontinental missiles.

16 ▶ A United DC-7 and a TWA Super-Constellation collide over New York City and 134 are killed, including six who were on the ground at the time of the crash. It is the first jet mishap in which more than 100 people are killed, establishing a grim baseline against which the drawbacks of the jet age will be measured.

20 ▶ Today marks the formation of the National Liberation Front of South Vietnam (the Viet Cong) and resumption of guerrilla war in that divided nation. There are quick reports that tunnel construction has been restarted in Cu Chi district and elsewhere.

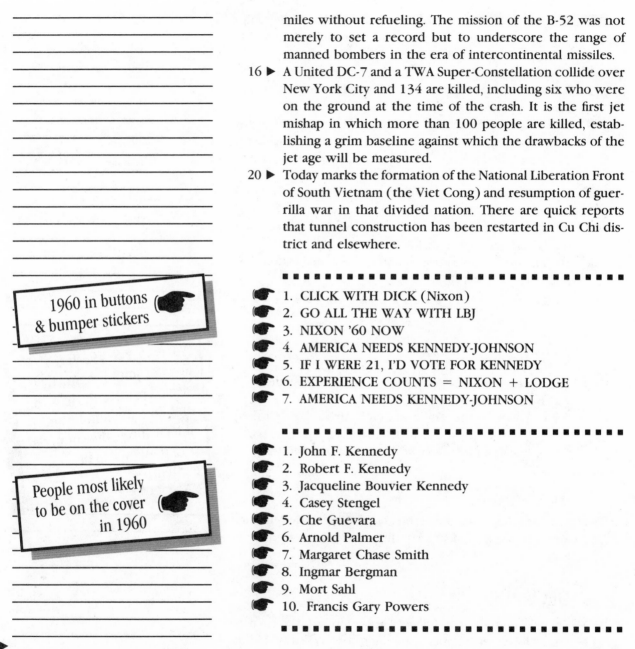

1960 in buttons & bumper stickers 👉

1. CLICK WITH DICK (Nixon)
2. GO ALL THE WAY WITH LBJ
3. NIXON '60 NOW
4. AMERICA NEEDS KENNEDY-JOHNSON
5. IF I WERE 21, I'D VOTE FOR KENNEDY
6. EXPERIENCE COUNTS = NIXON + LODGE
7. AMERICA NEEDS KENNEDY-JOHNSON

People most likely to be on the cover in 1960 👉

1. John F. Kennedy
2. Robert F. Kennedy
3. Jacqueline Bouvier Kennedy
4. Casey Stengel
5. Che Guevara
6. Arnold Palmer
7. Margaret Chase Smith
8. Ingmar Bergman
9. Mort Sahl
10. Francis Gary Powers

The year in which the ▶
Berlin Wall goes up and the ▶
United States is humbled ▶
at the Bay of Pigs ▶

1961

JANUARY

03 ▶ The United States breaks off diplomatic relations with Cuba.

20 ▶ President Kennedy is inaugurated in Washington, D.C. The morning's *Washington Post* carries the headline *SNOW CRIPPLES INAUGURAL CITY.*

FEBRUARY

01 ▶ The United States fires its first solid-fuel rocket, a Minuteman ICBM.

MARCH

01 ▶ By executive order President Kennedy creates the Peace Corps, sending American volunteers to meet "urgent needs for skilled manpower" in undeveloped countries and to "live at the same level as the citizens of the countries they are sent to." Over 1,000 will be on the job in the West Indies and Africa by September when Congress appropriates $40 million for the program.

13 ▶ President Kennedy proposes a ten-year plan of economic aid to Latin America, which he calls the Alliance for Progress.

March 1, 1961:
By executive order President Kennedy creates the Peace Corps, sending American volunteers to meet "urgent needs for skilled manpower" in undeveloped countries.

Fads and Trends for 1961 ☞

1. Bed racing is conducted mostly by collegians from Canada and California.

2. Hoffman-LaRoche introduces Valium.

3. There is a growing concern, especially in Congress, over the power of the right-wing, rabidly anti-Communist John Birch Society.

4. Old censorship barriers fall as Henry Miller's *Tropic of Cancer* and *Tropic of Capricorn* are published in the United States.

5. *Webster's Third New International Dictionary* is published by Merriam-Webster and sets off a debate as to what should and should not be in the dictionary. "Ain't no big thing."

6. Concern about civil defense remains high, and President Kennedy advises families to obtain—build or buy—a fallout shelter.

7. Thanks to the new president—and his doctor, Janet Travell, who orders him to use one—there is a revival in rocking chairs.

8. More and more men are sporting beards—full ones, like the folk singers grow.

9. A push for increased physical fitness begins in the White House and is felt all across the country, especially in the schools.

10. From its very beginning, the Peace Corps attracts many idealistic young people who see it as an army for peace.

April 12, 1961:
The USSR puts the first person in space, Yuri Gagarin – one orbit, 89.1 minutes.

APRIL

12 ▶ The USSR puts the first person in space, Yuri Gagarin—one orbit, 89.1 minutes.

17 ▶ In an attempt to "liberate" Cuba, 1,500 Cuban refugees land at the Bay of Pigs. All are killed or captured by the Cuban armed forces within three days. A major fiasco and

failure for the Kennedy administration, the operation's negative impact is not quickly diminished by time.

29 ▶ *Wide World of Sports* premieres, televising the Penn Drake Relays. On its twenty-fifth anniversary, Norman Chad of the *Washington Post* writes: "*Wide World,* in effect, created a new sports world—outside of baseball, basketball and football—and brought that world into our homes for the first time, establishing a foothold in our athletic culture for previously neglected games. Kids, suddenly, wanted to be gymnasts and figure skaters, and viewers were enchanted by the new pastimes."

MAY

01 ▶ A National Airlines plane bound for Miami is hijacked to Havana by an armed passenger.

04 ▶ Thirteen freedom riders leave Washington, D.C., for New Orleans to test the desegregation of public facilities along the way. Between May 15 and 20 the freedom riders, now two buses strong, are attacked in three cities in Alabama.

05 ▶ The first American astronaut goes into space today. Navy commander Alan B. Shepard, Jr., leaves Cape Canaveral and makes a suborbital flight that reaches 114 miles in altitude and reaches a top speed of 5,181 MPH. He is aboard the Mercury capsule *Freedom VII.*

11 ▶ President Kennedy dispatches 400 Special Forces soldiers and an additional 100 military advisors to Vietnam. He gives his authorization for clandestine warfare against the North by personnel of the South with American help.

JUNE

16 ▶ Soviet ballet dancer Rudolf Nureyev defects to the West while his troupe is in Paris.

May 11, 1961: President Kennedy dispatches 400 Special Forces soldiers and an additional 100 military advisors to Vietnam.

1961 by the numbers

1. U.S. patent number 3,000,000 is awarded to the General Electric Company for an automatic reading system.
2. At the end of the year there are 3,200 U.S. troops in Vietnam.
3. The packaging industry takes a dime out of every dollar spent on food. One of this year's packaging innovations is a see-through tray that allows shoppers to see both sides of a piece of meat.
4. The average American drinks 147 quarts of milk and cream—the lowest amount in twenty years. Cheese consumption is up, however, to 8.7 pounds per person.
5. There are 1,378,075 hospital beds in the United States, or 7.5 beds per thousand in population.
6. There are 1,292,000 marriages in the United States in 1961 and 171,933 divorces.
7. Cigarette manufacturers spend a cool $115 million on TV advertising.
8. The population of China reaches 650 million.
9. The John Birch Society claims to have 60,000 dues-paying members including three members of Congress.
10. Of the 14 million blind people in the world, 380,000 are in the United States and Canada.
11. Seventeen million acres of wilderness remain in the United States, down considerably from 55 million acres in 1926.

JULY

02 ► Author Ernest Hemingway, age sixty-one, shoots himself to death at his mountain-ringed home in Ketchum, Idaho. It is ruled accidental.

AUGUST

13 ► East Germany closes the Brandenburg Gate and seals off

the border between the eastern and western sectors of Berlin. As part of the closing, the government is about to begin building the Berlin Wall.

SEPTEMBER

01 ► The Soviet Union resumes testing of nuclear weapons in the atmosphere. Tests from now into November involve the largest weapons ever exploded.

05 ► In response to the first hijacking over American soil on September 5, 1961, President Kennedy signs a bill that makes hijacking a federal crime punishable by prison or death.

15 ► The U.S. resumes underground testing of nuclear weapons.

18 ► UN secretary-general Dag Hammarskjöld is killed in a plane crash in Africa. His death sets off a crisis within the world organization because it comes at a time when the Soviet Union is trying to abolish the office of secretary-general and replace it with a three-member board.

■■■■■■■■■■■■■■■■■■■■■■■■■■■■■■■■■■■■

☞ 1. *catch 22* (from the Joseph Heller novel of the same name. It alludes to a solution that is part of the problem.)

☞ 2. *freedom riders* (whites and blacks who head south to test and challenge segregation)

☞ 3. *cinéma verité* (a movement among filmmakers to create a new, spontaneous, unrehearsed realism)

☞ 4. *a vast wasteland* (The Federal Communications Commission chairman uses these words to describe television and threatens to deny new licenses unless more programming is offered in the public interest.)

☞ 5. *non-dairy creamer* (generic name for Coffee Mate)

☞ 6. *certificate of deposit* or *CD* (fixed-term interest generator pioneered by the First National City Bank of New York)

☞ 7. *like* (now can be used as a conjunction according to *Webster's Third New International Dictionary* published

August 13, 1961: East Germany closes the Brandenburg Gate and seals off the border between the eastern and western sectors of Berlin. As part of the closing, the government is about to begin building the Berlin Wall.

1961 in eleven words (& phrases)

this year. The new dictionary is important and well, *like* controversial.)

☞ 8. *Total* (a General Mills cereal promoted for its—this is a new one—nutritional qualities)

☞ 9. *recycle* (to take waste and scrap and turn it back into something of value—an old idea that gets a new name in 1961)

☞ 10. *Medicare* (short for medical care, an idea whose time is coming.)

☞ 11 *Bay of Pigs* (a place name that will live in infamy for years to come)

■■■■■■■■■■■■■■■■■■■■■■■■■■■■■■■■

OCTOBER

01 ► Roger Maris of the New York Yankees hits his sixty-first home run in the 162nd and last game of the season, breaking Babe Ruth's 154-game 1927 record.

NOVEMBER

14 ► President John F. Kennedy decides to increase the number of American advisors in Vietnam from 1,000 to 16,000 over the next two years.

DECEMBER

01 ► Nazi war criminal Adolf Eichmann is sentenced to death for crimes against the Jewish people, crimes against humanity, and war crimes. He is hanged at Ramie Prison on May 31, 1962.

11 ► Two U.S. Army helicopter companies, representing the first direct military support for South Vietnam, arrive in Saigon. These first two companies include 32 helicopters and 4,000 men. They are immediately assigned to Vietnamese combat units.

October 1, 1961:
Roger Maris of the New York Yankees hits his sixty-first home run.

December 11, 1961:
Two U.S. Army helicopter companies, representing the first direct military support for South Vietnam, arrive in Saigon.

▶ 1961

1. Marilyn Monroe
2. Sam Rayburn
3. Oscar Robertson
4. Chubby Checker
5. John F. Kennedy
6. Alan Shepard
7. Roger Maris
8. Robert S. McNamara
9. Yuri Gagarin
10. J. D. Salinger

People most likely to be on the cover in 1961

*The year in which ▶
the Cuban missile crisis ▶
plays out and an American ▶
orbits the earth ▶*

1962

JANUARY

29 ▶ An East-West Conference on Banning Nuclear Weapons Tests ends in deadlock in Geneva. It began in October 1958, and its collapse suggests a new round of testing by the USSR and the United States.

FEBRUARY

08 ▶ The U.S. establishes the Military Assistance Command (MACV) in South Vietnam. At this moment, some 5,000 U.S. troops are in Vietnam with the official mission of providing training and technical assistance. For instance, the U.S. Special Forces are training Montangnard tribesmen to fight the Viet Cong.

20 ▶ Lieutenant Colonel John Glenn orbits the earth three times in space capsule *Friendship* 7, becoming the first American in orbit. Television beams his flight to 135 million Americans.

MARCH

02 ▶ Basketball player Wilt Chamberlain scores 100 points—36 field goals and 28 foul shots—for the Philadelphia Warriors against the New York Knicks.

February 20, 1962:
Lieutenant Colonel John Glenn orbits the earth three times in space capsule Friendship 7, becoming the first American in orbit.

09 ▶ The Pentagon announces that U.S. pilots are now flying combat missions in Vietnam.

■■■■■■■■■■■■■■■■■■■■■■■■■■■■■■■

Fads and Trends for 1962

☞ 1. the bossa nova—both the music and the dance itself

☞ 2. the watusi—both the music and the dance itself

☞ 3. Biggest of all is the twist—both the music and the dance itself—which started in '61 but goes out of control in '62.

☞ 4. The romantic goings on between Richard Burton and Elizabeth Taylor on the set of *Cleopatra* in Rome consume a river of newspaper ink.

☞ 5. Compact model cars, or those called compact, burgeon to such a degree that some think the term "compact" no longer has any meaning.

☞ 6. Freeze-dried foods, including steaks and chops, are a novelty in the market.

☞ 7. There has been a sizeable reduction in drug abuse in the nation. The Federal Bureau of Narcotics reports that in 1930 one American in 1,070 was addicted, but in 1962 the ratio drops to approximately one in 4,000.

☞ 8. The altogether new New York Mets fascinate the nation through their ineptitude. Despite the leadership of Casey Stengel, they lose a record 120 games.

☞ 9. By mid-1962 the boom in fallout shelters has gone bust and manufacturers cannot sell them at any price.

☞ 10. Folk music is very popular thanks to Peter, Paul, and Mary, the New Christie Minstrels, and Joan Baez. Bob Dylan releases his first album.

☞ 11. This is the year of the doctor show on TV thanks to *Dr. Kildare* and *Ben Casey*.

☞ 12. Broadway is fascinated with Edward Albee's rough and four-letter-word-heavy play, *Who's Afraid of Virginia Woolf?*

■■■■■■■■■■■■■■■■■■■■■■■■■■■■■■■

► 1962

APRIL

07 ► Cuba sentences 1,179 captive invaders from the ill-fated Bay of Pigs mission to thirty years in prison.

20 ► The segregationist New Orleans Citizens' Council initiates a plan to give free one-way transportation to blacks wishing to move to northern cities. By October 7, ninety-six persons have taken the "reverse freedom rides."

25 ► The United States resumes testing nuclear weapons in the atmosphere at Christmas Island in the Pacific.

MAY

15 ► President Kennedy orders 4,000 troops into Thailand as Communist forces advance in Laos.

31 ► Adolf Eichmann is hanged in Israel's Ramie prison.

JUNE

22 ► The Soviet Union casts its one-hundredth veto in the United Nations Security Council.

25 ► The U.S. Supreme Court rules that the use of an unofficial, nondenominational prayer in New York State public schools is unconstitutional.

■ ■

☞ 1. The USSR and Great Britain each have thirty-nine nuclear reactors.

☞ 2. It is determined that 44 percent of the world's adult population is illiterate.

☞ 3. At year's end there are 11,300 U.S. troops in Vietnam—up from 3,200 the year before.

☞ 4. In 1961 paperbacks accounted for 14 percent of the books sold; in 1962 the total rises to 31 percent.

☞ 5. The birthrate falls by more than 130,000 from 1961 as the number of women of childbearing age declines.

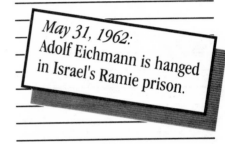

May 31, 1962:
Adolf Eichmann is hanged in Israel's Ramie prison.

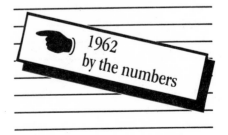

1962
by the numbers

6. For the first time ever, the life expectancy of the average American goes over seventy years.

7. The electronics industry is coming on like gangbusters; now the fifth-largest industry, sales for the year exceed $13.1 billion—up 30 percent from the year before.

8. Ninety percent of U.S. households have one television set; 13 percent have two or more.

9. The average American car is driven 120,000 miles and kept in operation for eleven years before being junked. In contrast, in the mid-1920s the average mileage was 25,000.

10. The Bureau of Labor Statistics estimates that 200,000 to 300,000 workers will lose their jobs each year for the next decade because of automation.

JULY

03 ► Algeria gets independence after 132 years of French rule.

10 ► The *Telstar* communications satellite is launched from Cape Canaveral, Florida, to relay TV and telephone signals between the United States and Europe.

► *Also today:* The first direct-dial long-distance telephone service goes into operation in the United States.

18 ► AT&T's *Telstar* relays the first TV programs across the Atlantic. Among other things, satellite transmission will everlastingly change the nature of television news.

AUGUST

05 ► Marilyn Monroe is found dead of a barbiturate overdose in her Los Angeles home. The death is officially ruled a suicide.

31 ► President Kennedy signs a law creating the Communications Satellite Corporation, or Comsat.

July 10, 1962:
The first direct-dial long-distance telephone service goes into operation in the United States.

▶ 1962

SEPTEMBER

02 ▶ The Soviet Union announces stepped-up aid to Cuba.

03 ▶ The last link in the trans-Canada highway is opened, making it, at 4,869 miles, the world's longest national highway.

30 ▶ Rioting among angry whites erupts when James Meredith, a black student, attempts to enroll at the University of Mississippi. By night's end 200 are arrested and two are dead, including French reporter Paul Guihard, who is shot in the back. It is quickly dubbed "the Battle of Ole Miss."

▪▪▪▪▪▪▪▪▪▪▪▪▪▪▪▪▪▪▪▪▪▪▪▪▪▪▪▪▪▪▪

☞ 1. *cryobiology* (the new science of very low temperatures)

☞ 2. *Astronaut Way* (the name for Fifth Avenue in New York on March 1 when 4 million New Yorkers turn out to salute John Glenn)

☞ 3. *blockade* (an old name for a particular act of war is brought back with nerve-wracking directness during the October Cuban missile crisis)

☞ 4. *corner back* (defensive halfback in football: the idea is old but the name is new)

☞ 5. *retrofire* (to fire a retrorocket)

☞ 6. *splashdown* (the landing of a spacecraft in the water, where it will float until recovered by a ship)

☞ 7. *the medium is the message* (the message from Marshall McLuhan, who sees salvation in television)

☞ 8. *diet cola* (now on the menu thanks to Diet-Rite Cola, which is introduced nationally)

☞ 9. *quarantine* (the term used by the White House to block the shipment of arms to Fidel Castro's Cuba)

☞ 10. *silent spring* (the title of Rachel Carson's book on the dangers of DDT and other pesticides becomes a metaphor for those dangers)

☞ 1962 in eleven words (& phrases)

☛ 11. *"You won't have Nixon to kick around anymore"* (former vice president's farewell to politics)

■■■■■■■■■■■■■■■■■■■■■■■■■■■■■■

OCTOBER

01 ▶ This evening Johnny Carson succeeds Jack Paar as the permanent host of the NBC *Tonight Show*.

19 ▶ China opens a heavy attack on India along the Himalayan frontier. The fighting lasts for thirty-three days.

23 ▶ The United States blockades—by air and sea—Cuba after announcing that it has photographs of Cuban-Russian missile bases capable of sending nuclear bombs 1,000 miles into the U.S. The U.S. threatens to invade Cuba if the bases are not dismantled. The Soviet Union threatens nuclear war.

28 ▶ Premier Khrushchev offers to take offensive weapons out of Cuba if the U.S. promises not to invade Cuba or allow others to invade. For all practical purposes, the Cuban missile crisis is over.

NOVEMBER

01 ▶ The Soviet Union launches an unmanned probe to Mars.

08 ▶ All known missile bases in Cuba have been dismantled and are on their way back to the USSR.

21 ▶ The U.S. ends its blockade of Cuba after the Soviet Union promises to have all of its jet planes off the island by December 20.

30 ▶ Burma's U Thant is elected to the post of secretary-general of the United Nations. This effectively ends the Soviet bid to change the structure of the world organization by installing a three-member board instead of the secretary-general.

October 1, 1962: Johnny Carson succeeds Jack Paar as the permanent host of the NBC *Tonight Show*.

November 1, 1962: The Soviet Union launches an unmanned probe to Mars.

▶ 1962

DECEMBER

23 ▶ In exchange for millions of dollars worth of prescription drugs, 1,113 Cuban prisoners are flown to the United States.

■■■■■■■■■■■■■■■■■■■■■■■■■■■■■■■■

☞ 1. John Glenn
☞ 2. Pope John XXIII
☞ 3. Tennessee Williams
☞ 4. Edward M. Kennedy
☞ 5. Maury Wills
☞ 6. Vince Lombardi
☞ 7. Joan Baez
☞ 8. Billie Sol Estes
☞ 9. Jack Nicklaus
☞ 10. Sophia Loren

■■■■■■■■■■■■■■■■■■■■■■■■■■■■■■■■

☞ People most likely to be on the cover in 1962

▶ 145

The year in which ▶ President Kennedy is ▶ assassinated in Dallas ▶ **1963**

JANUARY

14 ▶ George Wallace, sworn in as governor of Alabama, pledges, "segregation now, segregation tomorrow and segregation forever."

FEBRUARY

26 ▶ NASA announces that its *Mariner II* spacecraft has determined that Venus has no magnetic field and that its surface is too hot for manned exploration or life of any kind.

28 ▶ President Kennedy sends a major civil rights message to Congress in which he calls for new voting rights, job opportunities, and educational integration.

MARCH

20 ▶ The first major pop art exhibition opens at the Guggenheim Museum in New York, featuring such artists as Andy Warhol, Robert Rauschenberg, and Jasper Johns.

■ ■

☞ 1. Weight control becomes commodified with the introduction of Metracal, Tab (cola), and Weight Watchers.

☞ 2. *Beverly Hillbillies* is the top television show.

March 20, 1963: The first major pop art exhibition opens at the Guggenheim Museum in New York.

☞ Fads and Trends for 1963

3. Home saunas are the hot trend for those who can afford them.

4. Goofy elephant jokes are the rage. (Sample: Why do elephants have trunks? Because they don't have glove compartments.)

5. The Kodak Instamatic brings in film in a cartridge.

6. Pool comes on as a game for both men and women in large numbers. Pastel-colored streamlined tables in well-lit halls give the game of dim backrooms a new image.

7. The business of dying comes under fire with two scathing books: Jessica Mitford's *The American Way of Death* and Ruth M. Harmer's *The High Cost of Dying*.

8. The assassination and its aftermath give television a new place and distinction in the American scheme of things. "Through television," wrote Jack Gould of the *New York Times*, "the shock of history reverberated in every home."

9. Films like *Tom Jones* and *Lawrence of Arabia* pull a lot of people away from TV sitcoms.

10. Fashion focuses on the "young look"—sleeveless dresses, knee-high skirts, pleated trousers, etc.—and turtle neck shirts and sweaters.

APRIL

04 ► President Kennedy's Advisory Commission on Narcotic and Drug Abuse recommends a massive attack on importers of drugs.

10 ► The last message is received from the nuclear submarine *Thresher*. The loss of 129 men makes it the worst U.S. submarine disaster in history. It had been the navy's fastest, deepest-diving sub.

17 ► Pete Rozelle suspends Green Bay's Paul Hornung and Detroit's Alex Karras for gambling with known hoodlums. Fines for five others on the Detroit Lions are $2,000 each.

April 4, 1963: President Kennedy's Advisory Commission on Narcotic and Drug Abuse recommends massive attacks on importers of drugs.

29 ▶ The Supreme Court rules that racial segregation in courtrooms violates the Constitution.

MAY

03 ▶ Birmingham, Alabama, police attack young civil rights marchers with dogs and fire hoses.

15 ▶ The President's Science Advisory Committee calls for caution in the use of pesticides and asks for further research on their impact.

25 ▶ At a conference in Addis Ababa, Ethiopia, thirty African nations form the Organization of African Unity.

JUNE

12 ▶ Medgar Evers, a civil rights leader and secretary of the NAACP, is murdered by a sniper in Jackson, Mississippi.

17 ▶ By a vote of eight to one the Supreme Court declares Bible reading and the reciting of the Lord's Prayer in public schools to be unconstitutional.

26 ▶ President John F. Kennedy visits West Berlin, where he is greeted by more than 1 million residents of the divided city. In his speech he makes his famous declaration, *"Ich bin ein Berliner."* It proves to be one of the emotional high points of the Kennedy years.

30 ▶ Pope Paul VI is crowned the 262nd head of the Roman Catholic Church in an outdoor ceremony at St. Peter's Square.

☞ 1. The cost of mailing a first-class letter rises from four to five cents.

☞ 2. *Cleopatra* opens. At $37 million it is the most expensive movie to this date.

☞ 3. The number of American troops in Vietnam at the end of the year is 16,300—up from 11,300 at the end of 1962.

May 15, 1963: The President's Science Advisory Committee calls for caution in the use of pesticides and asks for further research on their impact.

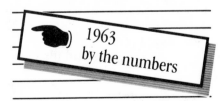

1963 by the numbers

4. Two-thirds of the automobiles in the world are in the United States.

5. For the first time in history, American workers earn an average of more than $100 per week.

6. For the first time, Americans spend more than a billion dollars on television sets in one year.

7. At $585 billion the gross national product outdistances the predictions of experts.

8. Eighty-two million cars, trucks, and buses are now crowding the American road.

9. There are now a million motel rooms in the nation— up from 60,000 in 1958.

10. The average farm worker now produces enough food for thirty-one others, a far cry from the 15.5 in 1950.

JULY

24 ► Cuba seizes the U.S. embassy in Havana.

AUGUST

07 ► The United Nations Security Council votes nine to zero to ban arms shipments to South Africa. Great Britain and France abstain.

28 ► More than 200,000 people take part in a massive march on Washington in the name of civil rights and racial equality. Dr. Martin Luther King, Jr., head of the Southern Christian Leadership Conference, delivers his stirring "I have a dream" speech to the mass of people assembled at the Lincoln Memorial. During the day, King and nine other black leaders meet with President Kennedy at the White House.

30 ► The first emergency hot line goes on line between the White House and the Kremlin. The purpose of the special line is to provide a means of emergency consultation that

August 30, 1963:
The first emergency hot line goes on line between the White House and the Kremlin.

can prevent accidental war. It is approved by a pact signed on June 20 by delegates from the two nations.

SEPTEMBER

02 ▶ Alabama governor George Wallace prevents the integration of Tuskegee High School by surrounding the building with state troopers.

10 ▶ Twenty black students enter public schools in Tuskegee, Birmingham, and Mobile following a standoff between Governor George Wallace and federal authorities. As the Alabama National Guard is federalized, Wallace gives up.

15 ▶ A black Baptist church is bombed in Birmingham, Alabama, killing four schoolgirls ages eleven to fourteen. The Sixteenth Street Baptist Church is the largest in the city and had been the site of several civil rights rallies. Two more blacks are killed in the ensuing riots, including a sixteen-year-old who is shot by the police for throwing rocks.

■■■■■■■■■■■■■■■■■■■■■■■■■■■■■■■■■■

☞ 1. *strategic hamlet* (South Vietnam proclaims that 39 percent of its people live in such enclaves.)

☞ 2. *The Fire Next Time* (the title of a James Baldwin book and a warning of possible black violence if things do not change)

☞ 3. *fail-safe* (The public learns the military term for the point at which a bomber pilot—alerted to the possibility of attack—is told whether to proceed or return to base.)

☞ 4. *General Hospital* (A new daytime soap opera gives this term a new, naughty meaning.)

☞ 5. *Pacem in Terris* (name for the encyclical issued by Pope John XXIII advocating peaceful settlement of issues between Catholics and non-Catholics)

☞ 6. *Surtsey* (an island that is being formed by an underwater volcano)

☞ **1963 in ten words (& phrases)**

7. *blister pack* (a dome of plastic covering products on a piece of cardboard. It gets you to buy thirty-six wing nuts when you need only four.)

8. *nitty-gritty* (the essential)

9. *hootenannies* (the continued success of folk music brings these about. Sing out!)

10. *wallpaper music* (background music of the kind heard in an elevator or in the dentist's chair)

■■■■■■■■■■■■■■■■■■■■■■■■■■■■■■■■■

OCTOBER

07 ► President Kennedy signs the nuclear test ban treaty after its ratification by the U.S. Senate.

11 ► The Commission on the Status of Women reports to President Kennedy, who concedes that there is discrimination against women in the United States.

NOVEMBER

01 ► President Ngo Dinh Diem is murdered in a military coup in Saigon, which results in a series of coups.

18 ► AT&T introduces the Touch-Tone telephone to a nation that is said to be obsessed with space-age speed and push-button convenience. Studies are released that show that people dial more quickly and more accurately with the Touch-Tone. To dial a seven-digit number takes an average of ten seconds on a rotary dial but only five seconds on the new push-button system.

22 ► President John F. Kennedy is shot by a sniper in Dallas, Texas. He dies within the half hour. Lee Harvey Oswald is arrested as the assassin after he shoots and kills patrolman J. D. Tippitt.

Aboard the presidential jet, Lyndon B. Johnson takes the oath of office, making him the thirty-sixth president of the United States.

October 11, 1963:
The Commission on the Status of Women reports to President Kennedy, who concedes that there is discrimination against women in the United States.

November 22, 1963:
President John F. Kennedy is shot by a sniper in Dallas, Texas.

▶ 1963

24 ▶ Lee Harvey Oswald is shot dead as he is transferred from the city to the county jail in Dallas. His assailant is nightclub owner Jack Ruby. The shooting is seen live on television by millions of viewers.

25 ▶ John F. Kennedy is buried at Arlington National Cemetery.

DECEMBER

07 ▶ The instant replay is born during a telecast of the Army-Navy game in Philadelphia. The first play to be shown again is a short touchdown run by Army quarterback Rollie Stichweh. "This is not live!" announcer Lindsey Nelson screams, "Ladies and gentlemen, Army did not score again."

■■■■■■■■■■■■■■■■■■■■■■■■■■■■■■■

☞ 1. GENERAL WALKER FOR PRESIDENT IN '64
☞ 2. MARCH ON WASHINGTON FOR JOBS AND FREEDOM
☞ 3. WE SAW NIAGARA FALLS

■■■■■■■■■■■■■■■■■■■■■■■■■■■■■■■

☞ 1. John F. Kennedy
☞ 2. Gordon Cooper
☞ 3. Sandy Koufax
☞ 4. Sonny Liston
☞ 5. Governor George Wallace
☞ 6. Martin Luther King, Jr.
☞ 7. Harold Wilson
☞ 8. Pope Paul VI
☞ 9. Christine Keeler
☞ 10. Cassius M. Clay

■■■■■■■■■■■■■■■■■■■■■■■■■■■■■■■

☞ 1963 in buttons & bumper stickers

☞ People most likely to be on the cover in 1963

The year in which the ▶
Civil Rights Act is passed ▶
and the government ▶
attacks smoking ▶

1964

JANUARY

08 ▶ Lyndon B. Johnson makes his first state-of-the-union address to Congress and uses it to call for greater efforts in civil rights and to declare his war on poverty. (See March 16.)

30 ▶ A coup in Vietnam topples the junta that deposed Diem in a late 1963 coup.

FEBRUARY

02 ▶ The U.S. *Ranger VI* hits the moon. American hardware is now on the lunar surface but fails to send back the photographs it is supposed to.

03 ▶ Some 465,000 students are absent from the schools of New York City in a one-day protest against de facto segregation. The boycott is repeated and the message underscored on March 16.

06 ▶ Fidel Castro cuts off the water supply—for twenty-three hours a day—to the American naval base at Guantanamo Bay.

09 ▶ The toy soldier known as GI Joe is introduced by Hasbro, Inc. Since then, Joe has rarely been out of the top ten most popular toys except for a brief furlough in the late 1970s. As far into the future as 1986, it will be the most popular toy of the year.

February 13, 1964:
The Beatles arrive in the United States for the first time.

▶ 155

————————————
————————————
————————————
————————————
————————————
————————————
————————————
————————————
————————————
————————————
————————————

Fads and Trends for 1964 ☞

————————————
————————————
————————————
————————————
————————————
————————————
————————————
————————————
————————————
————————————
————————————
————————————

13 ► The Beatles arrive in the U.S. for the first time. On the 15th they appear on the *Ed Sullivan* television show, and rock 'n' roll never is the same.

MARCH

16 ► President Johnson sends his War on Poverty program to Congress, calling for an Office of Economic Opportunity to administer it.

■■■■■■■■■■■■■■■■■■■■■■■■■■■■■■■■■■

☞ 1. The Beatles' popularity skyrockets with hit after hit and two U.S. tours.

☞ 2. Bob Dylan becomes very popular singing hitherto unpopular songs of protest.

☞ 3. Sperm banks open (the first two are in Tokyo and Iowa City), fueling jokes about this new human institution.

☞ 4. The success of *The Feminine Mystique* establishes the women's movement as a readers' movement.

☞ 5. The electric carving knife makes it easier to cut a roast or turkey.

☞ 6. Discotheques draw hordes to do the frug, monkey, and funky chicken.

☞ 7. The Rolling Stones break into the U.S. top forty.

☞ 8. The Berkeley free speech movement begins and attracts the attention of many campuses.

☞ 9. Rudi Gernreich introduces the topless bathing suit. It is more discussed than observed.

☞ 10. Two brands of electric toothbrush get the approval of the American Dental Association.

■■■■■■■■■■■■■■■■■■■■■■■■■■■■■■■■■■

APRIL

17 ► The Ford Mustang makes its debut and immediately turns heads. It spawns a generation of copycat small, high-per-

formance, V-8 powered cars that are known as "pony cars" in deference to the Mustang. Among its sires: the Plymouth Barracuda, Chevrolet Camaro, and Pontiac Firebird.

The car brings immediate fame to Lee Iacocca, who later becomes more famous when he revives the Chrysler Corporation.

MAY

21 ▶ The world's first nuclear lighthouse goes into operation in Baltimore with the promise that it can run without attention for ten years.

24 ▶ In Lima, Peru, 318 soccer spectators die in a riot.

JUNE

15 ▶ New York City comes out with a desegregation plan that is acceptable to black groups.

20 ▶ Freedom summer brings a thousand young civil rights workers to Mississippi.

21 ▶ Three civil rights workers disappear in Philadelphia, Mississippi. The three men are Andrew Goodman, a twenty-year-old white New Yorker, James Chaney, a twenty-one-year-old black Meridian resident, and Henry Schwerner, a twenty-four-year-old white New Yorker. The three men are conducting a black voter registration drive when they leave the site of a burned black church in Neshoba County. They are arrested on a traffic violation, taken to jail in Philadelphia, and later released. They disappear this day and their bodies are found forty-four days later buried in an earthen dam.

■■■■■■■■■■■■■■■■■■■■■■■■■■■■■■■■■■

☞ 1. California becomes the most populous state, dropping New York to second place.

☞ 2. U.S. airlines rack up $130 million in profits.

June 20, 1964: Freedom summer brings a thousand young civil rights workers to Mississippi.

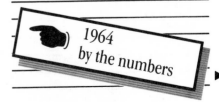

1964 by the numbers

☞ 3. The GNP soars to $625 billion.

☞ 4. It is determined that there are now more than 500 million radios in the United States.

☞ 5. CBS buys an 80 percent stake in the New York Yankees for $11.2 million.

☞ 6. Some 10 million Beatles records are sold in the U.S., and their *Hard Day's Night* reaps $5.6 million in its first six weeks in movie theaters.

☞ 7. Americans smoke 524 billion cigarettes, which averages out to 4,300 cigarettes, or 215 packs for every American over the age of eighteen.

☞ 8. Americans now pump $3.5 billion into vending machines per year.

☞ 9. A head of lettuce now costs twenty-five cents and a pound of coffee sets you back eighty-two cents.

☞ 10. The average American spends eighteen cents of his or her after-tax dollar for food.

■■■■■■■■■■■■■■■■■■■■■■■■■■■■■■■■■■

JULY

02 ► On the same day it is passed by Congress, President Johnson signs the Civil Rights Act into law. It is the most sweeping legislation of its kind since Reconstruction.

15 ► Senator Barry Goldwater of Arizona is nominated for president by the Republican National Convention in San Francisco.

18 ► Urban inner-city rioting breaks out in New York City and Rochester. They are the first in a long series of riots.

AUGUST

02 ► The president announces that the destroyers *Maddox* and *Turner Joy* have been attacked by North Vietnamese torpedo boats in the Gulf of Tonkin. He orders immediate retaliation.

July 18, 1964:
Urban inner-city rioting breaks out in New York City and Rochester.

► 1964

04 ► The bodies of the three civil rights workers, missing since June 21, are found buried in Mississippi.

07 ► Congress approves the Gulf of Tonkin Resolution, giving the commander-in-chief power "to take all necessary *measures* to repel any armed attack against the forces of the United States, and to prevent further aggression."

SEPTEMBER

27 ► The 888-page Warren Commission report summarizing the findings of the inquiry into the death of President Kennedy concludes that Lee Harvey Oswald acted alone. For years to come, critics insist that there is more to the story and Oswald was part of a larger conspiracy.

■■■■■■■■■■■■■■■■■■■■■■■■■■■■■■■■■■

☛ 1. *Beatlemania* (The fab four win eight gold records this year.)

☛ 2. *go-go* (as in "go-go girls," who are part of the attraction at the discotheques)

☛ 3. *supertanker* (a term attached to the launching of the 205,000-ton Japanese *Idemitsu Maru*)

☛ 4. *brain drain* (what happens as engineers and scientists move out of their own countries to work elsewhere. The term describes many British who come to the United States to work in the aerospace and computer industries.)

☛ 5. *Pop-Tarts* (toaster pastries that are new this year from Kellogg's)

☛ 6. *white backlash* (Caucasian hostility to the civil rights movement)

☛ 7. *frontlash* (Lyndon B. Johnson's term for disaffected Republicans who he predicted would vote Democratic)

☛ 8. *Goldwaterism* (reactionary Republicanism)

☛ 9. *quasar* (a distant object in space radiating strong radio waves)

☞ 1964 in ten words (& phrases)

► 159

► 10. *the new math* (a new approach to one of the basic subjects)

■■■■■■■■■■■■■■■■■■■■■■■■■■■■■■■■■■■■■

OCTOBER

15 ► Nikita Khrushchev is ousted as premier of the Soviet Union.

16 ► The Chinese detonate their first atomic bomb.

NOVEMBER

23 ► Today is the last day that Latin is used as the official language of the liturgy of the Roman Catholic church.

24 ► Congolese rebels kill eighteen white hostages in Stanleyville. This massacre is one bloody incident in a long and bloody year in which hundreds of white and black residents are slain.

DECEMBER

31 ► The first North Vietnamese regulars appear in South Vietnam as the war escalates. At this point there are 23,300 American troops in Vietnam.

■■■■■■■■■■■■■■■■■■■■■■■■■■■■■■■■■■■■■

► 1. LBJ FOR THE USA
► 2. WHAT'S WRONG WITH BEING RIGHT? (Goldwater item)
► 3. HENRY SABOTAGE FOR PRESIDENT (anti-Lodge item)
► 4. AuH₂O
► 5. NOBODY FOR PRESIDENT
► 6. ALLONS AVEC L'EAU D'OR
► 7. BE HAPPY GO ROCKY
► 8. THINK! PREVENT WALLACITIS
► 9. PANTIN' FOR SCRANTON
► 10. . . . and the great generic entry BUMPER STICKER

■■■■■■■■■■■■■■■■■■■■■■■■■■■■■■■■■■■■■

November 23, 1964:
Today is the last day that Latin is used as the official language of the liturgy of the Roman Catholic church.

1964 in buttons & bumper stickers ☞

The year in which ▶
the Great Society is unveiled ▶ **1965**

JANUARY

04 ▶ President Lyndon Johnson's state-of-the-union address calls for the creation of the Great Society, the most ambitious program of social legislation since the New Deal.

FEBRUARY

03 ▶ At the U.S. Air Force Academy, 105 cadets resign in a major cheating and exam-selling scandal.

07 ▶ The United States bombs North Vietnam in retaliation for a National Liberation Front (NFL) attack on U.S. ground troops in South Vietnam.

21 ▶ Malcolm X, leading spokesman among black nationalists, is shot and killed while speaking in New York City.

MARCH

07 ▶ Black marchers leaving Selma, Alabama, for the state capital at Montgomery are attacked and beaten back by 200 state police using tear gas, nightsticks, and whips.

09 ▶ The first of President Johnson's Great Society bills is signed into law: a billion-dollar package of aid for the eleven-state Appalachia area.

January 4, 1965:
The Great Society is launched in President Lyndon Johnson's state-of-the-union address.

▶ 161

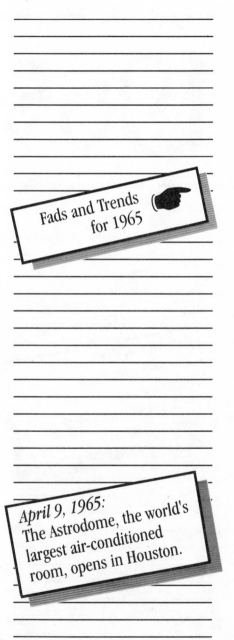

Fads and Trends for 1965

April 9, 1965:
The Astrodome, the world's largest air-conditioned room, opens in Houston.

23 ▶ America's first two-person space flight begins as *Gemini 3,* nicknamed the Molly Brown, blasts off from Cape Kennedy with astronauts Virgil Grissom and John Young on board.

25 ▶ The Selma to Montgomery civil rights march is completed, but on this day white volunteer Viola Gregg Liuzzo is killed by the Ku Klux Klan while transporting marchers.

1. James Brown establishes himself as soul brother number one.

2. Bellbottom trousers come into vogue.

3. Mary Quant, fashion designer, introduces the miniskirt.

4. The Great Society envisioned by LBJ moves ahead with the creation of new agencies and federal programs.

5. As if to show the distance the nation has come since World War II, CBS brings on a TV sitcom named *Hogan's Heroes.* It is set in a German POW camp and features nutty, fun-loving Nazis. NBC counters with the Oedipal oddity *My Mother the Car.*

6. This is the year in which the Frisbee flying disc comes on strong and they fill the air.

7. The lava lamp is born. To some they are tacky and ugly— but not, it would seem, to the 2.5 million who go out and buy one.

8. Thirty thousand new books appear this year. Daily newspaper circulation reaches an estimated 60,640,000.

9. The 007–James Bond mania inspires TV spy series, including *The Man from U.N.C.L.E.* and *Get Smart!*

10. Among the many items that come into fashion this year: poor boy sweaters, white Courrèges boots, bare knees, and white textured stockings.

▶ 1965

APRIL

06 ▶ The world's first commercial communications satellite, *Early Bird*, is launched. Regular use of the satellite by television networks begins on May 2.

09 ▶ The Astrodome, the world's largest air-conditioned room, opens in Houston.

MAY

02 ▶ President Johnson sends 14,000 troops to the Dominican Republic "to prevent another Communist state in this hemisphere."

15 ▶ A teach-in opposing the Vietnam War is broadcast to over 100 colleges.

JUNE

09 ▶ For the first time, the United States confirms that Americans are undertaking combat assignments in Vietnam.

■■■■■■■■■■■■■■■■■■■■■■■■■■■■■■■■

☞ 1. This is the first year of the Eastern Shuttle and the cost of a one-way ticket between New York and Washington is $18.

☞ 2. The nation is spending $654 per public school student—$262 billion in all.

☞ 3. The Watergate complex opens in Washington, D.C., where the price of a two-bedroom condominium is $38,500.

☞ 4. The biggest year yet for U.S. automakers: *profits* for the American manufacturers exceed $3 billion.

☞ 5. Color television arrives this year to the extent that 96 percent of NBC's programs, 50 percent of CBS's, and 40 percent of ABC's are in color.

☞ 6. At Tiffany's in Manhattan a full sterling silver service for eight, including gold-finished plates, sells for $9,000.

May 15, 1965: A teach-in opposing the Vietnam War is broadcast to over 100 colleges.

☞ 1965 by the numbers

July 15, 1965:
President Johnson signs the law requiring cigarette packages and ads to be printed with health warnings.

August 11, 1965:
Rioting breaks out in the Watts section of Los Angeles involving at least 10,000 Blacks, who burn and loot a 500-square-block area.

☛ 7. A record sales year for tuxedos, tail coats, and formal attire: $55 million.

☛ 8. Approximately 1 percent of the U.S. GNP ($670 billion) is earmarked for foreign aid.

☛ 9. Statistically, marriage and divorce are both hot: the former is up 5 percent over 1964 and the latter has increased by 7 percent.

☛ 10. Americans buy $60 million in prescription drugs designed to help them lose weight, up from $30 million worth five years ago.

JULY

15 ▶ U.S. scientists display close-up photographs of the planet Mars taken by the spacecraft *Mariner IV*.

▶ *Also today:* President Johnson signs the law requiring cigarette packages and ads to be printed with health warnings.

23 ▶ The president signs a coinage bill that eliminates silver from quarters and dimes and restricts its use in half-dollars.

28 ▶ President Johnson announces that soon 125,000 American troops will be in South Vietnam, up from the present level of 75,000, and that draft calls will be doubled. This announcement marks the moment of escalation that eventually leads to massive unrest across the United States.

30 ▶ Over the objections of the American Medical Association, the Social Security Act is amended to create Medicare, a government-funded health insurance plan for the elderly.

AUGUST

11 ▶ Rioting breaks out in the Watts section of Los Angeles involving at least 10,000 blacks who burn and loot a 500-square-block area. Fifteen thousand police and National Guardsmen are brought in to control the situation. The rioting lasts through the 16th.

▶ 1965

SEPTEMBER

09 ▶ President de Gaulle announces that France is withdrawing from NATO.

21 ▶ British Petroleum strikes oil in the North Sea. The rig from which the discovery is made collapses on December 27, 1965.

■■■■■■■■■■■■■■■■■■■■■■■■■■■■■

☞ 1. *Caution: cigarette smoking may be hazardous to your health* (the warning that Congress legislates for all cigarette packages)

☞ 2. *Vietnik* (one opposed to the war in Vietnam)

☞ 3. *pop-top* (a type of can that can be opened by lifting a small lid that stays attached to the can)

☞ 4. *charisma* (an old word that gets a new workout as glamour candidate John V. Lindsay is elected mayor of New York City)

☞ 5. *vodkatini* (a vodka martini in its first blush of popularity)

☞ 6. *teach-in* (a protest at which the issue being protested is discussed)

☞ 7. *folk rock* (a blend of two musical forms commonly associated with protest)

☞ 8. *clad coinage* (what they call the new coins that are not made, but rather coated, with silver)

☞ 9. *blackout* (Millions learned the modern meaning of this term on November 9.)

☞ 10. *EVA* (extravehicular activity—what an astronaut does outside the spacecraft)

■■■■■■■■■■■■■■■■■■■■■■■■■■■■■

☞ 1965 in ten words (& phrases)

OCTOBER

15 ▶ Anti–Vietnam War rallies are held in forty U.S. cities, the largest (10,000) in New York and Berkeley. In New York, police make the first arrest under a new federal draft-card-

November 9, 1965:
A massive power blackout hits the Northeast United States, Ontario, and Quebec. In New York City it hits during the evening rush hour.

People most likely to be on the cover in 1965

burning law. In Berkeley marchers are blocked from entering Oakland by police and then attacked by the Hell's Angels motorcycle gang.

NOVEMBER

09 ► A massive power blackout hits the Northeast U.S., Ontario, and Quebec. In New York City it hits during the evening rush hour.

DECEMBER

15 ► The *Gemini VII* and *Gemini IV* spacecraft rendezvous in space for the first such meeting in history.

■■■■■■■■■■■■■■■■■■■■■■■■■■■■■■■■

1. Lyndon B. Johnson
2. General William Westmoreland
3. The Beatles
4. Lady Bird Johnson
5. Sonny and Cher
6. Chris Kraft
7. Ho Chi Minh
8. John V. Lindsay
9. Barbra Streisand
10. Carl Albert

■■■■■■■■■■■■■■■■■■■■■■■■■■■■■■■■

The year in which a little ▶
war becomes a big one ▶
and unrest grows on the ▶
campus and in the ghetto ▶

1966

JANUARY

13 ▶ President Johnson nominates Dr. Robert Weaver to become the first black Cabinet member in U.S. history. Weaver, a Harvard graduate and head of the Housing and Home Finance Agency since 1961, becomes secretary of the new Department of Housing and Urban Development (HUD) when confirmed by the Senate on January 17.

FEBRUARY

06 ▶ In Honolulu President Johnson and Premier Ky of South Vietnam begin three days of meetings to discuss the war. Ky emerges from the meeting insisting that he will not negotiate with the Viet Cong or talk of a coalition government. He urges more bombing by the United States.

MARCH

16 ▶ Ten thousand Buddhists march in Saigon to protest the corruption of the U.S.-supported Ky regime.
25 ▶ Rallies against the war in Vietnam are staged in seven cities in the U.S. and Europe. The largest turnouts are in New York City and Washington, D.C.

March 16, 1966:
Ten thousand Buddhists march in Saigon to protest the corruption of the U.S.-supported Ky regime.

▶ 167

► 1966

Fads and Trends for 1966

■ ■

☞ 1. *The Quotations of Chairman Mao* (a.k.a. "The Little Red Book") finds a surprisingly large audience in the West.

☞ 2. A number of groups are being formed to advance the cause of women's rights, but one commands immediate attention—the National Organization of Women (NOW) headed by Betty Friedan.

☞ 3. Simon and Garfunkel are tops in pop music.

☞ 4. The use of consciousness-raising drugs—mainly lysergic acid diethylamide (LSD) and marijuana—gain national attention.

☞ 5. Ralph Nader, a young lawyer who published *Unsafe at Any Speed* in 1965, becomes the leader in the fight for consumerism and auto safety legislation.

☞ 6. The mod look arrives from London in full force replete with—women first—fishnet stockings, undershirt tops, mannish jackets, little girl shoes, and mini—but sometimes maxi—skirts. Men get to wear skinny fitted pants, wide colorful ties, and shirts with floral wallpaper style prints.

☞ 7. Rising food costs spark a series of picket and protest lines around supermarkets by groups with names like HELP (Housewives to Enact Lower Prices).

☞ 8. A big year for new food products—instant freeze-dried coffee, liquid margarine in plastic squeeze bottles, veggies packed in butter, and rows of goods marked "low calorie" or "reduced in calories."

☞ 9. TV's biggest hit—the twice-a-week *Batman* show. Holy phenomenon! By the end of the year the caped crusader has invaded the toy market with model kits, walkie-talkies, radios, puzzles, capes, and batmobiles.

☞ 10. As draft calls increase, a great deal of controversy surrounds the military draft. A major point in the controversy is the fact that 1.9 million college boys have been deferred from it.

■ ■

1966

APRIL

30 ▶ In China the cultural revolution begins as Premier Chou En-lai calls for a long struggle to drive out bourgeois ideology.

MAY

15 ▶ The protest against the Vietnam War gains momentum as 63,000 marchers to the Washington Monument pledge to vote only for antiwar candidates.

16 ▶ Stokely Carmichael is elected chairman of SNCC—Student Nonviolent Coordinating Committee—beginning a shift in emphasis from civil rights to black power among black activists. The idea is for blacks to organize blacks into their own political groups.

JUNE

02 ▶ *Surveyor I* makes a perfect soft landing on the moon—a key U.S. first.

08 ▶ After a series of secret meetings between the NFL and rival AFL, NFL Commissioner Pete Rozelle announces a merger of the two leagues (regular-season play to begin in 1970). The first Super Bowl is set for 1967.

13 ▶ The Supreme Court hands down a decision in *Miranda v. Arizona* ruling that criminal suspects must be advised of their rights before they can be interrogated.

29 ▶ The United States bombs fuel storage facilities near the North Vietnamese cities of Hanoi and Haiphong, thereby ending the policy of avoiding urban areas.

30 ▶ Today is Mississippi's last day of prohibition—making the nation's last dry state wet at midnight.

April 30, 1966:
In China the cultural revolution begins as Premier Chou En-lai calls for a long struggle to drive out bourgeois ideology.

June 13, 1966:
The Supreme Court hands down a decision in *Miranda v. Arizona* ruling that criminal suspects must be advised of their rights before they can be interrogated.

▶ 169

▶ 1966

1966
by the numbers ☞

July 1, 1966:
The Medicare federal medical insurance program for the elderly goes into effect with 17 million enrollees.

■■■■■■■■■■■■■■■■■■■■■■■■■■■■■■■■■

1. U.S. factory workers take home an average of $91.80 a week.

2. The Pentagon announces that 5,008 Americans died in Vietnam during the year.

3. There are 78 million passenger cars on the roads of America.

4. A record 52,500 Americans die on the roads and 9 million are injured in traffic accidents. A Labor Day weekend record is set with 614 deaths.

5. The consumer price index hits a record high in July, making this the most inflationary year since 1957.

6. *A GOOD MEAL IN 1966:* At Reade's Restaurant at Burgaw, North Carolina, a dinner of southern fried chicken, two vegetables, hot bread or rolls, dessert, and tea or coffee is $1.10. If you just want homemade pie—chocolate, lemon, coconut, or apple—it costs $.20, a dime extra for à la mode.

7. There are 2,377 corporate mergers in the United States in 1966, which is triple the 1960 rate.

8. The moon has eight unmanned visitors from earth this year that either orbit or soft-land (five carry the markings of the Soviet Union; three are American).

9. U.S. automakers offer 367 basic '67 models.

10. Baseball draws a record 25.2 million.

■■■■■■■■■■■■■■■■■■■■■■■■■■■■■■■■■

JULY

01 ▶ The Medicare federal medical insurance program for the elderly goes into effect with 17 million enrollees.

07 ▶ Despite his conviction for taking $250,000 in union funds and his status on bail pending appeal, Jimmy Hoffa is re-elected to a five-year term as Teamsters president by acclamation.

▶ 1966

08 ▶ A machinist's strike closes down five major U.S. airlines. It ends on August 19.

12 ▶ Rioting breaks out on Chicago's mostly black West Side and lasts for several days despite the presence of the National Guard.

14 ▶ Eight student nurses are murdered by Richard Speck in a Chicago dormitory.

23 ▶ In Vietnam, Buddhist Thich Thien Hoa says that suicide by fire must end as a means of protest because it is taking too many. Ten Buddhists have taken their lives in this manner in 1966.

AUGUST

01 ▶ In Austin, Texas, Charles Whitman shoots and kills sixteen people. Most are shot from a campus tower at the University of Texas. Whitman is shot by police.

05 ▶ Beatle John Lennon says the Beatles are more popular than Jesus, leading many U.S. radio stations to take Beatles songs off the air.

20 ▶ In China young Red Guards begin a series of violent demonstrations as part of the Great Proletarian Cultural Revolution. The demonstrations spread throughout the country.

29 ▶ The Beatles make their last concert appearance as a group. It takes place at Candlestick Park in San Francisco.

SEPTEMBER

08 ▶ *Star Trek* makes its television debut.

09 ▶ Sweeping automobile safety legislation is signed into law by President Johnson. This legislation establishes such things as anchored seat belts, emergency flashers, recessed dashboard knobs, and postsale safety notices and recalls.

11 ▶ In New York City the longest newspaper strike in a major city ends. It was against the new *World-Journal-Tribune*, which had been created from three failing papers.

August 5, 1966:
Beatle John Lennon says the Beatles are more popular than Jesus, leading many U.S. radio stations to take Beatles songs off the air.

12 ▶ A white mob attacks black pupils at a school in Grenada, Mississippi. As a result, a federal judge orders local officials to protect students at integrated schools.

■■■■■■■■■■■■■■■■■■■■■■■■■■■■■■■■■■■■■

1966 in ten words (& phrases)

1. *swinger* (Sexual liberation frees us from terms like *promiscuous.*)

2. *Star Trek* (name of a new television show that takes a while to catch on. It runs for seventy-eight episodes.)

3. *jumbo jet* (In April Boeing gets its first order for some of these 490-seaters to be delivered beginning in 1969.)

4. *suggested for mature audiences* (The movie *Georgie Girl* is the first to carry this label; the second is *A Funny Thing Happened on the Way to the Forum.*)

5. *utterly* (term used in determining obscenity following a Supreme Court decision that states that a proper test of obscenity is something "utterly" without redeeming social value)

6. *The Persecution and Assassination of Marat as Performed by the Inmates of the Asylum of Charenton under the Direction of the Marquis de Sade* (the longest title ever on a Broadway marquee and, with violence and sensational effects, proof that it was not "business as usual" in show business)

7. *hunter-killer* (This was the name for the kind of operation that military planners at the Pentagon said was needed to resolve the war in Vietnam.)

8. *body count* (These were becoming important as Pentagon briefers could report that October's Operation Irving yielded 1,973 enemy dead, 1,765 enemy captured, and 5,712 suspected enemy apprehended.)

9. *mass murder* (a term made stunningly graphic during a year in which three of the worst in U.S. history take place: Speck's killings of eight student nurses in Chicago, Charles Whitman's Texas tower massacre of fourteen, and Robert Benjamin Smith's slaughter of five in Mesa, Arizona. Smith says he was "inspired" by Speck and Whitman.)

▶ 1966

☞ 10. *GTO* (A Pontiac with this three-letter name hits the showrooms and middle-agers turn into teen-agers with the turn of the ignition key.)

☞ 11. *black power* (popularized by Stokely Carmichael along with the clenched fist)

■■■■■■■■■■■■■■■■■■■■■■■■■■■■■■■

OCTOBER

15 ▶ The president signs a bill creating the Department of Transportation and adding a twelfth member to the Cabinet, the secretary of transportation.

NOVEMBER

08 ▶ Elections in the U.S. give major gains to the Republicans.

12 ▶ With today's splashdown of *Gemini XII,* this extremely successful program comes to an end.

DECEMBER

02 ▶ A ruling becomes effective exempting U.S. Roman Catholics from meatless Fridays (except during Lent). The ruling was announced on November 18, 1966.

■■■■■■■■■■■■■■■■■■■■■■■■■■■■■■■

☞ 1. COMMIT LBJ, NOT THE USA

☞ 2. MARY POPPINS IS A JUNKIE

☞ 3. TROUBLE PARKING? SUPPORT PLANNED PARENT-HOOD

☞ 4. WAR IS A GOOD BUSINESS, INVEST YOUR SON

☞ 5. DRAFT BEER, NOT BOYS

☞ 6. SEND BATMAN TO VIETNAM

☞ 7. I LOVE MY CORVAIR

☞ 8. IF IT MOVES, FONDLE IT

☞ 9. GOD IS A 5,000 FOOT TALL JELLY BEAN

☞ 10. POODLE POWER

■■■■■■■■■■■■■■■■■■■■■■■■■■■■■■■

October 15, 1966:
The president signs a bill creating the Department of Transportation and adding a twelfth member to the Cabinet, the secretary of transportation.

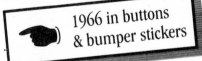
1966 in buttons & bumper stickers

The year race riots strike ▶
more than 100 cities and ▶
the U.S. and Soviet space ▶
programs experience tragedy ▶

1967

JANUARY

12 ▶ The first Super Bowl is staged in Los Angeles. The Green Bay Packers (NFL) beat the Kansas City Chiefs (AFL), thirty-five to ten.

27 ▶ During a ground test at Cape Kennedy, a flash fire inside an *Apollo* space capsule kills three American astronauts— Virgil I. Grissom, Edward H. White II, and Roger B. Chaffee. It is America's first space program disaster and a devastating and demoralizing blow to the program.

▶ *Also on this day:* The United States, Soviet Union, and sixty other nations sign a treaty agreeing to limit the military uses of space.

FEBRUARY

10 ▶ The twenty-fifth amendment to the Constitution is formally ratified. It deals with the disability and succession of the president.

13 ▶ The National Student Association admits that it has taken $3 million in secret aid from the Central Intelligence Agency.

February 13, 1967: The National Student Association admits that it has taken $3 million in secret aid from the Central Intelligence Agency.

▶ 175

▶ 1967

Fads and Trends for 1967 ☞

MARCH

01 ▶ Adam Clayton Powell, a congressman from Harlem who is a key to getting LBJ's Great Society bills passed, is denied his seat in Congress by a vote of 307 to 116 for using government money for private purposes. A House subcommittee denounces his "female-accompanied private pleasure jaunts at taxpayer expense."

18 ▶ A ship, *The Torrey Canyon,* is grounded off Land's End, England, spilling 34.9 million gallons of oil. It is the first of a long series of major oil spills (of 24 million gallons or more) that plague the world's waters.

21 ▶ Svetlana Alliluyeva, the daughter of Joseph Stalin, defects from the USSR and arrives in New York City.

■■■■■■■■■■■■■■■■■■■■■■■■■■■■■■■■■■

☞ 1. In Canada, Expo '67 opens to rave reviews and long lines.

☞ 2. Twiggy, the very thin boyish-looking model, becomes the darling of U.S. fashion.

☞ 3. Singles bars go into full swing across America.

☞ 4. *Blow-up* and *Bonnie and Clyde* set a new tone for movies with stylish presentation of frontal nudity and choreographic violence.

☞ 5. Andy Warhol breaks a number of taboos in a series of movies that bridge the gap between pornography and art film.

☞ 6. Nehru jackets are worn a few times and then placed in the back of the closet. Hula hoops make a short-lived comeback; this time they are loaded with metal beads that make an odd whirring sound.

☞ 7. Radio is changing. Droves are turning away from AM top-forty and tuning into FM "progressive" rock stations.

☞ 8. ABC makes *The Flying Nun* the centerpiece of its new season. It is at once a hit and proof positive that anything is possible in the world of television.

► 1967

☞ 9. The Monterey International Pop Festival is the first large gathering of the musical clan—Janis Joplin, The Grateful Dead, etc.—and becomes a watershed moment in rock 'n' roll history. The Who come from England to set off smoke bombs and smash their instruments.

☞ 10. As older institutions fall on hard times, new ones are cropping up. In November, *Rolling Stone* starts up on a $7,000 shoestring.

■■■■■■■■■■■■■■■■■■■■■■■■■■■■■■■■■■

APRIL

20 ► For the first time, U.S. planes bomb the North Vietnamese city of Haiphong.

24 ► The first human known to die in space is killed in a *Soyuz 1* mishap. Cosmonaut Vladimir M. Komarov dies as a parachute tangles during reentry.

MAY

30 ► Nigeria's eastern region secedes as the independent nation of Biafra.

JUNE

01 ► *Sgt. Pepper's Lonely Hearts Club Band* is released in Britain. By the end of the summer some 2.5 million copies are sold. For millions, it becomes a soundtrack for the time and the theme music for a rebellious generation's groovy coming-out party—1967's psychedelic summer of love. "Today," said *USA Today* on the twentieth anniversary of the record, "it remains an indelible musical and cultural totem of its time, in which The Beatles ushered in state-of-the-art rock by donning the costumes of an old-time oom-pah band."

02 ► Rioting breaks out in Roxbury, Boston's black district, following a welfare sit-in. Before the month is out there are

June 1, 1967:
Sgt. Pepper's Lonely Hearts Club Band is released in Britain.

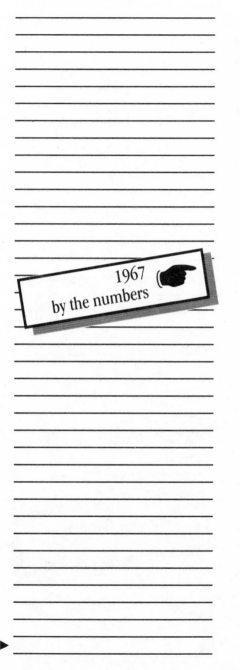

1967
by the numbers ☞

major disturbances in Tampa, Cincinnati, Buffalo, and Atlanta. A black man dies in the Atlanta riot of June 19–20.

05 ▶ The six-day Arab-Israeli War is fought. It quadruples the Israeli military occupation to four times its former size. It ends with an uneasy truce.

17 ▶ China explodes its first hydrogen bomb.

23 ▶ The Senate votes ninety-two to five to censure Senator Thomas J. Dodd for personal use of private funds, making him the sixth senator to be censured or condemned.

29 ▶ Jerusalem is reunified as Israel removes barricades separating the Old City from the Israeli sector.

■ ■

☞ 1. 100 million telephones are now in use in the United States.

☞ 2. Americans consume 12 billion cases of beer.

☞ 3. 9,419 die in Vietnam in 1967—more than died in all previous years of that war.

☞ 4. The cost of a Levittown, Long Island, home is $15,000, which is up from $6,990 in 1947.

☞ 5. The appropriation for defense is $69.9 billion. This is heaped on top of increased Social Security payments and new aid to education.

☞ 6. When the gross receipts are counted, it is shown that the movies are a billion-dollar industry without even counting exports. It is Hollywood's most prosperous year in a decade. It is coincidentally a year of great violence in the movies (*The Dirty Dozen, Bonnie and Clyde, Point Blank,* etc.).

☞ 7. With 700,000 welfare clients the city of New York cries for fiscal help.

☞ 8. For the seventh year in a row the poodle is the most popular dog in America. In order rounding out the other top breeds for the year—German shepherds, beagles, dachshunds, Chihuahuas, Pekinese, collies, miniature schnauzers, and cocker spaniels.

▶ 1967

☞ 9. Mickey Mantle hits his 500th career home run and Francis Chichester completes a one-man trip around the world in 226 days.

☞ 10. Boats and boating enjoy phenomenal popularity with sales over $3 billion.

■ ■

JULY

12 ▶ Race-related rioting breaks out in Newark, New Jersey. By the time the violence ends on July 17, twenty-seven people have been killed.

23 ▶ A week of racial rioting begins in Detroit and ends with thirty-nine people dead.

27 ▶ In response to widespread racial violence, President Johnson establishes a blue-ribbon panel on racial disorder and appoints Illinois Governor Otto Kerner, Jr., as its director.

30 ▶ Riots and fires break out in Milwaukee.

AUGUST

03 ▶ President Johnson asks for a 10 percent income tax surcharge to help pay for the war in Vietnam. He also announces that U.S. forces there would increase to 525,000 by June of 1968.

25 ▶ A former aide assassinates George Lincoln Rockwell, head of the American Nazi party.

SEPTEMBER

28 ▶ Walter E. Washington is appointed chief executive (commissioner) of the District of Columbia. He is the first black man to be given the key job in a predominantly black city.

> *August 3, 1967:*
> President Johnson asks for a 10 percent income tax surcharge to help pay for the war in Vietnam.

▶ 1967

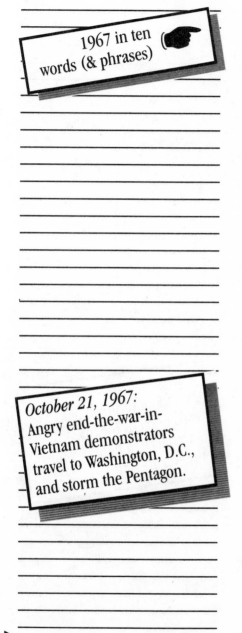

1967 in ten words (& phrases)

October 21, 1967:
Angry end-the-war-in-Vietnam demonstrators travel to Washington, D.C., and storm the Pentagon.

■■■■■■■■■■■■■■■■■■■■■■■■■■■■■■

☞ 1. *long hot summer* (phrase used for a stunning period of urban anger and violence. Not to be confused with . . .)

☞ 2. *summer of love* (one-time use for this term—this is the summer)

☞ 3. *love beads* (Even Sammy Davis, Jr., wore them in '67. Some were worn atop Nehru jackets.)

☞ 4. *Electric Prune* (the name of a rock group and just one of a number of surrealistic names that emerged in a surrealistic year)

☞ 5. *microwave* (a term that is on its way to household name status with the introduction of the first home microwave oven by Amana. It becomes a noun and a verb.)

☞ 6. *endangered species* (With the passage of laws protecting them, the term has new relevance.)

☞ 7. *ASH* (acronym for Action on Smoking and Health. This group posts many gains in the fight against tobacco.)

☞ 8. *do-little Congress* (President Johnson's name for the Ninetieth Congress. It reflects the national inertia over events and LBJ's declining popularity.)

☞ 9. *anatomically correct* (words used to describe the unflinching realism of the new dolls for children)

☞ 10. *draft-card burning* (a ritual of protest and anger)

■■■■■■■■■■■■■■■■■■■■■■■■■■■■■■■■

OCTOBER

02 ▶ Thurgood Marshall is sworn in as the first black Supreme Court justice.

09 ▶ The Bolivian army reports that Cuban revolutionary Ernesto Che Guevara has been killed in that country.

18 ▶ The Soviet *Venus IV* probe lands on Venus. It is the first successful landing on the planet.

21 ▶ Angry end-the-war-in-Vietnam demonstrators travel to Washington, D.C., and storm the Pentagon.

NOVEMBER

07 ▶ The United Nations adopts a rights for women declaration by unanimous vote in the General Assembly. It calls for "equal rights for women in employment, politics and cultural life."

10 ▶ Today, according to the Census Bureau, the population of the United States is 200 million. It has doubled in fifty years. More than one editorialist uses this milestone to point out that it means that there are 200 million people frustrated with inflation, urban rioting and violence, and the quagmire of Vietnam.

22 ▶ U.S. forces take Hill 875 in Vietnam after nineteen days of fighting and a cost of 290 American and 1,600 North Vietnamese lives.

DECEMBER

03 ▶ The world's first successful heart transplant operation is performed in Capetown, South Africa, by Dr. Christiaan Barnard. The patient, Louis Washkansky, lives until the 21st of the month.

09 ▶ For the first time since 1914, the daughter of a U.S. president is married in the White House. Lynda Bird Johnson and Charles S. Robb marry in the East Room.

■ ■

☞ 1. WHEN GUNS ARE OUTLAWED, ONLY OUTLAWS WILL HAVE GUNS

☞ 2. HOW DO TAXI DRIVERS GET TO WORK?

☞ 3. UNZIPPED MAIL IS IMMORAL

☞ 4. WHAT HAPPENED TO SMOKEY THE BEAR MATCHBOOKS?

☞ 5. JULIA CHILD EATS TV DINNERS

December 3, 1967: The world's first successful heart transplant operation is performed in Capetown, South Africa, by Dr. Christiaan Barnard.

1967 in buttons & bumper stickers

▶ 1967

■ ■

1968

JANUARY

02 ▶ World's second heart transplant is performed by Dr. Christiaan Barnard in Capetown, South Africa, on retired dentist Philip Blaiberg. (The first was performed there December 3, 1967, on Louis Washkansky, who died eighteen days later of pneumonia.)

05 ▶ The United States loses its 10,000th aircraft in Vietnam.

22 ▶ Rowan and Martin's *Laugh-In* series makes its regular television debut.

30 ▶ A national Tet Offensive by Viet Cong in Saigon and other towns is followed by sieges at Hue and Khe Sanh. Even though the Communist forces later retreat with heavy losses, it serves to intensify opposition to the war in the United States.

FEBRUARY

01 ▶ Richard Nixon declares his presidential candidacy.

08 ▶ Violence erupts during a racial protest by black students at South Carolina State College in Orangeburg. Police open fire, killing three students and wounding twenty-seven in what comes to be called the Orangeburg massacre.

08 ▶ Alabama Governor Wallace announces he will run for president on the newly formed American Independent party ticket.

January 5, 1968:
The United States loses its 10,000th aircraft in Vietnam.

12 ▶ Eldridge Cleaver's *Soul on Ice* is published. The book is hailed for its power in exploring a black's rage at the injustice he finds in society.

28 ▶ George Romney withdraws from the presidential race after being hurt by his own statement that he was "brainwashed" on Vietnam.

29 ▶ The Kerner Commission, headed by Illinois Governor Otto Kerner and appointed by the president to investigate civil disorders, issues a celebrated report warning that the United States is moving toward two societies, "one black, one white—separate and unequal." Among other things, it calls for financial aid to black communities. Ironically, many of those communities are seriously damaged in riots following the assassination of Martin Luther King, Jr., less than a month later on April 4.

MARCH

12 ▶ Johnson leads the New Hampshire Democratic primary with 48 percent (all write-ins). Minnesota senator Eugene McCarthy gets 42 percent but is widely regarded as the "winner." Nixon gets 79 percent on the Republican side to Rockefeller's 11 percent.

16 ▶ U.S. soldiers line up between 300 and 500 old men, women, and children in a ditch in the Vietnamese village of My Lai and shoot them. This massacre is covered up by the army until November 1969.

27 ▶ Soviet cosmonaut Yuri Gagarin, the first man to orbit Earth, dies in a plane crash.

31 ▶ LBJ announces that he will not seek reelection, creating a primary battle among Hubert Humphrey, Eugene McCarthy, and Robert Kennedy. Johnson also orders a halt to U.S. bombing of most of North Vietnam, excluding its southern 170 miles, and calls for negotiations.

▶ *Also:* A judge rules that Karen Anne Quinlan can be disconnected from her life support system.

March 31, 1968:
LBJ announces that he will not seek reelection.

1. Unisex is in, and as look-alike couples wear long hair, bellbottoms, and beads, sociologists scratch their heads.

2. It is a year of dissent and polarization—not a great time to be a public official, cop, or any other kind of authority figure.

3. The waterbed makes it big on the West Coast and the rest is history.

4. Physical fitness is termed the nation's newest fad.

5. New rock groups—including the Doors, Cream, and the Jefferson Airplane—emerge to challenge the dominance of the Beatles.

6. A movie, *The Graduate,* and a song from it, *Mrs. Robinson,* have a spellbinding effect on the young.

7. A nationwide boycott of table grapes is called by labor organizer Cesar Chavez. Many join as Chavez holds long fasts in support of his cause.

8. Military fatigues and combat boots are, paradoxically, in vogue for civilians opposed or just trying to avoid the war in Southeast Asia.

9. Stanley Kubrick's *2001* is the ultimate cinematic trip: is it a space opera, is it self-discovery, or does it represent a drug trip?

10. The paperwork backlog on Wall Street reaches such a level that the New York Stock Exchange is forced to close on Wednesdays.

Fads and Trends for 1968

April 4, 1968: Civil rights leader Martin Luther King, Jr., is shot and killed in Memphis by James Earl Ray just before 7 P.M.

APRIL

03 ▶ The North Vietnamese agree to begin peace talks in Paris.

04 ▶ Civil rights leader Martin Luther King, Jr., is shot and killed in Memphis by James Earl Ray just before 7 P.M. Within two hours, 125 cities across the nation are in flames with 46 deaths, 21,270 arrests, and 55,000 federal troops and

▶ 1968

1968
by the numbers ☞

national guard used to control riots, the biggest of which occur in Washington, D.C., Chicago, Baltimore, and Kansas City.

06 ▶ Relief forces arrive at the marine combat base at Khe Sanh, Vietnam, ending a seventy-seven-day siege.

23 ▶ Students at Columbia University seize five buildings in protest against Columbia's plan to build a new gymnasium in an adjacent ghetto area and against the university's connections with the Pentagon-sponsored Institute of Defense Analysis.

29 ▶ The rock musical *Hair* opens in New York.

MAY

02 ▶ In Washington, D.C., civil rights demonstrators hold a Poor People's March on the capital. Their base camp is Resurrection City, a shantytown of tents and shacks on the mall.

04 ▶ In Vietnam there are coordinated Viet Cong attacks. It is dubbed mini-Tet after the Tet Offensive of January 30–31.

JUNE

05 ▶ Robert Kennedy, age forty-two, is fatally shot in a Los Angeles hotel after winning the California primary. He dies early the next day.

14 ▶ Dr. Benjamin Spock, the Reverend William Sloane Coffin of Yale, and two others are convicted for counseling and aiding draft evasion.

■■■■■■■■■■■■■■■■■■■■■■■■■■■■■■■■■■■

☞ 1. The cost of mailing a first-class letter rises one cent to six cents.

☞ 2. The gross national product exceeds $846 billion.

☞ 3. The median family income in the U.S. is approaching $8,000 a year—about $2,000 over Sweden, which ranks second in the world after the United States. Meanwhile,

29,700,000 Americans live below the poverty line, which is now $3,335 a year.

☞ 4. Since 1940 and into 1968 it is determined that 4 million blacks along with uncounted poor whites have left the South for what they hoped would be a better life in the West and North.

☞ 5. At the supermarket—per an ad for Safeway, December 27, 1968—one can expect to pay $.79 a pound for ground chuck, $1.19 for choice beef roast, and $.63 for loin pork roast. Franks cost $1.09 for a two-pound package and two 8-ounce packages of fishsticks cost $.69.

☞ 6. The nation's jobless rate declines to 3.6 percent, which is a fifteen-year record. The number of hard-core unemployed is 323,000.

☞ 7. The average American now eats eleven pounds of fish per year.

☞ 8. ITT goes on a spending spree—$112 million for the Pennsylvania Sand Company, $200 million for the Sheraton Hotel Corporation, $293 million for Rayonier Corporation, and $280 million for Continental Baking.

☞ 9. The number to call in New York City in an emergency is 911. The number is adopted gradually across the country.

☞ 10. The nickel Hershey Bar is a thing of the past. It now costs a dime but weighs in at a fuller 1.5 ounces.

■ ■

June 5, 1968:
Robert Kennedy, age forty-two, is fatally shot in a Los Angeles hotel after winning the California primary.

JULY

01 ► The United States, USSR, and fifty-eight nations without nuclear weapons sign a treaty prohibiting the proliferation of such weapons.

► *Also on this date:* The United Automobile Workers separate from the AFL-CIO. The divorce takes place after years of squabbling.

05 ► Desecration of the American flag is made a federal offense.

September 30, 1968: U. S. strength in Vietnam is 537,800 – the highest level.

1968 in ten words (& phrases) ☛

AUGUST

20 ▶ The Soviet Union and other Warsaw Pact nations begin invading Czechoslovakia to crush the Prague spring liberalization drive of Alexander Dubcek's regime.

26 ▶ Riots occur at the Democratic National Convention in Chicago.

SEPTEMBER

16 ▶ Presidential candidate Richard Nixon appears on Rowan and Martin's *Laugh-In* and says, "Sock it to me!"

30 ▶ U.S. strength in Vietnam is 537,800—the highest level.

■■■■■■■■■■■■■■■■■■■■■■■■■■■■■■■■■

☛ 1. *yippie* (short for Youth International Party, a revolutionary notion with few members and great momentary impact)

☛ 2. *Chinese restaurant syndrome* (temporary symptoms from MSG; something else to fret about)

☛ 3. *zero population growth* (the goal and name of a group based in Washington, D.C., that wants to stabilize population. It is founded by Paul Ehrlich.)

☛ 4. *earthrise* (what you call an image of the earth rising above the lunar surface—à la *Apollo 8*)

☛ 5. *aerobics* (appropriate term as the fitness craze gets down to business)

☛ 6. *don't trust anyone over thirty* (motto of the young and the angry)

☛ 7. *Tet* (For Americans this means more than Vietnamese New Year.)

☛ 8. *Hey! Hey! LBJ! How many kids did you kill today?*

☛ 9. *crime capital* (new and unwanted slogan for the District of Columbia)

☛ 10. *Sock it to me* (the signature cry of *Laugh-In*)

■■■■■■■■■■■■■■■■■■■■■■■■■■■■■■■■■

▶ 1968

OCTOBER

19 ▶ Jacqueline (Mrs. John F.) Kennedy and shipping magnate Aristotle Onassis are married on the island of Skorpios.

31 ▶ President Johnson halts the bombing of North Vietnam and invites South Vietnam and the Viet Cong (National Liberation Front) to the expanded Paris peace talks.

NOVEMBER

05 ▶ Richard Nixon is elected president and promises to restore law and order in the nation, to stage a U.S. troop withdrawal in Southeast Asia, and to bring about the Vietnamization of the war. Nixon wins by a slim margin and third-party candidate George Wallace receives 13.5 percent of the vote.

14 ▶ "National Turn in Your Draft Card Day" features draft card burning at many campuses and at rallies in several major cities.

DECEMBER

14 ▶ The U.S. death toll in Vietnam passes 30,000.

21 ▶ *Apollo 8* makes the first of ten manned lunar orbits and allows the first human eyes to see the dark side of the moon. Before this, the highest altitude flown by a manned craft was 851 miles, but *Apollo 8* rises 240,000 miles.

24 ▶ The crew of the U.S. spy ship *Pueblo* is released after eleven months of brutal captivity by North Korea.

29 ▶ A spectacular image of the earth rising above the lunar surface is broadcast from *Apollo 8* to the world's televisions.

■ ■

☞ 1. HAPPINESS IS A WARM MUSKIE
☞ 2. HUMPHREY–NIXON–WALLACE—THREE STRIKES
☞ 3. EUGENE McCARTHY IS A PEACEMONGER
☞ 4. SUPPORT YOUR CHURCH—PLAY BINGO

November 5, 1968: Richard Nixon is elected president and promises to restore law and order in the nation.

December 29, 1968: A spectacular image of the earth rising above the lunar surface is broadcast from *Apollo 8* to the world's televisions.

1968 in buttons & bumper stickers

▶ 1968

☛ 5. BOYCOTT PAY TOILETS

☛ 6. BAN THE BOMB—SAVE THE WORLD FOR CONVEN-
TIONAL WARFARE

☛ 7. WE ARE THE PEOPLE OUR PARENTS WARNED US
ABOUT

☛ 8. CAUTION: MILITARY SERVICE MAY BE HAZARDOUS
TO YOUR HEALTH

☛ 9. TARZAN AND JANE ARE LIVING IN SIN

☛ 10. PRESERVE DEMOCRACY, SEAL IT IN PLASTIC

■■■■■■■■■■■■■■■■■■■■■■■■■■■■■■

The year in which ▶
Neil Armstrong becomes ▶
the first man to ▶
walk on the moon ▶

1969

JANUARY

10 ▶ After 147 years the *Saturday Evening Post* ceases publication today.

28 ▶ Oil suddenly gushes out of an underwater fissure beneath Union Oil Company's platform A, staining Santa Barbara's lovely beaches with a black tide and suffocating thousands of grebes, loons, and cormorants. It is, says former U.S. Secretary of the Interior Stewart Udall later, "a conservation Bay of Pigs." The leak continues for ten more days, providing many alarming images of dying birds on television news shows. Thanks to the media, this local accident becomes a national event, one that helps to set the stage for the environmental decade of the 1970s.

FEBRUARY

09 ▶ The Boeing 747 flies for the first time, ushering in the era of the wide-body, jumbo, and stretch jets.

■ ■

☞ 1. Rowan and Martin's *Laugh-In,* a 1968 TV hit—goofy comedy for an unfunny time—seems even more popular in its second season.

☞ 2. Baseball introduces divisional playoffs, creating a major stir among traditionalists.

Fads and Trends for 1969

▶ 191

3. See-through fashions reveal themselves.

4. A hoax of the first order is put over with the publication of David Rorvik's *In His Image: The Cloning of a Man,* in which it is claimed that an American millionaire has been cloned—duplicated—in Switzerland.

5. Inflation becomes a major international phenomenon.

6. Burglar alarms become a common household appliance: fear of crime is seen as powerful and widespread.

7. In a new aspect of the fitness craze, people begin riding bicycles to work.

8. In response to a growing number of antiwar vehicle displays, American flag decals are seen everywhere. Gulf Oil hands out 22 million of them at their gas stations—one for every third car in the country.

9. Machines for making yogurt at home are big sellers in gourmet and department stores.

10. The moon landing is celebrated widely and with a certain whimsy: Baskin-Robbins introduces a new flavor called lunar cheesecake.

APRIL

03 ▶ The Vietnam War death roll reaches 33,641 today—a dozen more than were killed in the Korean War. Vietnam is now the third costliest foreign war in American history.

MAY

14 ▶ In Canada abortion and homosexuality are made legal as part of a new Omnibus Crime code.

JUNE

08 ▶ President Nixon orders the first troops out of Vietnam.

17 ▶ The erotic musical *Oh! Calcutta!* opens in Manhattan. The

critics hate it ("With all my heart," writes Brendan Gill in *The New Yorker,* "I recommended staying away from the slick and repulsive come-on called *Oh! Calcutta!*" but it is immensely popular. Save for a moment of frontal nudity in *Hair* (1967), it signals the debut of the human body as a stage costume. It also serves to graphically underscore the nation's changing attitude towards sex.

■■■■■■■■■■■■■■■■■■■■■■■■■■■■■■■■

1969 by the numbers

☞ 1. A one-day sale of Alaska oil field leases nets $900,220,590.

☞ 2. The crime rate has more than doubled since 1960— 2,747 major felonies per 100,000 population in 1969, compared to 1,126 in 1960.

☞ 3. The president proposes the first national budget in excess of $200 billion.

☞ 4. The Federal Aviation Administration reports sixty-five hijackings; most of the planes end up in Cuba.

☞ 5. The prime rate reaches a record 8.5 percent.

☞ 6. The world's population is determined to be growing at the rate of 2 percent a year.

☞ 7. The rate of inflation for the year is pegged at 6.1 percent—the highest since 1951.

☞ 8. *The Reader's Digest* sells 17 million copies a year, *Life* 8.5 million, and *Look* 7.7 million. At the moment of its death (January 1) the *Saturday Evening Post* has 3.5 million subscribers.

☞ 9. The cost of the Nixon-Agnew inauguration is $2.5 million, up from the $2.1 million it cost to inaugurate Lyndon Johnson in 1965.

☞ 10. The United States now possesses 7,500 H-bombs.

☞ 11. The total annual salaries of the astronauts on the *Apollo 11* moon mission are Neil Armstrong—$30,054, Edwin E. Aldrin—$20,607, and Michael Collins—$18,648.

■■■■■■■■■■■■■■■■■■■■■■■■■■■■■■■■

JULY

14 ► Peter Fonda and Dennis Hopper star in an iconoclastic biker film called *Easy Rider,* which opens today. It is a disturbing entertainment for the summer of the moon landing, Chappaquiddick, and Woodstock.

16 ► 9:32 A.M., Eastern Standard Time: After a twenty-eight-hour countdown, *Apollo 11* blasts off from Cape Kennedy, Florida, atop the 363-foot Saturn 5 rocket. Commander Neil A. Armstrong, Command Pilot Michael Collins, and lunar module pilot Edwin E. (Buzz) Aldrin are aboard. Midway through its second Earth orbit, the craft is boosted toward the moon.

18 ► After leaving a party at about 11:15 P.M. this Friday night, Senator Edward M. Kennedy drives his Oldsmobile off Dike Bridge on Chappaquiddick Island, Massachusetts, into Poucha Pond around midnight. Mary Jo Kopechne, a twenty-eight-year-old Washington secretary, is found dead in the back seat about ten hours later. Kennedy, then thirty-seven, did not notify police until 9:30 A.M., long after he returned to his hotel, across the water on Martha's Vineyard.

Most Americans do not hear of this event until they get their newspapers on Sunday morning, when it appears in stunning juxtaposition. For instance, the first and second headlines in the *Washington Post* read *APOLLO IN ORBIT, SET FOR LANDING. KENNEDY PASSENGER DIES IN CAR PLUNGE.*

19 ► John Fairfax of Britain arrives at Fort Lauderdale, Florida, having become the first person to row across the Atlantic alone.

20 ► Two U.S. astronauts, Neil Armstrong and Edwin Aldrin, land the lunar module *Eagle* on the moon. At 10:56 P.M. Neil Armstrong sets foot on the moon: "That's one small step for a man, one giant step for mankind." Buzz Aldrin joins him on the surface twenty minutes later. They set up three experiments, unveil a plaque on the leg of the lander, and plant the American flag in lunar soil.

July 20, 1969:
Two U.S. astronauts, Neil Armstrong and Edwin Aldrin, land the lunar module *Eagle* on the moon at 10:56 P.M..

▶ 1969

21 ▶ Astronauts Neil Armstrong and Edwin (Buzz) Aldrin climb back into the lunar module *Eagle* and lift off from the surface of the moon.

24 ▶ Splashdown for *Apollo 11,* 825 nautical miles southwest of Honolulu: *ASTRONAUTS BACK SAFE ON EARTH AFTER HISTORIC WALK ON MOON,* says the *Washington Evening Star.* The astronauts are picked up and taken to a quarantine trailer aboard the USS *Hornet.* They remain in the trailer until they arrive at the Lunar Receiving Laboratory in Houston early July 27.

25 ▶ Senator Kennedy is given a two-month suspended sentence after pleading guilty to the charge of leaving the scene of an accident. He is also placed on a year's probation, which is required under Massachusetts law.

AUGUST

01 ▶ In response to the Chappaquiddick incident and sentencing Senator Edward Kennedy says, "I do not seek to escape responsibility for my actions by placing the blame either on physical or emotional trauma brought on by the accident or anything else. I regard as indefensible the fact that I did not report the accident to the police immediately."

08 ▶ Five people are murdered in the Hollywood Hills mansion that actress Sharon Tate, among the murdered, shared with film director Roman Polanski. On December 1 arrest warrants are issued for Charles Manson and his accomplices.

14 ▶ British troops arrive in Northern Ireland to intervene in the sectarian violence between Protestants and Roman Catholics. The conflict since has claimed the lives of more than 2,700 people.

15 ▶ About half a million people gather on a 600-acre farm near Woodstock, New York, to hear rock music. The Woodstock music festival features such performers as Santana, Janis Joplin, Jimi Hendrix, and Crosby, Stills, and Nash and is seen as emblematic of the values, taste, and morality of America's disaffected youth. The name Woodstock increas-

August 15, 1969: About half a million people gather on a 600-acre farm near Woodstock, New York, to hear rock music.

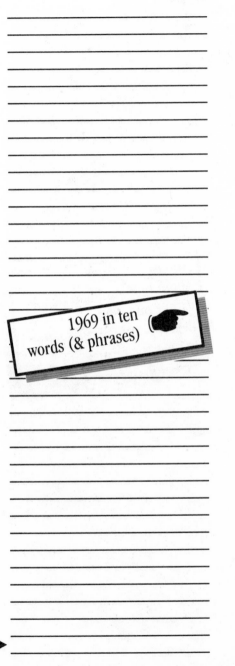

ingly is seen as synonymous with the turbulent counter-cultural period that lasts from 1965 through 1975.

17 ► Hurricane Camille slams into the Gulf Coast with winds clocked at more than 170 MPH and gusts over 200 MPH. More than 250 people die, most of them in the Mississippi Delta after warnings about the storm apparently go largely unheeded.

► ***Also occurring today:*** The Woodstock Music and Art Fair concludes.

SEPTEMBER

01 ► A Libyan coup brings Moammar Gadhafi to power.
03 ► Ho Chi Minh dies in Hanoi.

■ ■

☞ 1. *fern bar* (the first of these opens in San Francisco and is called Henry Africa. The bar has a long and famous life, finally closing in the summer of 1986.)

☞ 2. *If we can put a man on the moon, why can't we . . .* (the rallying cry for anything that is out of order; sample: *If we can put a man on the moon, why can't we build affordable housing?*)

☞ 3. *enemy sanctuaries* (the stated target of U.S. Cambodian incursions)

☞ 4. *LEM* (the Lunar Excursion Module, which puts Americans on the moon)

☞ 5. *Chappaquiddick* (Since the nation hears this geographic name in a new and tragic context on Sunday morning July 20, 1969, it has been with us.)

☞ 6. *Concorde* (the Anglo-French supersonic transport that begins trials in 1969)

☞ 7. *bubble memory* (It allows computers to remember things even when they are shut down.)

☞ 8. *the silent majority* (the group that President Nixon calls on for support with the war until Vietnamization has been accomplished)

☛ 9. *Mars by the '80s* (In the wake of the moon landing this was a popular slogan with NASA, the aerospace industry, and many members of Congress, who saw a manned landing on Mars as the next goal of the space program.)

☛ 10. *This is the greatest week since the beginning of the world, the creation* (statement made by President Nixon after the lunar landing, which invites much commentary. Billy Graham suggests that Nixon neglected the first Christmas, the crucifixion, and the first Easter.)

■ ■

OCTOBER

04 ▶ According to a Gallup poll released today, 58 percent of the American people believe the war in Vietnam is a mistake.

NOVEMBER

03 ▶ President Nixon asks the silent majority for their support while the Vietnamese take over the war.

10 ▶ *Sesame Street* makes its debut on television. It is immediately seen for what it is—a radical new departure in children's programming.

14 ▶ The second manned lunar landing takes place without a hitch. The crew of *Apollo 12* will return to Earth with parts of the unmanned *Surveyor 3* probe.

15 ▶ In the largest antiwar demonstration in U.S. history, an estimated 250,000 people, an admittedly modest police estimate, march in Washington, D.C., to protest the war in Vietnam. The *Washington Post* calls it "One of the immense crowds of American political history."

20 ▶ The Department of Agriculture bans the insecticide DDT in residential areas.

November 20, 1969: The Department of Agriculture bans the insecticide DDT in residential areas.

DECEMBER

12 ▶ The Boeing 747—first flown on February 9—makes its first public flight from Seattle to New York.

22 ▶ A major—the most far-reaching to date—tax reform bill is passed by Congress removing 9 million poor people from the rolls of the taxed.

■■■■■■■■■■■■■■■■■■■■■■■■■■■■■■■

☞ 1. FLYING SAUCERS ARE REAL, THE AIR FORCE DOESN'T EXIST

☞ 2. MARCH AGAINST DEATH (slogan of the November Vietnam moratorium)

☞ 3. OUR GOD IS NOT DEAD—SORRY ABOUT YOURS

☞ 4. HELP YOUR POLICE FIGHT CRIME

☞ 5. KEEP AMERICA BEAUTIFUL: SWALLOW YOUR BEER CANS

☞ 6. EAT THE RICH

☞ 7. TRUST GOD! SHE PROVIDES

☞ 8. CUSTER WORE AN ARROW SHIRT

☞ 9. WE ARE THE SILENT MAJORITY

☞ 10. BURN POT, NOT PEOPLE

■■■■■■■■■■■■■■■■■■■■■■■■■■■■■■■

1969 in buttons & bumper stickers ☞

The year in which the ▶
Beatles break up and four ▶
students are killed by the ▶
National Guard at Kent State ▶

1970

JANUARY

01 ▶ President Nixon signs a bill creating the Council on Environmental Quality. He promises to fight air and water pollution and turn the '70s into the decade in which America regains "a productive harmony between man and nature."

FEBRUARY

20 ▶ The Chicago Seven—Abbie Hoffman, Jerry Rubin, Tom Hayden, Rennie Davis, David Dellinger, Lee Weiner, and John Froines—are convicted of a conspiracy to cross state lines and instigate a riot at the Democratic convention of 1968.

MARCH

06 ▶ A Greenwich village townhouse explodes killing three young radicals, who police say were manufacturing bombs. One young woman has ties to the Weatherman faction of the Students for a Democratic Society.

23 ▶ President Nixon calls out the National Guard to alleviate delays caused by the first widespread postal workers' strike.

March 6, 1970: A Greenwich Village townhouse explodes, killing three young radicals, who police say were manufacturing bombs.

▶ 199

■■■■■■■■■■■■■■■■■■■■■■■■■■■■■■■

☞ 1. *Monday Night Football* is an immediate hit on ABC-TV.

☞ 2. Domestic terrorism is a fact of life and characterized by white radicals with bombs and black radicals who attack the police.

☞ 3. Great numbers of hippies are abroad in the land. *Newsweek* later typifies the year as one in which drug-age Bedouins roam the land.

☞ 4. Sexually explicit massage parlors show up in all major—and many minor—cities.

☞ 5. The April 1970 issue of *Penthouse* is the first national magazine to show pubic hair in photographs. It creates much talk about how far the newsstand skin magazines will go to titillate their readers.

☞ 6. Male long hair seems to be at its longest this year, and many schools are forced to change their dress codes to accommodate the fashion.

☞ 7. Women's liberation displays strength, size, and no uncertain anger through many protests and demonstrations.

☞ 8. Most of the big Hollywood studios are swallowed by giant conglomerates.

☞ 9. Sex is big, both between the sheets and between the covers of books (*The Sensuous Woman* by J., *Everything You Wanted to Know about Sex, but Were Afraid to Ask*, etc.)

☞ 10. Several states liberalize their abortion laws.

■■■■■■■■■■■■■■■■■■■■■■■■■■■■■■

April 29, 1970:
American troops begin what President Nixon will call an "incursion" into Cambodia.

APRIL

11 ▶ A third lunar landing attempt is aborted due to an oxygen tank explosion in the service module. The crew of *Apollo 13* returns safely.

29 ▶ American troops begin what President Nixon will call an "incursion" into Cambodia. It is an invasion and is initially kept from the public.

▶ 1970

30 ▶ The government announces the Cambodian invasion, which touches off violence and widespread demonstrations in the days ahead. Before the end of this day there are major clashes between students and police and/or National Guard. Forty-two are injured at Stanford.

MAY

01 ▶ President Nixon refers to student protesters as "these bums" who burn books and "blow up buildings."

04 ▶ National Guardsmen kill four students at Kent State University in Ohio after a campus protest against the Cambodian invasion. President Nixon says, "This should remind us all once again that when dissent turns to violence it invites tragedy." The vice president calls it a predictable tragedy.

05 ▶ A nationwide student strike, supported on the majority of campuses in the country, protests the extension of the war and the killing of students at Kent State. At least 223 campuses are involved by the night of the 6th.

06 ▶ Interior Secretary Walter J. Hickel sends a letter to the president in which he says that the administration has turned its back on youth, thereby contributing to student revolt.

09 ▶ Before dawn, President Nixon visits antiwar demonstrators convening at the Lincoln Memorial and chats with them for an hour. Later 100,000 march against the war and the Cambodian invasion.

15 ▶ Two black students are killed by police gunfire at Jackson State College in Mississippi.

JUNE

16 ▶ Kenneth A. Gibson of Newark, New Jersey, becomes the first black to win a mayoral election in a major northeastern city.

May 5, 1970:
A nationwide student strike, supported on the majority of campuses in the country, protests the extension of the war and the killing of students at Kent State.

▶ 1970

■■■■■■■■■■■■■■■■■■■■■■■■■■■■■■■■■■

☞ 1. Federal authorities put the number of American marijuana users at over 8 million.

☞ 2. No deaths from polio are recorded in 1970. This is the first year without a polio fatality since record keeping began in 1955.

☞ 3. Due to campus unrest throughout the year 448 U.S. colleges and universities are closed or go on strike.

☞ 4. The size of the federal workforce is 441,410.

☞ 5. The free market price of gold drops below the standard $35 an ounce.

☞ 6. The cost of an average day of hospital care is $85 per patient.

☞ 7. The National Gallery of Art in Washington, D.C., is visited by 1,824,452 people.

☞ 8. Between 1960 and 1970, 3,321,677 migrate to the United States from other countries; more than half are from other countries in the Americas.

☞ 9. The population of the United States, according to the 1970 Census, is 203,211,926. The population center of the nation is now five miles east southeast of Mascoutah in St. Claire County, Illinois.

☞ 10. Japanese automakers produce 3.2 million cars this year, up from 79,000 in 1958 and 110 in 1947.

■■■■■■■■■■■■■■■■■■■■■■■■■■■■■■■■■■

JULY

04 ▶ J. Willard Marriott, Sr., organizes Honor America Day on the Washington Monument grounds. Bob Hope is the master of ceremonies; Billy Graham leads an interdenominational service.

▶ 1970

AUGUST

02 ▶ The first known racial intermarriage in Mississippi takes place.

SEPTEMBER

06 ▶ On this day four commercial jetliners are hijacked by Arab commandos. Three of the planes land in Arab nations; the fourth lands in London after security guards kill one hijacker and wound another.

15 ▶ As will be fully revealed five years from now with the release of a report from the Senate Intelligence Committee, this is the moment when President Nixon tells CIA Director Richard M. Helms that the eleven-day-old regime of Salvador Allende of Chile is unacceptable to the United States. Nixon instructs the CIA to play a direct role in a military coup.

22 ▶ Richard Nixon signs legislation authorizing a nonvoting delegate from the District of Columbia to the U.S. House of Representatives. The District has not been represented in Congress since 1875.

28 ▶ President Nasser of Egypt dies of a heart attack.

■ ■

☞ 1. *fragging* (term from the combat zone for killing one's own officers or NCOs)

☞ 2. *future shock* (Alvin Toffler's book title and name for the phenomenon by which it is hard to deal with rapidly unfolding events)

☞ 3. *greening* (becoming gentler; less competitive—from the best-selling *Greening of America*)

☞ 4. *Vietnamization* (Richard Nixon's word for what would get us out of Southeast Asia)

☞ 5. *benign neglect* (espoused administration policy toward African-Americans, which is expressed by presidential aide Daniel Patrick Moynihan. Black leaders see it as a calculated

August 2, 1970: The first known racial intermarriage in Mississippi takes place.

☞ *1970 in ten words (& phrases)*

effort to wipe out the advances of the civil rights movement.)

☞ 6. *peace symbol jewelry* (from Swank at leading department stores for today's "with it" man)

☞ 7. *smoke detector* (Introduced this year, they are suddenly a household necessity.)

☞ 8. *pig* (radical term for police, politicians, the whole system, etc.)

☞ 9. *electronic smog* (popular name for electronic radiation, which is now being seen as a problem. "Urban living is doomed, unless we can do something about it," says one expert.)

☞ 10. *Kent State* (both an event and a rallying cry: "Remember Kent State!")

■ ■

OCTOBER

04 ► Popular blues singer Janis Joplin, twenty-seven, dies of a drug overdose in Hollywood.

18 ► War powers are invoked in Canada to control the Front for the Liberation of Quebec.

NOVEMBER

09 ► Former French president Charles de Gaulle dies at his home.

23 ► Defense Secretary Laird reveals that there has been a daring but unsuccessful raid on a POW camp near Hanoi in an attempt to free American prisoners. The camp was deserted when the raiders got there.

October 4, 1970:
Popular blues singer Janis Joplin, twenty-seven, dies of a drug overdose in Hollywood.

► 1970

DECEMBER

15 ► Protests break out in Poland, and, before they come to an end on the 19th, 300 demonstrators are killed. Labor unrest and rising food prices are behind the demonstrations.

■■■■■■■■■■■■■■■■■■■■■■■■■■■■■■■■

1970 in buttons & bumper stickers

☞ 1. FIGHT INFLATION—HIBERNATE

☞ 2. IF YOU DON'T LIKE THE POLICE, NEXT TIME YOU'RE IN TROUBLE CALL A HIPPIE

☞ 3. HOW MANY VIETNAMESE FOUGHT IN *OUR* CIVIL WAR?

☞ 4. HORMONES ARE A BIG BUST

☞ 5. VISIT BEAUTIFUL VIETNAM BY SOUTHEAST ASIA AIR-LINES

☞ 6. POT: HOBBY NOT HABIT

☞ 7. KEEP YOUR CITY CLEAN, EAT A PIGEON

☞ 8. STRIKE THE WAR MACHINE

☞ 9. TOMORROW IS CANCELLED DUE TO LACK OF IN-TEREST

☞ 10. STOP THE WAR NOW

■■■■■■■■■■■■■■■■■■■■■■■■■■■■■■■■

The year in which the ▶
Supreme Court orders busing ▶
to end segregation ▶
in the public schools ▶

1971

JANUARY

01 ▶ A ban on radio and television advertising of tobacco products goes into effect after a New Year's Eve during which the nation's eyes and ears are blitzed with tobacco ads.

18 ▶ Senator George McGovern (D., S.D.) announces his candidacy for the presidency, vowing to get the United States out of Southeast Asia.

FEBRUARY

08 ▶ South Vietnamese troops with U.S. air support cross into Laos for a forty-four-day assault against the Ho Chi Minh Trail. It later is described as the bloodiest fighting of the war.

MARCH

01 ▶ A bomb explodes in a men's room in the Senate wing of the Capitol, causing $300,000 in damages but no injuries. Half an hour before the blast, the Capitol receives a warning phone call saying the bomb is "in retaliation for the Laos decision." The Weather Underground claims responsibility. The Capitol was first bombed in 1915 and is not hit again until 1983.

January 18, 1971:
Senator George McGovern announces his candidacy for the presidency.

▶ 1971

Fads and Trends for 1971

25 ▶ East Pakistan proclaims its independence, taking the name Bangladesh.

1. *The Whole Earth Catalog* gives a new look, feel, and direction to product consumption.

2. Smiley-faced buttons show up everywhere: Have a nice day!

3. The staid Commonwealth of Virginia creates a stir with its "Virginia Is for Lovers" ad campaign.

4. A television show about a lovable bigot named Archie Bunker makes *All in the Family* the surprise hit of the year.

5. Conceptual art sweeps the art world.

6. Gay liberation bursts from the closet.

7. The issue of day care looms large; a number of day-care centers—but not nearly enough to fill the demand—come into being.

8. Hot pants are very short and, as it turns out, short-lived.

9. Nostalgia time on Broadway with Ruby Keeler in *No, No, Nanette* and Alexis Smith in *Follies.*

10. Acupuncture and needlepoint make this a vintage year for needles.

11. The movie car chase scene is brought back with a bang thanks to *The French Connection.*

12. The unrest and violence of the street, ghetto, and campus cool off in 1971, while gay liberation takes an increasingly militant turn and prisons erupt tragically.

13. *Mariner 9* sends back the first out-of-this-world photos from Mars.

14. London Bridge is moved to the Arizona desert and Frank Sinatra says farewell to show business: things seem out of place. The Bridge will stay, Sinatra will return.

1971

APRIL

09 ▶ An American ping-pong team enters the People's Republic of China for a series of exhibition matches. It is the first time an official delegation of Americans enters mainland China in almost twenty years. It is widely and correctly seen as evidence of warming relations between the two countries.

19 ▶ The Reverend Walter Fauntroy, a young, Yale-trained disciple of Martin Luther King, Jr., is sworn in as the District of Columbia's elected, nonvoting delegate to Congress.

20 ▶ The Supreme Court, in a unanimous decision, upholds busing as the prime method for achieving racial integration. Opposition to this decision is widespread when schools open in the fall.

MAY

01 ▶ The 182 trains of the National Railroad Passenger Corp.—better known as Amtrak—provide service to 300 cities.

▶ *Also today:* Nearly 10,000 protesters are arrested during May Day, an antiwar protest aimed at paralyzing the government by clogging Washington roads and shutting down offices. More than 5,000 District police officers, 1,500 National Guardsmen, and 8,000 federal troops make mass arrests as an estimated 50,000 protesters swarm through the streets, starting fires, blocking traffic, and causing commuters to arrive hours late for work. After civil libertarians charge that police arrested people without noting names or details of alleged offenses—for instance, herding 2,000 protesters into RFK Stadium—Judge Harold Greene orders authorities to justify the dragnet arrests or release the suspects. The courts later throw out almost all the arrests.

12 ▶ In Stockholm, Sweden, police clash with youngsters protesting the felling of elm trees in Kungstradgarden, an urban royal park, and the socialist establishment learns

April 20, 1971:
The Supreme Court, in a unanimous decision, upholds busing as the prime method for achieving racial integration.

June 30, 1971:
The twenty-sixth amendment to the Constitution, lowering the minimum voting age to eighteen, is ratified as Ohio becomes the thirty-eighth state to approve it.

1971 by the numbers ☞

that traditional passivity toward insensitive government, no matter what its political color, might be over.

JUNE

30 ► The twenty-sixth amendment to the Constitution, lowering the minimum voting age to eighteen, is ratified as Ohio becomes the thirty-eighth state to approve it. The new age for voting goes into effect immediately.

■ ■

☞ 1. Billie Jean King becomes the first woman athlete in history to earn more than $1 million in a single year.

☞ 2. The largest seagoing tanker to this point in history is built by the Japanese—378,377 tons.

☞ 3. The cost of mailing a first-class letter goes up to eight cents from six cents.

☞ 4. The first hand-held calculator is marketed by Bowmar Instruments Corporation. List price is $249.

☞ 5. Jasper Johns's painting "Map" sells for $200,000—the highest price paid to this date for the work of a living American artist.

☞ 6. A bottle of Château Lafite Rothschild sells for a cool $5,000, enraging more than a few who deem the purchase excessive.

☞ 7. Big bucks are appropriated for fighting crime through the Omnibus Crime Control Act—$3.6 billion.

☞ 8. The National Cancer Act is signed into law and authorizes $1.5 billion per year for the battle against the nation's second-leading cause of death.

☞ 9. Advertising bans notwithstanding, Americans are puffing down 547.2 billion cigarettes.

☞ 10. For the first time this century, America imported more than it exported. Nearly 30 percent of all petroleum is imported, up from 20 percent in 1967.

☞ 11. The Department of Agriculture gives schools permission to use up to 30 percent soybean substitute in meat and fish dishes in hot lunch programs.

■ ■

JULY

15 ▶ A major diplomatic surprise takes place as President Richard Nixon announces that he accepts "with pleasure" an invitation to visit mainland China in 1972 and reveals that this invitation was arranged by Henry Kissinger on a secret trip to Beijing. It is understood the visit will lead to diplomatic recognition.

AUGUST

15 ▶ President Richard Nixon orders a ninety-day wage-price-rent freeze and announces imposition of a 10 percent surcharge on foreign imports.

SEPTEMBER

03 ▶ The Plumbers burglarize the office of Daniel Ellsberg's psychiatrist.

08 ▶ The $72 million Kennedy Center opens, highlighted by the world premiere of Leonard Bernstein's *Mass*, a theater piece commissioned for the event and requiring more than 200 performers. The Nixon crowd squirms at the antiwar overtones of the work as well as the glittery appearance of the Kennedy clan.

09 ▶ In the New York state prison at Attica a prisoners' rebellion breaks out, and 1,200 inmates control the institution for four days.

13 ▶ As 1,500 police and prison guards retake control of the Attica prison, thirty-one prisoners and nine of their hostages are killed.

July 15, 1971:
A major diplomatic surprise takes place as President Richard Nixon announces that he accepts "with pleasure" an invitation to visit mainland China in 1972.

▶ 1971

1971 in ten words (& phrases) ☞

■■■■■■■■■■■■■■■■■■■■■■■■■■■■■■■■

☞ 1. *workaholic* (the invention of psychologist Wayne E. Oates and a word that immediately works itself into the language)

☞ 2. *black hole* (the term jumps into common parlance as astronomers claim proof of their existence. However, the term is often applied to things like teenagers' rooms.)

☞ 3. *ping-pong diplomacy* (improved relations through an exchange of teams, experts, etc.) (See April 9.)

☞ 4. *exorcist* (an archaic religious term brought back by William Peter Blatty, who puts a new spin on it)

☞ 5. *dare to be great* (motto of pitchman Glenn Turner, even while charges are pending against him in thirty of the fifty states)

☞ 6. *the female eunuch* (Germaine Greer and her book, in the words of *Life* magazine, "stormed the halls of fame in record time.")

☞ 7. *Jesus freak* (This term gets quite a workout in the year of *Jesus Christ, Superstar,* but traditional Christians are not comfortable with the new zealots.)

☞ 8. *junk food* (finally an antonym for *health food.* Within moments of first hearing this term many people declare themselves to be . . .)

☞ 9. *junk food junkies*

☞ 10. *granola* (a health food that becomes synonymous with the natural life)

■■■■■■■■■■■■■■■■■■■■■■■■■■■■■■■■

OCTOBER

25 ▶ Over the strong protests of the United States, the United Nations General Assembly seats the People's Republic of China and expels Nationalist China.

▶ 1971

NOVEMBER

15 ▶ The People's Republic of China becomes a member of the United Nations.

DECEMBER

28 ▶ The U.S. stages a massive five-day bombing offensive on North Vietnam—the largest escalation of the war since 1968.

■■■■■■■■■■■■■■■■■■■■■■■■■■■■■

☞ 1. DOWN WITH HOT PANTS
☞ 2. HAVE A NICE DAY
☞ 3. GO AHEAD—DO YOUR OWN THING
☞ 4. AMERICA—LOVE IT OR LEAVE IT
☞ 5. AMERICA—CHANGE IT OR LOSE IT
☞ 6. IF JESUS RETURNS TODAY, SOMEBODY GRAB MY STEERING WHEEL
☞ 7. GOD BLESS THE SUPREME COURT
☞ 8. WHEN YOU'VE SEEN ONE ATOMIC WAR YOU'VE SEEN 'EM ALL
☞ 9. VIETNAM: LOVE IT OR LEAVE IT
☞ 10. CLEAN AIR SMELLS FUNNY

■■■■■■■■■■■■■■■■■■■■■■■■■■■■■

November 15, 1971: The People's Republic of China becomes a member of the United Nations.

☞ 1971 in buttons & bumper stickers

The year in which we ▶
all learn to say "detente" ▶
and combat troops are ▶
withdrawn from Vietnam ▶

1972

JANUARY

23 ▶ Gloria Steinem and thirteen other founders put out the first issue of *Ms.* Fearing that the feminist magazine will linger on the newsstands, the editors put a spring date on that first issue. In fact, all 300,000 copies of that issue sell out in a mere nine days and the idea of a woman's magazine is never the same.

28 ▶ The first presidential drug war is declared as President Nixon orders a "concentrated assault on the street-level heroin addict." He appoints Myles J. Ambrose to be the first federal drug czar.

FEBRUARY

01 ▶ A wildcat strike against speed-up and arbitrary management rules begins at the Lordstown, Ohio, General Motors plant. The strike's significance is that the issue is *not* pay, benefits, or other traditional reasons. The workers—whose average age is twenty-four—strike over the issue of dehumanizing, hard, and monotonous work: as 101.6 Chevrolet Vegas come off the line per hour, each man or woman is allowed only thirty-six seconds to perform the same fragmented job.

January 28, 1972:
The first presidential drug war is declared as President Nixon orders a "concentrated assault on the street-level heroin addict."

▶ 215

05 ► After numerous hijacking incidents, United States airlines begin mandatory inspection of passengers and luggage.

MARCH

30 ► In an effort to stem the violence there, Great Britain imposes direct rule on Northern Ireland, ending fifty-one years of semi-autonomous rule by the Ulster government.

■■■■■■■■■■■■■■■■■■■■■■■■■■■■■■■■

Fads and Trends for 1972 ☞

☞ 1. A naked Burt Reynolds shows up in a *Cosmopolitan* centerfold.

☞ 2. The slap-on decal rainbow replaces the smiley face as the logo of cheeriness. Once again, have a nice day!

☞ 3. The black, red, and green Afro tricolors show up on everything from decals to flags.

☞ 4. Strict antihijacking measures are implemented at U.S. airports.

☞ 5. As the first *Landsat* satellite is put into orbit to photograph Earth, there is widespread interest in satellite images and their ability to reveal earthly problems.

☞ 6. Metro in the Washington, D.C., area and BART, the San Francisco Bay Area Rapid Transit System, both begin operation, giving regional mass transit an enormous boost.

☞ 7. Don McLean's *American Pie* reveals nostalgia for rock 'n' roll (as opposed to rock music). There is a quick revival of ragtime music as well, especially the work of Scott Joplin.

☞ 8. For the first time in American history vodka outsells whiskey.

☞ 9. *The Godfather* is the movie we can't refuse. It is a lavishly produced, extremely violent film that fascinates the critics and public alike.

☞ 10. *Jonathan Livingston Seagull* becomes the biggest best seller since *Gone with the Wind.* It is the best-selling book in human history about a bird.

☛ 11. *All in the Family* takes its place as the leading television show in the United States.

■■■■■■■■■■■■■■■■■■■■■■■■■■■■■■■

APRIL

30 ► A major offensive against South Vietnam is mounted by the North Vietnamese and Viet Cong.
   ► *Also:* Seven nuns are arrested protesting the war in front of St. Patrick's Cathedral in New York City.

MAY

15 ► Alabama Governor George Wallace is shot during a political rally in a Laurel, Maryland, shopping center by Arthur Bremer, a twenty-one-year-old busboy and janitor from Milwaukee. Wallace is paralyzed from the waist down and drops out of the presidential race.
29 ► President Nixon and Premier Brezhnev of the Soviet Union end talks in Moscow in which they pledge to do their utmost to avoid any kind of military confrontation.

JUNE

03 ► Sally Preisand, America's first woman rabbi, is ordained at the Isaac M. Wise Temple in Cincinnati.
17 ► Police apprehend five men attempting to electronically bug the Democratic National Committee headquarters in the Watergate complex in Washington. The men turn out to be employees of the Committee to Reelect the President, or CREEP. Despite this, in August Nixon announces that an investigation by White House counsel John Dean reveals that no administration officials are involved.

May 15, 1972:
Alabama Governor George Wallace is shot during a political rally in a Laurel, Maryland, shopping center.

June 17, 1972:
Police apprehend five men attempting to electronically bug the Democratic National Committee headquarters in the Watergate complex in Washington.

1972
by the numbers

August 11, 1972:
The United States withdraws its last combat unit — the Third Batallion of the Twenty-first Infantry — from Vietnam.

1. Women constitute 40 percent of the delegates to the Democratic National Convention—up from 13 percent in 1968.

2. A 969.8-carat diamond—the largest ever discovered—is found in Sierra Leone.

3. The bottom is dropping out of the baby boom as parents now average 2.1 children per couple.

4. While 753 daily newspapers support Richard Nixon in his reelection bid, a mere 56 endorse George McGovern.

5. Writer Clifford Irving demands and gets $750,000 from McGraw-Hill for a bogus autobiography of reclusive billionaire Howard Hughes.

6. Americans got sick or injured about 450 million times in 1972, according to the Department of Health, Education, and Welfare. This amounts to about twice for every person in the country.

7. At a May half-gallon sale at the Calvert Liquor Store in Washington, D.C., Tanqueray gin costs $10.98 and the same size White Horse scotch is $10.98. A case of beer (Pabst or Schaefer's) is $3.28.

8. There are 2.3 million new cases of gonorrhea this year and 100,000 cases of infectious syphilis. This is the greatest increase since the introduction of antibiotics.

9. At 3,225 performances (June 17) *Fiddler on the Roof* becomes the longest-running Broadway play ever.

10. President Nixon's revenue sharing plan puts $30.2 billion into the hands of local government.

JULY

25 ► Democratic vice presidential nominee Senator Thomas Eagleton of Missouri discloses he underwent psychiatric treatment in the 1960s.

▶ 1972

31 ▶ Senator Thomas Eagleton withdraws from the vice presidential race following disclosure that he once received electroshock therapy. Presidential nominee George McGovern replaces him on the ticket with Sargent Shriver.

AUGUST

11 ▶ The United States withdraws its last combat unit—the Third Batallion of the Twenty-first Infantry—from Vietnam.

12 ▶ American B-52 bombers deliver the largest twenty-four-hour bombing raid of the war.

SEPTEMBER

04 ▶ Mark Spitz wins a record seventh Olympic gold medal in the summer Olympics in Munich, West Germany.

05 ▶ In Munich at the Olympic Games eight Arab commandos raid the dormitory housing the Israeli team and take eleven hostages. Later in the day the Arabs arrange to be transported with their hostages to the airport where a plane is waiting. In an airport gun battle with German police all of the hostages, all but three of the commandos, and one policeman are killed.

■ ■

☛ 1. *godfather* (Thanks to the movie, the gangland meaning of this term dominates the traditional.)

☛ 2. *open marriage* (disarming the nuclear family)

☛ 3. *Peace is at hand* (Henry Kissinger's slogan for disengagement from Southeast Asia)

☛ 4. *designated hitter* or *DH* (a tenth baseball player allowed in the American League)

☛ 5. *the best and the brightest* (The title of David Halberstam's book on U.S. involvement in Vietnam comes to describe those who blundered into the war.)

> *September 5, 1972:*
> In Munich at the Olympic Games eight Arab commandos raid the dormitory housing of the Israeli team and take eleven hostages.

☛ 1972 in ten words (& phrases)

6. *breeder reactor* (Plans are made to create the first nuclear reactor that creates more fuel than it consumes.)

7. *Gray Panthers* (Formed by Margaret Kuhn, this group fights against discrimination against the elderly.)

8. *CAT scan* (A medical imager introduced in England, CAT stands for computerized axial tomography.)

9. *universal product code* (a bar code for all supermarket products that is recommended by a panel studying electronic scanners able to read and record prices)

10. *SX-70* (Polaroid's name for a camera that produces color prints outside the camera while the snapshooter watches)

■ ■

OCTOBER

18 ▶ Over the veto of President Nixon, the Water Pollution Control Act is passed by Congress. It requires industry to halt discharges by 1985 and allots federal money for new sewage treatment plants.

NOVEMBER

07 ▶ Voters go to the polls and reelect Richard M. Nixon in a landslide. George McGovern is only able to carry the District of Columbia and the Commonwealth of Massachusetts.

14 ▶ The Dow Jones Industrial Average reaches a milestone of 1,003.16 points, breaking through 1,000 for the first time in its history.

22 ▶ The State Department announces an end to the twenty-two-year ban on travel to mainland China.

DECEMBER

07 ▶ *Apollo 17* makes the sixth and last manned lunar landing, during which its crew collects 243 pounds of lunar rock

November 14, 1972: The Dow Jones Industrial Average reaches a milestone of 1,003.16 points, breaking through 1,000 for the first time in its history.

samples. When they leave, astronaut Eugene Cernan utters the last words spoken on the lunar surface for decades to come: "We leave as we came and, God willing, we shall return—with peace and hope for all mankind."

19 ▶ With the successful splashdown of *Apollo 17,* the U.S. manned lunar program comes to an end.

23 ▶ A government report on *Work in America* concludes that American people at all levels are becoming more dissatisfied with the quality of their working lives and cites two reasons for this state of affairs—adherence to the dehumanizing principles of scientific management and diminishing opportunities for people to be their own bosses.

29 ▶ *Life* magazine ceases publication following the demise of other traditional, weekly magazines, such as *Look, Saturday Evening Post, Colliers,* and the *Saturday Review.*

■ ■

☞ 1. HONK IF YOU LOVE JESUS
☞ 2. HONK IF YOU ARE JESUS
☞ 3. WILL ROGERS NEVER MET McGOVERN
☞ 4. BAN BUMPER STICKERS
☞ 5. McGOVERN-EAGLETON
☞ 6. HAVE A NICE FOREVER
☞ 7. DIRTY OL' MEN NEED LOVE TOO
☞ 8. TEEN-AGERS: STRAIGHTEN YOUR ROOM, THEN THE WORLD
☞ 9. McGOVERN-SHRIVER
☞ 10. TEDDY IN '72

■ ■

December 19, 1972: With the successful splashdown of *Apollo 17,* the U.S. manned lunar program comes to an end.

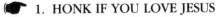 1972 in buttons & bumper stickers

The year in which the ▶
Watergate scandal grows ▶
and the United States ▶
gets out of Vietnam ▶

1973

JANUARY

08 ▶ Five defendants plead guilty as the Watergate burglary trial begins.

22 ▶ In the matter of *Roe v. Wade* the Supreme Court in a seven-to-two vote for the first time legalizes abortion nationwide. The ruling is based on a woman's constitutional right to privacy and guarantees an unqualified right to an abortion only during the first three months, or trimester, of pregnancy.

Today the Court also rules in the matter of *Roe v. Bolton,* voting seven to two to strike down restrictions on places that can be used to perform abortions, a decision that gives rise to the abortion clinic.

23 ▶ President Nixon announces that the war in Vietnam will end on January 28 and that America's last 23,700 troops will be removed within sixty days.

27 ▶ A cease-fire agreement is signed in Paris by Henry Kissinger and Le Duc Tho.

30 ▶ James W. McCord, Jr., and G. Gordon Liddy, members of Nixon's reelection committee, are found guilty of the 1972 Watergate burglary and wiretapping. The significance of the trial does not become evident, however, until March 19.

January 22, 1973:
In the matter of *Roe v. Wade* the Supreme Court in a seven-to-two vote for the first time legalizes abortion nationwide.

▶ 223

► 1973

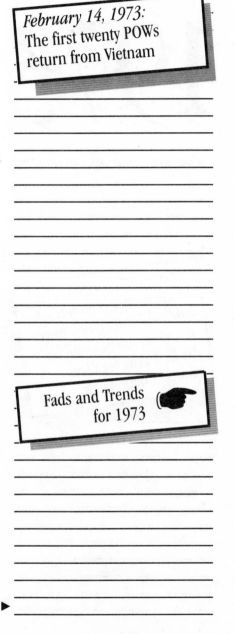

February 14, 1973:
The first twenty POWs
return from Vietnam

Fads and Trends
for 1973

FEBRUARY

14 ► The first twenty POWs return from Vietnam.

15 ► The U.S. and Cuba sign a memorandum of agreement aimed at curbing hijacking at sea and in the air.

MARCH

19 ► Watergate burglar James W. McCord, Jr., writes a letter to trial judge John J. Sirica saying that the defendants in the actual break-in pleaded guilty under pressure. McCord also writes that perjury was committed and that others were involved in the conspiracy.

23 ► Judge Sirica reveals the March 19 letter from McCord. At this moment it becomes clear that a much broader scandal is waiting to be uncovered.

28 ► In a bid to end interagency bickering, President Nixon announces the creation of a new super agency, the Drug Enforcement Agency, to fight drugs. He reports that the administration has made "very encouraging" progress against traffickers.

■■■■■■■■■■■■■■■■■■■■■■■■■■■■■■■■■■■■

☛ 1. Long gas lines, closed service stations, and tales of renegade line busters become irritating facts of life for Americans.

☛ 2. Hot tubs . . .

☛ 3. . . . hang-gliding and . . .

☛ 4. yoga spread across the country moving West to East.

☛ 5. The movie *American Graffiti* gives an added spur to a growing revival of interest in early rock 'n' roll.

☛ 6. A graphically illustrated new sex manual, *The Joy of Sex,* is a monster hit and a major source of "new" sexual information.

☛ 7. From the use of pronouns to the language of job application forms, written material is examined for the treatment of gender and sexual bias. Dr. Benjamin Spock, for instance, denounces his early child-care books as sexist.

☞ 8. The Gatsby look is inspired by a movie remake of *The Great Gatsby*.

☞ 9. As the Watergate scandal unfolds, a new fascination with investigative journalism grows, especially that modeled on the work of the *Washington Post*'s Carl Bernstein and Bob Woodward.

☞ 10. Woody Allen's movie *Sleeper* puts an entirely new spin on the future.

■■■■■■■■■■■■■■■■■■■■■■■■■■■■■■■■

APRIL

30 ► On national TV, Nixon accepts the resignations of advisors H. R. Haldeman and John Ehrlichman and Attorney General Richard Kleindienst. He fires John Dean. The Watergate scandal enters a new realm: to quote the next day's banner headline in the *New York Times, NIXON ACCEPTS ONUS FOR WATERGATE, BUT SAYS HE DIDN'T KNOW ABOUT PLOT.*

MAY

09 ► Hearings for the impeachment of President Richard M. Nixon are begun by the House Judiciary Committee.

10 ► Former Nixon Cabinet members John Mitchell and Maurice Stans and financier Robert Vesco are indicted on charges arising from Vesco's illegal $200,000 contribution to Nixon's campaign.

11 ► East and West Germany establish formal diplomatic relations.

17 ► The televised Senate hearings into Watergate begin. Senator Sam Ervin, the special Watergate committee chairman, is quoted during the hearings: "O what a tangled web we weave, when first we practice to deceive!" Because they

May 1, 1973: New York Times headline: "Nixon accepts onus for Watergate, but says he didn't know about plot."

are televised and followed closely, the Senate hearings become the vehicle that seals the fate of the Nixon presidency and gives the nation a close look at the nature of political corruption.

JUNE

16 ► Valentina Tereshkova becomes the first female space traveler when *Vostok 6* is launched from the Soviet Union on a three-day mission.

25 ► John Dean testifies in front of the Senate Select Committee, implicating himself, Nixon, Ehrlichman, Mitchell, and others and revealing the use of "hush money" and an "enemies' list." The most damaging revelation comes when Dean outlines the operation of a political espionage program run by the White House and says that Nixon was participating in the Watergate cover-up within a few days of the actual burglary.

■ ■

☛ 1. The federal budget deficit is $14.8 billion.

☛ 2. Jackson Pollock's painting "Blue Poles" sells for a record $2 million.

☛ 3. President Nixon reveals that he has become a millionaire while in office but paid less than $1,000 in taxes in 1970 and 1971. (In 1974 the IRS declares that Nixon owes $432,787 in back taxes.)

☛ 4. The median price of a single-family home is $28,900.

☛ 5. Army beats Navy in this year's football classic, fifty to zero.

☛ 6. This year's Arab-Israeli war is the fourth in twenty-five years.

☛ 7. It is discovered that nations in the Arab League have $10 billion in Western banks—$8.5 billion in the United States.

☛ 8. Willie Mays retires with 3,283 career hits.

June 16, 1973:
Valentina Tereshkova becomes the first female space traveler when *Vostok 6* is launched from the Soviet Union on a three-day mission.

1973
by the numbers ☛

▶ 1973

☞ 9. A collector pays $153,000 for Adolf Hitler's car at auction. It is a record price for a car bought at auction.

☞ 10. The Sears Tower is completed as the tallest building in the world: 1,454 feet.

■■■■■■■■■■■■■■■■■■■■■■■■■■■■■■■■■

JULY

10 ▶ The Bahamas become independent after three centuries of British colonial rule.

16 ▶ Former White House aide Alexander Butterfield inadvertently reveals to Senate Watergate investigators that President Nixon maintains a tape-recording system. Nixon's secret recording system—not suspected before this moment—is now exposed and immediately recognized as the ultimate witness.

It is a stunning day because President Nixon's personal lawyer, Herbert W. Kalmbach, reveals that former presidential assistant John D. Ehrlichman gave explicit approval for the payment of $200,000 to the defendants in the Watergate burglary.

26 ▶ Nixon defies prosecutors' subpoenas of his tapes and appeals his case until October 19.

AUGUST

15 ▶ U.S. bombing of Cambodia ends, marking the official halt to twelve years of combat in Southeast Asia.

21 ▶ In Richmond, Virginia, a four-bedroom, trilevel home replete with family room is ready for occupancy. It is built primarily of recycled materials to demonstrate the practicality of recycling. The project involves thirty companies coordinated by Reynolds Metals.

29 ▶ President Richard Nixon is ordered by Judge John Sirica to turn over secret Watergate tapes. He refuses and appeals the order.

> *August 15, 1973:* U.S. bombing of Cambodia ends, marking the official halt to twelve years of combat in Southeast Asia.

► 1973

1973 in ten words (& phrases) ☞

SEPTEMBER

11 ► In a violent coup, the elected Marxist government of Salvador Allende is overthrown by a military junta in Chile. Allende dies defending the presidential palace. The police say he committed suicide rather than surrender to the new regime.

■■■■■■■■■■■■■■■■■■■■■■■■■■■■■■■■

☞ 1. *Watergate* (Last year this was the name of an apartment complex and the site of a robbery, but this year it emerges as the name of the major political scandal of the twentieth century. Even lesser post-Watergate scandals will be given a *-gate* suffix.)

☞ 2. *gulag* (The horrors of Soviet imprisonment are evoked by one word after the release of Alexander Solzhenitsyn's *Gulag Archipelago.*)

☞ 3. *Kahoutek* (comet first spotted this year by Lubos Kahoutek of the Hamburg Observatory. It passes closest to Earth in 1974.)

☞ 4. *inoperative statements...*

☞ 5. *...stonewall...*

☞ 6. *...and executive privilege* (terms that are heard repeatedly in connection with the Watergate hearings)

☞ 7. *Wounded Knee* (a place name of historic importance given new meaning when it is seized by American Indians in a February demonstration)

☞ 8. *Saturday night massacre* (A turning point in American political history surrounding the Nixon firing of special Watergate prosecutor, Archibald Cox, is given a name out of the Wild West.)

☞ 9. *battle of the sexes* (reduced to a tennis tournament in which woman—Billy Jean King—triumphs over man—Bobby Riggs)

► 1973

☞ 10. *gene-splicing* (first accomplished by splicing a human gene into the molecules of a bacterium's DNA)

■■■■■■■■■■■■■■■■■■■■■■■■■■■■■■■■

OCTOBER

06 ► War erupts in the Middle East between Israel and Syria and Egypt.

10 ► Spiro T. Agnew resigns as vice president. In return for the Justice Department's dropping all charges against him, he pleads no contest to charges of income-tax evasion while governor of Maryland. He is fined $10,000 and put on three years' probation.

12 ► Nixon nominates House minority leader Gerald Ford as vice president. Ford quips: "I'm a Ford, not a Lincoln."

► *Also:* The U.S. Circuit Court of Appeals orders President Nixon to surrender his secret Watergate tapes.

17 ► Arab nations begin an oil embargo against the United States in an attempt to raise prices and alter U.S. support of Israel. It is a particularly unpleasant surprise in a year of unpleasant surprises.

20 ► In a quick succession of events that become known as the Saturday night massacre, Nixon fires special Watergate prosecutor, Archibald Cox. Because they will not personally fire Cox, Attorney General Elliot Richardson resigns and Deputy Attorney General William Ruckelshaus is fired.

23 ► Eight impeachment resolutions are introduced in the House.

NOVEMBER

05 ► The president appoints a new special Watergate prosecutor, Leon Jaworski.

17 ► Richard Nixon declares, "I'm not a crook." The line comes on the first day of a whirlwind tour of the South in which Nixon tries to regather public support. In context, he says,

October 10, 1973: Spiro T. Agnew resigns as vice president.

"People have got to know whether or not their President is a crook. Well, I'm not a crook."

21 ► An inexplicable eighteen-and-a-half-minute gap is discovered in a subpoenaed tape. This gap works strongly against the president's case.

24 ► Richard Nixon signs the District of Columbia Self-Government and Reorganization Act, allowing election of a mayor and city council the following year.

DECEMBER

15 ► The American Psychiatric Association reverses its traditional position and declares that homosexuality is not a mental illness.

23 ► Heralding a revolution in professional baseball, labor arbitrator Peter M. Seitz rules that a player cannot be bound indefinitely to one team without his consent. Seitz rules that Andy Messersmith and Dave McNally, two pitchers who have been playing without contracts, are now "free agents" who can sell their services to any team.

■ ■

☛ 1. CANCER CURES SMOKING

☛ 2. ARCHIE BUNKER FOR PRESIDENT

☛ 3. BEAUTIFY AMERICA—GET A HAIRCUT

☛ 4. ONE DOWN, ONE TO GO (this after vice president Agnew's resignation)

☛ 5. THE DEVIL MADE ME BUY THIS CAR

☛ 6. SAVE WATER—SHOWER WITH A FRIEND

☛ 7. DRUGS ARE FOR SICK PEOPLE

☛ 8. DON'T LAUGH—YOU DON'T KNOW IF YOUR DAUGHTER IS IN THE BACK OF THIS VAN

☛ 9. OPEC IS A FOUR-LETTER WORD

☛ 10. And a number of anti-Nixon auto stickers, including IMPEACH WITH HONOR; SAY GOODBYE DICK!; HELP NIXON OUT; NIXON HAS A STAFF INFECTION; IF YOU THINK HE'S GUILTY, HONK; WATERGATE—NIXON'S

December 15, 1973:
The American Psychiatric Association reverses its traditional position and declares that homosexuality is not a mental illness.

1973 in buttons & bumper stickers ☛

WATERLOO; YOU CAN'T FOOL ALL OF THE PEOPLE ALL
OF THE TIME; IMPEACH THE MAD BOMBER; OUT OF
ASIA, OUT OF OFFICE; NIXON BUGS ME; SEE YOU LATER
WATERGATER; DON'T BLAME ME, I'M FROM MASSA-
CHUSETTS; IMPEACH TAPEWORM; SAVE ENERGY, UN-
PLUG NIXON; VISIT SAN CLEMENTE, YOU PAID FOR IT;
BEHIND EVERY WATERGATE THERE'S A WATERGATE,
etc.

■■■■■■■■■■■■■■■■■■■■■■■■■■■■■■■■■■

JANUARY

23 ▶ Beginning with today's report from Exxon, all of the major oil companies show sharp rises in fourth-quarter income from 1973—in the range of 50 to 70 percent.

FEBRUARY

13 ▶ The Soviet Union deposes writer Alexander Solzhenitsyn for his unrelenting criticism of the Soviet system. He eventually emigrates to the United States.

MARCH

01 ▶ An indictment is returned against seven former presidential aides in the Watergate conspiracy. The president is named as an unindicted coconspirator.

18 ▶ The Arab oil embargo ends.

■ ■

☛ 1. In an effort to minimize the effects of the energy crisis, year-round daylight savings time goes into effect.

☛ 2. Running naked in public—termed "streaking"—forever punctuates people's recollections of 1974.

March 18, 1974:
The Arab oil embargo ends.

Fads and Trends for 1974

► 1974

3. Transcendental meditation (or TM) gathers bevies of believers.

☞ 3. Transcendental meditation (or TM) gathers bevies of believers.

☞ 4. Shaven, saffron-robed Hare Krishnas are found chanting on the streets of most American cities.

☞ 5. Digital watches show their faces everywhere.

☞ 6. Swedish star Bjorn Borg nets a new interest in tennis as spectator sport.

☞ 7. Rowdyism becomes a problem at sports events. Drunken baseball fans cause a forfeit in Cleveland as they attack players on the field.

☞ 8. There is growing fear that the change in sexual mores will create long-term health problems. However, the International Red Cross releases a study that predicts that because of medical advances, "In twenty years' time there may well be a permissive society that is relatively free from venereal diseases." (Ironically, in 1987 it is reported that the first American to die of AIDS was a St. Louis teenager in 1969, a decade before the first case is diagnosed as such.)

☞ 9. Books with nothing in them but blank paper are sold under *The Nothing Book* title. People buy them.

☞ 10. Puka shell necklaces are the big unisex jewelry item. (Only the powerful pull of the mood ring eclipses this fad.)

■■■■■■■■■■■■■■■■■■■■■■■■■■■■■■■■■■

APRIL

08 ► Hank Aaron hits his 715th home run, breaking Babe Ruth's forty-seven-year-old record.

MAY

09 ► The House Judiciary Committee opens impeachment hearings against the president.

18 ► India becomes the sixth nation with a nuclear weapon.

April 8, 1974:
Hank Aaron hits his 715th home run, breaking Babe Ruth's record.

1974

JUNE

30 ▶ Mrs. Martin Luther King, Sr., mother of the slain civil rights leader, is shot and killed in church by an apparently insane gunman.

■ ■

☛ 1. The cost of mailing a first-class letter rises to ten cents.

☛ 2. Electricity rates rise a record 30 percent during the year.

☛ 3. The economy slides into crisis as inflation exceeds 10 percent and unemployment climbs past 7 percent.

☛ 4. Ten people are murdered in separate incidents in the District of Columbia and its suburbs in one summer weekend.

☛ 5. The Democratic National Committee is awarded $775,000 as a result of a civil suit for damages in the Watergate break-in.

☛ 6. The sale price on a Brooks Brothers "346" tropical suit ranges from $112.50 to $127.50 (normally $150.00).

☛ 7. NBC pays $10 million for one airing of the movie *The Godfather* and charges $225,000 a minute to run commercials during the airing.

☛ 8. Americans are dying on the roads at a rate of 3.57 for every 100 million miles traveled, down considerably from the 6.28 rate in 1956.

☛ 9. Among the oddities uncovered during the Watergate scandal are the ways things are paid for. For instance, on October 10 James R. Polk reports in the *Washington Star-News* that the break-in at Daniel Ellsberg's psychiatrist's office was funded with $5,000 from the dairymen's fund and paid unwittingly and paradoxically through a group called People United for Good Government.

☛ 10. Consumer prices rise by 12.2 percent, the largest yearly increase since 1946.

■ ■

1974 by the numbers

JULY

11 ▶ The House Judiciary Committee releases volumes of evidence it has gathered in its Watergate inquiry.

12 ▶ John Ehrlichman, a former aide to President Richard Nixon, and three others are convicted of conspiring to violate the civil rights of Daniel Ellsberg's former psychiatrist.

15 ▶ Sarasota, Florida, TV commentator Chris Chubbuck finishes reading the news to her audience and then says, "And now, in keeping with Channel 40's policy of always bringing you the latest in blood and guts, in living color, you're about to see another first—an attempted suicide." She then shoots herself in the head and dies later in a hospital.

24 ▶ The U.S. Supreme Court unanimously rules that President Richard M. Nixon must turn over subpoenaed White House tape recordings to the Watergate special prosecutor.

27 ▶ The House Judiciary Committee votes twenty-seven to eleven to recommend President Richard M. Nixon's impeachment on a charge that he has personally engaged in conduct designed to obstruct justice in the Watergate case.

30 ▶ The Supreme Court upholds the subpoena of Nixon's tapes. He turns them over on July 30 and August 5.

The House Judiciary Committee goes further and is now recommending three articles of impeachment, charging Nixon with obstruction of justice, failure to uphold the law, and refusal to produce subpoenaed material.

AUGUST

05 ▶ Nixon releases transcripts of three conversations held six days after the Watergate break-in. The taped conversations reveal that Nixon had ordered the FBI to abandon its investigation of the break-in, fearing that such an investigation would reveal that his reelection campaigners were involved.

08 ▶ President Nixon announces on TV that he is resigning.

09 ▶ Gerald Ford is sworn in as the thirty-eighth president. Rich-

July 24, 1974:
The U.S. Supreme Court unanimously rules that President Richard M. Nixon must turn over subpoenaed White House tape recordings to the Watergate special prosecutor.

August 8, 1974:
President Nixon announces on TV that he is resigning.

▶ 1974

ard M. Nixon becomes the first U.S. president to resign from office. Gerald Ford, appointed vice president by Nixon after Spiro Agnew's resignation, becomes the first president to reach the position without a national election.

SEPTEMBER

08 ▶ Ford grants a "full, free, and absolute pardon" to Nixon.

■■■■■■■■■■■■■■■■■■■■■■■■■■■■■■■■■■■■

☞ 1. *smoking gun* (the metaphor for anything that links the president directly to the Watergate scandal. It turns out to be a tape.)

☞ 2. *expletive deleted* (stand-in for obscenities in the White House Watergate transcripts)

☞ 3. *full, free, and absolute* (terms of the pardon that President Gerald Ford gives President Nixon)

☞ 4. *shuttle diplomacy* (travel-intensive negotiating in the style of Henry Kissinger)

☞ 5. *Nader's raiders* (term created by journalist William Greider for the foot soldiers in Ralph Nader's crusade to improve the lot of the average American)

☞ 6. *thong* (a.k.a. the string bikini, a fad not meant for everyone)

☞ 7. *freon* (a fluorocarbon fingered as an enemy of the fragile ozone level)

☞ 8. *our long national nightmare* (what was over when President Ford took over on August 9)

☞ 9. *green revolution* (belief that new agricultural strains will dramatically increase yield and feed more people)

☞ 10. *Heimlich maneuver* (a new way of saving a choking victim is introduced by Dr. Henry M. Heimlich, who says it will save thousands of lives a year)

■■■■■■■■■■■■■■■■■■■■■■■■■■■■■■■■■■■■

1974 in ten words (& phrases)

December 19, 1974:
Former New York Governor Nelson Rockefeller is sworn in as vice president of the United States.

1974 in buttons & bumper stickers ☞

OCTOBER

03 ▶ Frank Robinson is named manager of the Cleveland Indians baseball team, making him baseball's first black manager.

NOVEMBER

29 ▶ Following two Birmingham bombings, the House of Commons approves legislation outlawing the Irish Republican Army and giving the police extraordinary powers of arrest and detention.

DECEMBER

19 ▶ Former New York Governor Nelson Rockefeller is sworn in as vice president of the United States. Rockefeller is appointed VP by Gerald Ford, who had been appointed VP by Richard Nixon, whose election in 1972 proves to be the result of illegal campaign tactics.

■■■■■■■■■■■■■■■■■■■■■■■■■■■■■■■■■

☞ 1. LADY GODIVA WAS A STREAKER
☞ 2. A WOMAN'S PLACE IS IN THE WORLD
☞ 3. WIN (acronym for President Ford's "whip inflation now" slogan)
☞ 4. LOSE (acronym for the counternotion: "let others suffer the loss")
☞ 5. HAVE YOU THANKED A GREEN PLANT TODAY?
☞ 6. A PILL A DAY KEEPS THE STORK AWAY
☞ 7. I'M NOT A DIRTY OLD MAN, I'M A SEXY SENIOR CITIZEN
☞ 8. LSD IS OUT; IUD IS IN
☞ 9. BE ALERT: THIS COUNTRY NEEDS MORE LERTS
☞ 10. MARIJUANA—NATURE'S WAY OF SAYING "HI"

■■■■■■■■■■■■■■■■■■■■■■■■■■■■■■■■■

The year in which ▶
two assassination attempts ▶
are made on the president ▶ **1975**

JANUARY

08 ▶ In Connecticut, Ella T. Grasso becomes the first woman governor of a state whose husband did not precede her in office.

12 ▶ Several insurance companies announce that they will no longer offer medical malpractice insurance because of some very costly court awards. The "serious crisis" touched off by the announcement sparks doctors' strikes and slow-downs and eventually is resolved by higher rates.

FEBRUARY

03 ▶ Layoffs announced today in the automotive industry put a record 274,380 workers out of work. Poor car sales are responsible.

MARCH

13 ▶ A report released today by the National Science Foundation concludes that the American lead in science is slipping.

March 13, 1975:
A report released by the National Science Foundation concludes that the American lead in science is slipping.

Fads and Trends for 1975 ☞

1. Mood rings—green for stability, purple for ecstasy, etc.—sell in the millions.
2. *Jaws,* the movie, is a monster hit.
3. The pet rock is the extraordinary novelty gift item for Christmas 1975.
4. Atari Corporation brings out the first line of mass-produced video games.
5. It is a period of particular fascination for the feline, brought on, at least in part, by B. Kliban's paperback hit *Cat.*
6. Assertiveness training and est come on strong.
7. Paté is the new high-status hors d'oeuvre.
8. Pie killing comes into its own as people hire third parties to hit a victim of choice in the face with a custard pie.
9. Soaring food prices prompt many to turn to gardening and home canning. The government estimates 6 million new Victory gardens.
10. Bruce Springsteen and the E Street Band break into the top forty.

APRIL

12 ▶ As Communist Khmer Rouge insurgents take control, the official U.S. presence in Cambodia comes to an abrupt end. Four marine helicopters land in the capital city of Phnom Penh and evacuate 276 persons—a handful of Cambodians and the rest Americans—including U.S. Ambassador John Gunther Dean and fifty members of his embassy staff, as well as forty journalists (three newsmen choose to remain behind).

30 ▶ Today marks the fall of Saigon to North Vietnamese troops. An emergency helicopter evacuation removes the last 1,000 Americans from South Vietnam, ending over two decades of U.S. military involvement. A few hours later the

April 30, 1975:
Saigon falls to North Vietnamese troops.

South Vietnamese government surrenders, and soldiers representing the Communist-led Provisional Revolutionary Government occupy Saigon, which soon is renamed Ho Chi Minh City.

MAY

14 ▶ President Ford orders the rescue of the cargo ship *Mayaguez,* which has been captured by the Cambodian Khmer Rouge. The mission is successful but thirty-eight U.S. servicemen are killed.

JUNE

26 ▶ The Supreme Court bars the confinement of mental patients against their will, providing that the patients are able to care for themselves and are not a danger to others. This decision is cited again and again as the number of homeless people living on the streets of American cities grows.

■■■■■■■■■■■■■■■■■■■■■■■■■■■■■■■■■■

☛ 1. The U.S. unemployment rate reaches 9.2 percent, the highest since 1941.

☛ 2. The cancer death rate per 100,000 is placed at 176.3 by the National Center for Health Statistics—up from 169.9 in 1974.

☛ 3. The cost of mailing a first-class letter rises to thirteen cents from ten cents.

☛ 4. A new galaxy, given the name 3C123, is discovered and determined to be 8 billion light-years from Earth.

☛ 5. New York City comes close to default on $450 million in notes; the White House arranges for $2.3 billion in short-term loans.

☛ 6. For the first time in history, there are more than a million divorces a year in the United States.

☛ 7. There are now more than 4 billion people in the world.

☛ 8. The federal government demands that women have

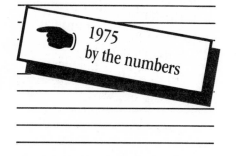

June 26, 1975: The Supreme Court bars the confinement of mental patients against their will.

☛ 1975 by the numbers

equal access to sports in schools because of numbers like these: of the $3 million spent by UCLA on sports for the 1984–1985 academic year, only $180,000 is earmarked for women's sports.

☛ 9. The Internal Revenue Service announces that in one recent year twenty-four people who earned $1 million or more paid no federal taxes. In addition fifty-four with adjusted gross incomes of between $500,000 and $1 million paid no taxes.

☛ 10. In an attempt to help fight inflation, the Senate votes to limit its own pay increase to 5 percent.

☛ 11. In the first U.S.-China track and field meet, the Americans win ninety-one of ninety-nine events.

JULY

15 ► Three American astronauts blast off aboard an *Apollo* spacecraft hours after Soviet cosmonauts head into orbit in a *Soyuz* spacecraft.

17 ► Three Americans and two Soviets link their orbiting *Apollo* and *Soyuz* spacecrafts for historic handshakes and expressions of goodwill 140 miles above Earth. In both symbol and reality, the space race between the two superpowers has come to an end.

30 ► Teamster boss Jimmy Hoffa is seen for the last time at Manchu's Red Fox restaurant in Detroit, Michigan.

AUGUST

06 ► The Voting Rights Act of 1975 abolishes literacy requirements for voting.

27 ► A grand jury acquits the governor of Ohio and members of the National Guard in the Kent State killings.

July 30, 1975:
Teamster boss Jimmy Hoffa is seen for the last time at Manchu's Red Fox restaurant in Detroit, Michigan.

▶ 1975

SEPTEMBER

01 ▶ The last episode of *Gunsmoke* is run after twenty seasons on the air.

05 ▶ An assassination attempt is made against President Ford in Sacramento, California, and is thwarted by an alert Secret Service agent, who pulls a revolver from the hands of Lynette A. "Squeaky" Fromme. She is a member of the small, violent cult that follows Charles Manson.

06 ▶ Czech tennis star Martina Navratilova, in the United States for the U.S. Open, requests political asylum in New York City.

22 ▶ For the second time this month, a woman makes an assassination attempt against President Ford in California. This time it occurs in San Francisco and the president is actually shot at by one Sara Jane Moore.

■■■■■■■■■■■■■■■■■■■■■■■■■■■■■■■■

☛ 1. *right to die* (term given new meaning through the Karen Anne Quinlan case)

☛ 2. *T-shirt advertising* (This is the year in which everybody carries a message.)

☛ 3. *no frills* (A new kind of airline ticket can be sold for the first time this year and allows the passenger to forgo food and drink for a lower fare.)

☛ 4. *Glomar Explorer* (name of the ship that was used by the CIA in 1974 to bring up a Soviet submarine. The mission is revealed this year along with its $250 million price tag.)

☛ 5. *malpractice crisis* (insurance problem that gets doctors to go on strike)

☛ 6. *rebate* (Detroit finds a new way to get people into the showroom.)

☛ 7. *elderhostel* (a new concept in education and housing for the elderly)

☛ 8. *garbology* (term created to describe the *National Enquirer*'s use of Henry Kissinger's trash cans as a source of news)

September 6, 1975: Czech tennis star Martina Navratilova, in the United States for the U.S. Open, requests political asylum in New York City.

☛) 1975 in ten words (& phrases)

9. *World Football League* (a term that goes from active to passive this year)

10. *Jaws* (the name of a movie that keeps people who ought to know better out of the water)

■■■■■■■■■■■■■■■■■■■■■■■■■■■■■■■■

OCTOBER

11. ▶ *Saturday Night* makes its first appearance on NBC. It is an irreverent, determinedly controversial show that changes the face and limits of television comedy overnight. It later is renamed *Saturday Night Live.*

22. ▶ Sergeant Leonard Matlovitch is given a general (less than honorable) discharge from the air force when he publicly declares his homosexuality. (He later is given an honorable discharge.)

NOVEMBER

20. ▶ Dictator Francisco Franco of Spain dies after thirty-six years of dictatorship.

22. ▶ Juan Carlos is proclaimed king of Spain.

DECEMBER

21. ▶ Palestinian terrorists raid the meeting of the Organization of Oil Exporting Countries (OPEC) in Vienna killing three. Some eighty-one hostages are taken but are later released.

■■■■■■■■■■■■■■■■■■■■■■■■■■■■■■■■

1. EAT BEANS—AMERICA NEEDS GAS
2. FAST IS FUELISH
3. ABORTION: A WOMAN'S RIGHT
4. THANKS MOM FOR NOT HAVING AN ABORTION
5. SUPPORT THE RIGHT TO ARM BEARS

■■■■■■■■■■■■■■■■■■■■■■■■■■■■■■■■

October 11, 1975: Saturday Night Live makes its first appearance on the National Broadcasting Company network.

1975 in buttons & bumper stickers ☞

The year in which the nation ▶
celebrates the bicentennial ▶
and Jimmy Carter is ▶
elected president ▶

1976

JANUARY

21 ▶ The Concorde Super Sonic Transport begins regular commercial operation after years of controversy over its economic and environmental significance. The commercial Concorde is a joint project of Air France and British Airways.

FEBRUARY

04 ▶ A Senate subcommittee reports that Lockheed Aircraft Company has paid $22 million in overseas bribes to sell its planes. This will occasion indictments and resignations overseas including former Japanese Premier Kakuei Tanaka of Japan and Dutch Prince Bernhard.

MARCH

31 ▶ Following a legal struggle on the part of Karen Anne Quinlan's parents to free her from an irreversible condition, the New Jersey Supreme Court gives permission for her respirator to be shut off. (Quinlan, however, stays alive without the respirator.)

January 21, 1976: The Concorde Super Sonic Transport begins regular commercial operation.

▶ 245

▶ 1976

Fads and Trends for 1976

1. The logo of the bicentennial is everywhere.
2. Exotic indoor plants are the rage along with the conviction that it is salutary to talk with said plants.
3. The CB—for citizen's band—radio jumps out of the trucker's cab and into the family car.
4. The short hairstyle of Dorothy Hamill, the gold medal Olympic skater, displaces long hair on many women.
5. Shredded currency is marketed in all sorts of novelty items, including bottled money: what was formerly $10,000 can be crammed into a small bottle.
6. Harlequin Romances and other lines of that genre create a new category of book aimed at a large, clearly defined audience.
7. Personal ads—the kind aimed at securing romance in all its different modes—start showing up in a variety of periodicals.
8. There is a fascination with the kitsch of the bicentennial and nobody seems terribly shocked by a garbage can that celebrates the event in red, white, and blue. Alexander Calder redesigns the exteriors of Braniff's planes in a wavy abstraction of the American flag (replete with Calder's immense signature over the cockpit) and Braniff takes out ads declaring the flag design art.
9. The monumentally tasteless *Gong Show* debuts in both a daytime and nighttime version. It is a variety show that seems to feature obese women doing suggestive dances in string bathing suits.
10. As the first drive-in window funeral home opens in New Roads, Louisiana, there is a new metaphor for the American attachment to the car.

▶ 1976

APRIL

04 ▶ In China a mass demonstration is held in Tiananmen Square against the Gang of Four, headed by Mao's wife. It is the first protest incident in the square.

MAY

28 ▶ The United States and USSR sign a five-year treaty limiting the size and nature of underground nuclear tests.

JUNE

01 ▶ In the matter of *Planned Parenthood v. Danforth,* the Supreme Court says that states cannot give a husband the right to veto his pregnant wife's decision to abort a pregnancy. The court also said that parents of minor, unwed daughters cannot be given absolute veto over their abortions.

16 ▶ When a riot breaks out in the township of Soweto, South Africa, police fire on 5,000 unarmed schoolchildren, killing and wounding fourteen students in this black residential area outside Johannesburg. The incident touches off a series of riots throughout the country that finally end in 1977 after 575 people have died.

■ ■

☞ 1. At the time of the bicentennial, the average American is 28.7 years old, has completed 12.4 years of school, has 2.3 children, and owns a house with 5.3 rooms.

☞ 2. We have clustered around metropolitan areas—of which thirty-three have populations of over a million—to the extent that three-quarters of all Americans live on 1.5 percent of the country's land mass.

☞ 3. The American suburbs are 95 percent white.

☞ 4. In trying to determine ethnicity, the Census Bureau finds the dominant nationality (14.4 percent) is English, fol-

May 28, 1976:
The United States and USSR sign a five-year treaty limiting the size and nature of underground nuclear tests.

1976
by the numbers

► 1976

lowed by German and Irish, but that 17 million Americans (or 8.5 percent) do not know their ethnic origin.

☞ 5. At about the same time, the Tandy Corporation and a fledgling outfit known as Apple market the first personal computers, and a new era is underway. Sales are not great the first year, but the excitement has begun.

☞ 6. The average American consumes 128.5 pounds of beef—up from 85.1 pounds in 1960.

☞ 7. At the time of his death on April 5, Howard Hughes's net worth is estimated at $1.5 billion.

☞ 8. Headline in the *Washington Star* for November 3, 1976: *A SQUEAKER FOR CARTER—SWITCH OF 5,000 VOTES WOULD HAVE GIVEN VICTORY TO FORD.*

☞ 9. Almost 70 percent of all U.S. cars come with a V-8 engine.

☞ 10. Almost half of all American babies wear Pampers, the disposable diapers manufactured by Procter & Gamble.

■■■■■■■■■■■■■■■■■■■■■■■■■■■■■■■

JULY

02 ► The unified Socialist Republic of Vietnam is proclaimed, and Saigon is officially named Ho Chi Minh City.

03 ► Israel launches its daring mission to rescue about 100 passengers and Air France crew members held at Entebbe Airport in Uganda by pro-Palestinian hijackers.

20 ► America's *Viking I* robot spacecraft makes the first successful landing on Mars.

28 ► An earthquake in China's Tangsham province kills an estimated 695,000 people.

AUGUST

07 ► Iran and the U.S. announce that Iran will buy $10 billion in arms from America.

July 20, 1976:
America's *Viking 1* robot spacecraft makes the first successful landing on Mars.

▶ 1976

SEPTEMBER

09 ▶ Communist Chinese leader Mao Tse-tung dies at the age of eighty-two in Beijing, setting off a power struggle between the hard-line Gang of Four and moderates.

24 ▶ Rhodesian Prime Minister Ian Smith announces that his country will immediately install a biracial government and that it will have majority (black) rule within two years.

30 ▶ California enacts the first right-to-die law, permitting adults to have life-support systems shut off when death is imminent.

■■■■■■■■■■■■■■■■■■■■■■■■■■■■■■■■■■

☛ 1. *adultery in my heart* (confessional phrase made by candidate Carter in a *Playboy* interview)

☛ 2. *PC* (thanks to two machines, the Tandy TRS 80 and the Apple 1)

☛ 3. *Las Vegas of the East* (the inevitable tag for Atlantic City after New Jersey approves casino gambling in the faded resort)

☛ 4. *telekinetic power* (a term we are taught most graphically by a movie named *Carrie*)

☛ 5. *Legionnaire's disease* (which kills twenty-seven attending an American Legion convention in Philadelphia)

☛ 6. *Yo!* (This is the year of the first *Rocky*.)

☛ 7. *handle* (one's CB nickname. More than a few suburban mothers become Big Mama during this period.)

☛ 8. *bear* (one of many CB terms—such as *big brother* and *John Law*—for law enforcers)

☛ 9. *sex and tennis* (A *Time* cover calls these two "the new battleground.")

☛ 10. *the tall ships* (The dynamic image presented on July 4, 1976, is of schooners and sails—an ancient flotilla on the Hudson. The official name for this is Operation Sail, but everybody calls them the tall ships.)

■■■■■■■■■■■■■■■■■■■■■■■■■■■■■■■■■■

1976 in ten words (& phrases)

November 2, 1976:
Jimmy Carter is elected president by a narrow margin over President Ford.

1976 in buttons & bumper stickers ☞

OCTOBER

04 ▶ Secretary of State Earl Butz resigns today because of public outrage at a racial slur that he made.

NOVEMBER

02 ▶ Jimmy Carter is elected president by a narrow margin over President Ford.

DECEMBER

16 ▶ The government halts a swine flu immunization program when it is discovered that fifty inoculated people experienced temporary paralysis. Over 35 million had been injected with the vaccine.

■■■■■■■■■■■■■■■■■■■■■■■■■■■■■■■■■

☞ 1. HAVE YOU HUGGED YOUR KID TODAY?
☞ 2. BOZO FOR PRESIDENT
☞ 3. HAPPY BIRTHDAY AMERICA!
☞ 4. RECALL RALPH NADER
☞ 5. REAL PEOPLE WEAR FAKE FURS
☞ 6. THIS CAR CLIMBED MOUNT WASHINGTON
☞ 7. NIXON'S FORD—A LEMON
☞ 8. NURSES ARE PANHANDLERS
☞ 9. UNEMPLOYMENT ISN'T WORKING
☞ 10. ANIMALS ARE KIND TO DUMB PEOPLE

■■■■■■■■■■■■■■■■■■■■■■■■■■■■■■■■■

JANUARY

01 ▶ Jacqueline Means is ordained the first woman Episcopal priest in the United States.

21 ▶ President Jimmy Carter offers a pardon to most Vietnam-era draft resisters. The controversial move appears to go a long way toward resolving some of the divisiveness of the war.

FEBRUARY

24 ▶ President Jimmy Carter announces that his administration's foreign aid contributions will be guided by the recipients' human rights records.

MARCH

09 ▶ The Food and Drug Administration proposes a ban on the artificial sweetener saccharin because laboratory tests suggest it may cause cancer.

27 ▶ In aviation's worst disaster 582 people are killed when a KLM Boeing 747 attempts to take off and crashes into a Pan Am 747 on a runway on the Canary Island of Tenerife.

March 9, 1977:
The Food and Drug Administration proposes a ban on the artificial sweetener saccharin because laboratory tests suggest it may cause cancer.

▶ 251

■ ■

☞ 1. Liquid protein diets are the rage.

☞ 2. The punk era begins in Britain with outrageous bands like the Sex Pistols.

☞ 3. Joggers seem to be everywhere.

☞ 4. Billy Beer, named for the president's brother, is a novelty hit beverage.

☞ 5. Anything blessed with the *Star Wars* logo seems anointed for commercial success.

☞ 6. Volkswagen discontinues the Beetle, which touches off an immediate wave of nostalgia for the last great, good, cheap car.

☞ 7. The television miniseries *Roots* is not only a hit but creates a great interest in genealogy.

☞ 8. The traveling show of Tutankhamen's treasures attracts overnight lines in many places.

☞ 9. Walking gets a great boost this year thanks in part to President Carter's walk back from his own inauguration.

☞ 10. Yogurt is declared to be part of the new American culture.

■ ■

April 18, 1977:
President Carter calls for a national effort for energy conservation that is the "moral equivalent of war."

APRIL

18 ▶ President Carter calls for a national effort for energy conservation that is the "moral equivalent of war."

28 ▶ The Department of Health, Education, and Welfare bans discrimination against the nation's 35 million handicapped individuals.

MAY

25 ▶ An obscure movie producer by the name of George Lucas releases a movie by the name of *Star Wars* that changes the movie business. Few give the film much hope of suc-

cess, but it becomes the second-highest-grossing movie in history, and its name enters the language permanently.

JUNE

29 ▶ The Supreme Court rules that capital punishment for rape is unconstitutional.

■■■■■■■■■■■■■■■■■■■■■■■■■■■■■■■■■■

☞ 1. British scientists determine that smoking one cigarette shortens the habitual smoker's life by five and a half minutes an hour.

☞ 2. The trans-Alaska pipeline opens. Total cost: $7.7 billion.

☞ 3. Gordie Howe becomes the first hockey player to score 1,000 points.

☞ 4. The number of adult Americans living alone has doubled since 1970.

☞ 5. Professional basketball attendance in the United States rises to over 10 million.

☞ 6. The miniseries *Roots* attracts 80 million viewers.

☞ 7. There are 120 million cases of malaria reported worldwide.

☞ 8. The retail price of a pound of coffee reaches $5 in some areas, a rise blamed on a killing frost in South America.

☞ 9. Movie revenues hit a record $2.3 billion thanks to hits like *Close Encounters of the Third Kind, Annie Hall,* and *Star Wars.*

☞ 10. Apprentice jockey Steve Cauthen wins 524 races with a combined purse value of $4.3 million.

■■■■■■■■■■■■■■■■■■■■■■■■■■■■■■■■■■

1977
by the numbers

May 25, 1977:
An obscure movie producer by the name of George Lucas releases a movie called *Star Wars* that changes the movie business.

JULY

05 ▶ Pakistan's army, led by General Mohammad Zia ul-Haq, seizes power from President Zulfikar Ali Bhutto. Bhutto is executed in 1979.

August 16, 1977:
Rock 'n' roll idol Elvis Presley dies of heart failure at his home in Memphis, Tennessee, at age forty-two.

1977 in ten words (& phrases) ☞

11 ▶ The Medal of Freedom is awarded posthumously at the White House to the Reverend Martin Luther King, Jr.

13 ▶ The New York City area is plunged into darkness after lightning strikes upstate power lines. Incidents of looting and violence break out before power is fully restored twenty-five hours later.

18 ▶ Vietnam is admitted to the United Nations.

19 ▶ Bohemian-born Jon Nepomucene Neumann, who was bishop of Philadelphia from 1852 to 1860, is canonized by Pope Paul VI as the first American male saint.

AUGUST

04 ▶ President Carter appoints the nation's first secretary of energy, James R. Schlesinger. With Cabinet status, the importance of energy for the future is underscored.

10 ▶ The United States and Panama come to an agreement to transfer the Panama Canal to Panama by the year 2000.

▶ *Also:* David Berkowitz is accused of being the mysterious Son of Sam who has terrorized the New York metropolitan area with a series of six murders and seven woundings.

16 ▶ Rock 'n' roll idol Elvis Presley dies of heart failure at his home in Memphis, Tennessee, at age forty-two.

20 ▶ The United States launches *Voyager 2,* an unmanned spacecraft carrying a twelve-inch copper phonograph record that contains greetings in dozens of languages, samples of music, and natural sounds.

SEPTEMBER

13 ▶ General Motors introduces the first American-made diesel cars.

■■■■■■■■■■■■■■■■■■■■■■■■■■■■■■■■■■■

☞ 1. *May the force be with you* (spirit-invoking incantation from the movie *Star Wars*)

▶ 1977

☞ 2. *neutron bomb* (progress in arms—a device that can kill thousands without harming property)

☞ 3. *genetic engineering* (something for public discussion—achieves full status as a "controversial subject")

☞ 4. *dress for success* (concept that promises advancement through power neckties for men and plain pumps in dark colors for women)

☞ 5. *downsizing* (what Detroit is doing to the American automobile)

☞ 6. *fresh faith in an old dream* (what President Carter asks for at his inauguration)

☞ 7. *androgyny* (the hot topic. The question of the hour is "Are men becoming more like women and vice versa?")

☞ 8. *energy czar* (immediate name applied to the first secretary of energy)

☞ 9. *May the floss be with you* (the ultimate blessing, from the dentist)

☞ 10. *urbank* (Short for "urban bank," it is the central idea in President Carter's urban plan—a government-funded bank to spur inner-city development. It does not fly.)

▪ ▪

OCTOBER

26 ▶ Bethlehem Steel posts third-quarter losses of $477 million, which is believed to be the largest quarterly loss in American corporate history.

NOVEMBER

01 ▶ The law raising the minimum wage from $2.30 to $3.35 an hour by 1981 is signed by the president.

October 26, 1977: Bethlehem Steel posts third-quarter losses of $477 million, which is believed to be the largest quarterly loss in American corporate history.

DECEMBER

20 ► Legislation is signed by the president that will significantly increase the Social Security tax.

■■■■■■■■■■■■■■■■■■■■■■■■■■■■■■■

☞ 1. I FOUND IT!

☞ 2. I NEVER LOST IT!

☞ 3. I FONDLED IT!

☞ 4. HONK IF YOU LOVE CHEESES

☞ 5. NO COMMENT!

☞ 6. PREPARE FOR THE RAPTURE

☞ 7. THE CZECHS REGISTERED THEIR GUNS

☞ 8. CLASS OF '77—HIGHER THAN HEAVEN

☞ 9. FLORIDA: ARRIVE STONED

☞ 10. PROTECT FARMLAND: YOU CAN'T EAT TOWN-HOUSES

■■■■■■■■■■■■■■■■■■■■■■■■■■■■■■■

1977 in buttons & bumper stickers ☞

The year in which ▶
there is a mass suicide ▶
in Guyana ▶
1978

JANUARY

29 ▶ Sweden becomes the first nation to curb the use of aerosol cans.

FEBRUARY

16 ▶ China and Japan sign a $20 billion trade pact that is seen as the most important new opening to China since 1972's initial diplomatic opening.

MARCH

22 ▶ Karl Wallenda, patriarch of the Flying Wallendas high-wire act, falls to his death while attempting to walk a cable strung between two hotels in San Juan, Puerto Rico. He is seventy-three.

■ ■

☞ 1. *Dallas* premieres on television and the nighttime soap is born.

☞ 2. College toga parties are a side-effect of the movie *Animal House*.

☞ 3. There is growing revulsion with the punk movement in music and style, underscored by the arrest in October of

Fads and Trends
for 1978

Fads and Trends for 1978 👉

Sid Vicious of the Sex Pistols for the murder of his girlfriend.

👉 4. *Saturday Night Fever* gives a big send-off to disco—music meant to be danced to. In the wake of the movie . . .

👉 5. Discotheques crop up everywhere.

👉 6. A television series called *The Holocaust* draws a large audience in the United States and is shown in Germany and Israel.

👉 7. *Space Invaders* brings America into the age of the video game.

👉 8. Hundreds of thousands of hot tubs are sold—and not just in California—at prices from $1,000 up.

👉 9. This is the year for the Muppets. Miss Piggy and Kermit the frog are everywhere—in the movies, on TV, and on every conceivable kind of merchandise.

👉 10. *The Deer Hunter* and *Coming Home* demonstrate that war movies in the wake of the Vietnam War are vastly different from those that followed earlier wars.

👉 11. Reggie Jackson introduces a candy bar with his name on it—the Reggie Bar.

■ ■

APRIL

06 ► President Carter signs a bill that gives most American workers the option of retiring at age seventy rather than the traditional mandatory retirement age of sixty-five.

MAY

26 ► The Resorts International Hotel Casino opens in Atlantic City, New Jersey. It is the first legal casino to open in the continental U.S. outside of Nevada.

May 26, 1978:
The Resorts International Hotel Casino opens in Atlantic City, New Jersey. It is the first legal casino to open in the continental U. S. outside of Nevada.

1978

JUNE

06 ▶ Proposition 13, a California constitutional amendment reducing property taxes by 57 percent, is approved by a large majority (65 percent) of the state's voters. This is the surest sign to date that the nation is in revolt against high taxes.

■■■■■■■■■■■■■■■■■■■■■■■■■■■■■■■■

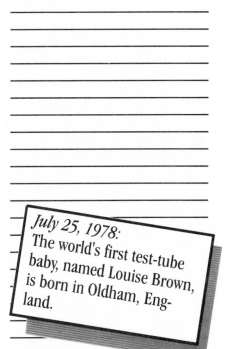

1. The life expectancy of an American born this year is 73.5—69.6 for men and 77.2 for women.
2. The cost of mailing a first-class letter is now fifteen cents.
3. Population of the world is now 4.4 billion and growing at a rate of 200,000 a day.
4. The city of Cleveland defaults on short-term notes to the tune of $15 million and becomes the first city to default since the Great Depression.
5. The stunning new East Building of the National Gallery in Washington opens; it costs $94.4 million.
6. There are 76 million households in the United States.
7. 20,000 people write to suggest that Miss Piggy win the Academy Award for best actress for 1978.
8. Major league baseball draws a record 40 million fans.
9. IBM introduces a 64,000-bit memory chip.
10. There are now 204 nuclear power plants in the world.

■■■■■■■■■■■■■■■■■■■■■■■■■■■■■■■■

JULY

10 ▶ Soviet dissident Anatoly Shcharansky goes on trial in Moscow, charged with espionage.
13 ▶ Lee Iacocca is fired as president of Ford Motor Company by chairman Henry Ford II.
25 ▶ The world's first test-tube baby, named Louise Brown, is born in Oldham, England. The event is hailed as a medical

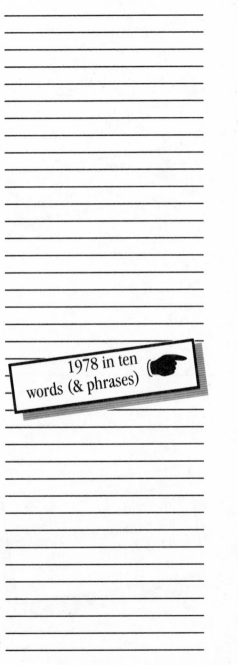

1978 in ten words (& phrases)

breakthrough on the order of the first heart transplant. As the first human conceived outside the womb, she gives hope to millions of childless couples.

AUGUST

04 ▶ Evacuation of the Love Canal neighborhood in Niagara Falls, New York, begins. Used as a toxic waste dump from 1947 to 1952, it is now deemed to be unfit for human habitation.

17 ▶ Three Americans complete the first successful crossing of the Atlantic by balloon, landing their helium-filled *Double Eagle II* near Paris.

SEPTEMBER

17 ▶ An accord between Egypt and Israel is signed at Camp David, Maryland, after negotiations overseen by President Jimmy Carter.

■ ■

☞ 1. *boat people* (Indochinese refugees from Communism)

☞ 2. *off the wall* (What appears to be a squash/handball term becomes a description for the odd and unusual.)

☞ 3. *tax revolt* (what the nation is in the midst of)

☞ 4. *spirit of Camp David* (name given to the desire for Mideast peace following the September meetings between the leaders of the United States, Egypt, and Israel)

☞ 5. *Speak and Spell* (hot educational plaything from Texas Instruments)

☞ 6. *moi* (in the mouth of Miss Piggy this French pronoun becomes a term of high vanity)

☞ 7. *sixteen-game season* (new description of pro football—up from fourteen games)

☞ 8. *hot tubbing* (what you do in a hot tub, formerly known as soaking)

☞ 9. *interferon* (Clinical tests get underway on this promising drug.)

▶ 1978

☛ 10. *intelligent typewriter* (Word processing meets the old technology.)

■■■■■■■■■■■■■■■■■■■■■■■■■■■■■■■

OCTOBER

06 ▶ As supporters continue to work toward winning the required thirty-eight states needed for ratification, Congress grants an extension on the equal rights amendment to the Constitution.

NOVEMBER

18 ▶ Shortly after 5:00 P.M. cult leader James Jones gives the order for the "White Night." This is no rehearsal. The cult settlement, known as Jonestown, Guyana, is to destroy itself. Jonestown's toll: 914 suicides and murder victims swollen and stacked like lengths of wood; a metal vat on a platform with purple, cyanide-laced Kool-Aid at its bottom. Earlier in the day, Congressman Leo J. Ryan and his party are attacked by members of the settlement. The assailants, firing pistols and automatic weapons, kill Ryan and four others.

27 ▶ Former San Francisco supervisor Dan White kills Mayor George Moscone and Supervisor Harvey Milk at City Hall.

DECEMBER

15 ▶ The People's Republic of China and the U.S. announce that they will resume full diplomatic relations on January 1, 1979.

■■■■■■■■■■■■■■■■■■■■■■■■■■■■■■■

☛ 1. LIVE DANGEROUSLY: TAKE A DEEP BREATH
☛ 2. I FIGHT POVERTY, I WORK
☛ 3. THE GAS WAR IS OVER—GAS WON

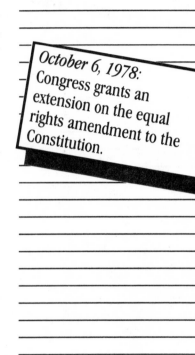

October 6, 1978: Congress grants an extension on the equal rights amendment to the Constitution.

1978 in buttons & bumper stickers

1978 bumper sticker:
Live Dangerously:
Take a Deep Breath.

☞ 4. NUKE THE TALL SHIPS
☞ 5. RUNNERS MAKE BETTER LOVERS
☞ 6. THE METRIC SYSTEM DOESN'T MEASURE UP
☞ 7. THIS VEHICLE STOPS AT MOOSE HOMES
☞ 8. DON'T COMPLAIN ABOUT FARMERS WITH YOUR MOUTH FULL
☞ 9. NO CANAL GIVEAWAY
☞ 10. IF I FOLLOW YOU HOME, WILL YOU KEEP ME?

■■■■■■■■■■■■■■■■■■■■■■■■■■■■■■■

1979

JANUARY

11 ▶ Pushing the warning to a new level, Surgeon General Julius B. Richmond terms smoking the "most important environmental factor contributing to early death."

16 ▶ The shah of Iran is forced to leave his country.

29 ▶ The United States, represented by President Carter, and China, represented by Vice Premier Teng Hsiao-ping, celebrate a day of reconciliation in Washington.

FEBRUARY

14 ▶ The American ambassador to Afghanistan is kidnapped and then killed when Afghan government forces try to free him.

26 ▶ The Ayatollah Khomeini makes a triumphant return to Iran.

MARCH

26 ▶ The Camp David peace treaty is signed by Israeli Prime Minister Menachem Begin and Egyptian President Anwar Sadat during a White House ceremony, with President Jimmy Carter signing as a witness. As thirty years of hostility come to an end, Carter pledges to "wage peace." It is a—some say *the*—great moment of the Carter presidency.

28 ▶ A near-monumental disaster occurs at the Three Mile Island

February 26, 1979:
The Ayatollah Khomeini makes a triumphant return to Iran.

nuclear power plant near Harrisburg, Pennsylvania. There are no fatalities, but radiation is released and the governor orders pregnant women and young children out of the area. Because of what almost happened it is regarded as America's worst nuclear accident.

■ ■

Fads and Trends for 1979

1. Great jumps in the price of gold—triggered by fears of inflation—create a new infatuation with the precious metal.
2. Comic strip character Superman makes a comeback thanks to the movie *Superman.*
3. The Three Mile Island accident and a prophetic movie, *The China Syndrome,* give new strength to the antinuclear movement.
4. This is the disco summer. From the beginning of June through the end of August number-one songs in the land include *Hot Stuff* by Donna Summer, *Love You Inside Out* by the Bee Gees, *Ring My Bell* by Anita Ward, and *Good Times* by Chic.
5. Slit skirts and baggy pants make fashion news for the umpteenth time.
6. Roller skating makes a dramatic but short-lived comeback.
7. The Susan B. Anthony dollar is introduced with great hoopla, but the public rejects it, probably because it feels too much like a quarter.
8. When high ratings are earned by a film on Charles Manson, made-for-television movies take a turn toward the violent and macabre. CBS announces plans for a film on the mass suicide in Guyana.
9. Americans take out their frustration with the hostage situation by wearing anti-Iranian T-shirts and buying things like dart boards covered with the face of the Ayatollah Ruhollah Khomeini.
10. Broadway has a great year at the box office, but record

sales are down as higher oil prices mean higher prices for vinyl recordings.

■■■■■■■■■■■■■■■■■■■■■■■■■■■■■■■

APRIL

03 ▶ Jane Byrne becomes the first woman mayor of Chicago.

MAY

04 ▶ The Conservative Party is declared winner of the May 3 general election in Great Britain and Margaret Thatcher becomes prime minister. Under Thatcher the nation marches away from its postwar socialism.

JUNE

18 ▶ President Jimmy Carter and Chairman Leonid Brezhnev sign the SALT II agreement (Strategic Arms Limitation Treaty) limiting long-range missiles and bombers to 2,250 for each country.

28 ▶ The Organization of Petroleum Exporting Countries raises world crude oil prices to a range of $18 to $23.50 a barrel, the biggest increase in five years. OPEC's power is still considerable.

■■■■■■■■■■■■■■■■■■■■■■■■■■■■■■■

1. Hurricane Frederic—September 12 to 14—racks up $752.5 million in insurance losses, making it the most costly hurricane to date and for years to come.

2. The *Voyager 1* spacecraft locates the hottest spot in the solar system—an area between Jupiter and Mars where the temperature is between 300 and 400 million degrees Celsius.

3. The consumer price index rises 13.3 percent, which is the largest jump in thirty-three years.

April 3, 1979: Jane Byrne becomes the first woman mayor of Chicago.

1979 by the numbers

☞ 4. The bank prime rate goes to 14.5 percent.

☞ 5. A haircut in the House of Representatives barber shop costs $3.50.

☞ 6. In March of this year 3.4 million families (representing 10.4 million individuals) are getting Aid to Families with Dependent Children (AFDC). About 40 percent of all black families with children under eighteen are involved compared to 6.8 percent of white families with children.

☞ 7. The consumer price index jumps 13.3 percent, the largest increase in thirty-three years.

☞ 8. In the benchmark palimony case, Michelle Marvin, actor Lee Marvin's longtime companion, is awarded $104,000 for reconstructing her life after they split up.

☞ 9. Henry Allen of the *Washington Post* notes that there are fifty-eight books in print on Virginia Woolf.

☞ 10. The White House invites 5,835 guests to see the Pope on the White House lawn. The official list of invitees includes fifty-four Murphys.

■ ■

JULY

01 ▶ The first Sony Walkman is unveiled as the Stowaway.

02 ▶ The new Susan B. Anthony dollar is introduced to the public. It is slightly larger than a quarter, 8.1 grams in weight, and features a portrait of the famous suffragist on one side and an image of an eagle landing on the moon on the other. Despite its grand debut, it does not attract broad public support.

11 ▶ The abandoned U.S. space station *Skylab* makes a spectacular return to Earth, burning up in the atmosphere and showering debris over the Indian Ocean and the Australian outback. Millions of people heave a collective sigh of relief as it comes down far from population centers.

31 ▶ After reporting the largest quarterly loss in corporate his-

July 1, 1979:
The first Sony Walkman is unveiled as the Stowaway.

▶ 1979

tory ($207 million) Chrysler asks for a $1 billion loan from the federal government. (See January, 1980.)

AUGUST

15 ▶ Andrew Young resigns as the U.S. delegate to the United Nations as disapproval is expressed over his unofficial meetings with members of the Palestine Liberation Organization.

SEPTEMBER

01 ▶ The *Pioneer 2* probe passes Saturn sending back evidence of two new rings and an additional moon.

■■■■■■■■■■■■■■■■■■■■■■■■■■■■■■■

☛ 1. *stagflation* (term invoked to describe this year's combination of inflation and lagging economic activity)

☛ 2. *palimony* (alimony for the unmarried)

☛ 3. *dollar-a-gallon gas* (It hurts to say this.)

☛ 4. *laetrile* (A cancer cure that wasn't.)

☛ 5. *Chrysler bail-out* (new term for corporate welfare)

☛ 6. *Ultrasaurus/Supersaurus* (names given to what is believed to be the largest dinosaur ever discovered. Its bones suggest a living weight of eighty tons.)

☛ 7. *irage* (nonce word created to describe the rage that Americans felt over the American hostages held in Iran)

☛ 8. *justice has no gender* (controversial sign carried by a nun during the Pope's visit to Washington)

☛ 9. *MX* (name of a new missile system approved by President Carter and estimated to cost $30 billion)

☛ 10. *acid rain* (serious discussion of this problem gets underway in 1979)

■■■■■■■■■■■■■■■■■■■■■■■■■■■■■■■

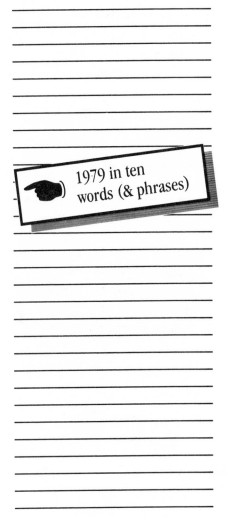

1979 in ten words (& phrases)

► 1979

November 4, 1979:
Iranian militants seize the American embassy in Tehran and take ninety hostages, including sixty-three Americans.

1979 in buttons & bumper stickers

OCTOBER

02 ► Charlie Smith, who has claimed to be America's last living slave, dies at age 137.

06 ► President Carter meets Pope John Paul II in Washington and becomes the first American chief executive to officially receive a Catholic pontiff.

NOVEMBER

04 ► Iranian militants seize the American embassy in Tehran and take ninety hostages, including sixty-three Americans. They demand the return of the shah of Iran, who is in the U.S. being treated for cancer. The militants hold fifty hostages for more than a year.

DECEMBER

04 ► President Carter announces that he will run for reelection.

1. JIMMY WHO?
2. CARS AREN'T THE ONLY THINGS BEING RECALLED BY THEIR MAKER
3. IF YOU CAN READ THIS, THANK A TEACHER
4. IF YOU CAN READ THIS, YOU'RE TOO DAMN CLOSE
5. THE SKYLAB IS FALLING! THE SKYLAB IS FALLING
6. CHICKEN LITTLE WAS RIGHT—SKYLAB '79
7. HAVE YOU HUGGED YOUR MISTRESS TODAY?
8. THE BEST THINGS IN LIFE ARE FREE, WHILE SUPPLIES LAST
9. WARNING: I DON'T BREAK FOR LIBERALS
10. THIS IS A GOD SQUAD CAR

1980

JANUARY

07 ▶ President Carter signs a bill—passed by Congress on December 21, 1979—that bails out the Chrysler Corporation to the tune of $1,500,000,000.

14 ▶ According to a report from the surgeon general, lung cancer in women is increasing dramatically and soon will overtake breast cancer as the leading cancer that kills women. The report raises the question of whether one cost of women's economic equality might be reduced life expectancy.

FEBRUARY

02 ▶ The FBI makes public its two-year long sting to catch corrupt politicians. In all, thirty-one public officials are named as targets of the probe including a senator and six members of the House of Representatives.

MARCH

23 ▶ Swedes vote in a national referendum on the future of nuclear power, deciding to keep the country's twelve reactors until the year 2010, by which time it is hoped they will be replaced by alternative power sources.

1980 by the numbers:
A million people visit the Picasso retrospective at the Museum of Modern Art.

▶ 269

Fads and Trends for 1980 ☞

April 11, 1980:
The U.S. Equal Opportunity Commission issues regulations making sexual harassment of women illegal in the workplace.

■ ■

☞ 1. A book called *The Official Preppie Handbook* and a movie called *Urban Cowboy* help elevate the preppie and the urban cowboy as the odd couple of the year.

☞ 2. A boardless, role-playing game called Dungeons and Dragons, which was created in 1974, becomes a big hit. The kids call it D&D, while the TV preachers see Satan's influence at work.

☞ 3. Cable News Network debuts.

☞ 4. The Moral Majority declares itself.

☞ 5. Professional women wearing running shoes are a common urban sight.

☞ 6. The question "Who shot J.R.?" from the television show *Dallas* keeps the nation guessing during the summer reruns. This is the year *Dallas* manifests itself from board games to Sue Ellen dolls.

☞ 7. The revival of the musical *42nd Street* brings on toe-tapping nostalgia.

☞ 8. Chocolate chip cookies inspire their own boutiques.

☞ 9. A New York transit strike puts a lot of professional men and women in running shoes.

☞ 10. 3M introduces its Post-it Notes, which stick to anything flat and come off easily without making a mark. They are soon as common in the office as paperclips and rubberbands and people are taking them home to leave messages on the refrigerator door.

■ ■

APRIL

11 ► The U.S. Equal Opportunity Commission issues regulations making sexual harassment of women illegal in the workplace.

24 ► The United States makes an attempt to land in Iran and rescue the hostages held at the U.S. embassy. It is a disaster in which eight American servicemen are killed.

1980

MAY

01 ▶ According to the Tax Foundation, today is tax freedom day 1980—the day on which workers theoretically get to start keeping all their earnings. It assumes that all money earned before this date went to pay federal, state, and local taxes.

08 ▶ Smallpox, once a great scourge, is declared to be totally eradicated by the World Health Organization. It is hailed as one of the century's greatest medical accomplishments.

18 ▶ Mount St. Helens, a volcano in Washington, erupts violently and remains in the news for many weeks to come.

JUNE

03 ▶ It is revealed that more than 100,000 Cuban refugees have arrived in the United States since April with the knowledge of Cuban authorities.

16 ▶ In a major advance for genetic engineering, the Supreme Court rules that biological organisms created in the laboratory can be patented.

■■■■■■■■■■■■■■■■■■■■■■■■■■■■■■■

☛ 1. The U.S. population stands at 226,547,000 with the population center now just west of DeSoto, Missouri.

☛ 2. The cost of a Levittown, Long Island, home is $60,000, up from $15,000 in 1967.

☛ 3. A million people visit the Picasso retrospective at the Museum of Modern Art.

☛ 4. Inflation reaches 12.4 percent at year's end, which is down from the 18 percent it hit last year.

☛ 5. The Libertarian candidate in November's presidential election, Ed Clark, wins more than a half million votes.

☛ 6. The oldest known biological cells are found and are estimated to be 3.5 million years old.

☛ 7. Damage caused by Mount St. Helens is estimated at $2.7 billion.

☛ 8. Hockey star Gordie Howe hangs up his skates at age

May 18, 1980: Mount St. Helens, a volcano in Washington, erupts violently and remains in the news for many weeks to come.

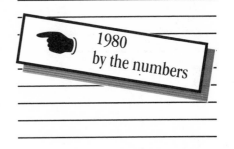

1980 by the numbers

▶ 271

fifty-two after playing in 1,687 National Hockey League games.

☞ 9. In a move against the Soviet Union for its invasion of Afghanistan, President Carter cancels a Soviet order for 17 million metric tons of American grain.

☞ 10. There are 2.41 million marriages in 1980 and 1.18 million divorces.

☞ 11. U.S. automakers lose an estimated $3 billion this year. The losses are blamed on imported cars.

■ ■

JULY

19 ▶ The Moscow summer Olympic games begin, minus dozens of nations boycotting the games because of the Soviet intervention in Afghanistan. The United States is most noticeable for its absence.

27 ▶ On day 267 of the Iranian hostage crisis, Mohammed Reza Pahlavi—the deposed, cancer-riddled shah of Iran—dies in a military hospital outside Cairo, Egypt, at age sixty.

AUGUST

13 ▶ President Jimmy Carter is nominated for a second term by the Democratic National Convention in New York and picks Vice President Walter Mondale as his running mate. They lose in November to Ronald Reagan and George Bush.

SEPTEMBER

22 ▶ Under the leadership of Lech Walesa Polish workers form a union that they call Solidarity.

■ ■

☞ 1. *gridlock* (a menacing word that comes out of Manhattan during the summer. *Newsweek* defines it this way: "The

September 22, 1980:
Under the leadership of Lech Walesa Polish workers form a union that they call Solidarity.

1980 in ten words (& phrases) ☞

ultimate traffic jam in which city streets are so clogged with vehicles that all intersections become blocked and traffic is hopelessly paralyzed in every direction.")

☞ 2. *marielito* (name for the 125,000 Cuban outcasts sent to the U.S. from Mariel)

☞ 3. *ABSCAM* (FBI term for a plan to catch legislators taking bribes. The name is derived from "Arab Scam" since some of those setting the trap pose as rich Arabs.)

☞ 4. *dawk* (term created for the person waffling between being a hawk [hardliner] and a dove [peace advocate])

☞ 5. *free base* (a method of drug abuse involving cocaine and ether that most Americans first hear about when comedian Richard Pryor almost kills himself when the mixture blows up in his face)

☞ 6. *toxic shock syndrome* (a sometimes fatal disease that makes news when linked to a popular brand of tampons)

☞ 7. *Olympic boycott* (a poke at the Russians and a disappointment to American athletes)

☞ 8. *Zimbabwe* (the new name for Rhodesia at the moment of independence)

☞ 9. *windfall profits tax* (how you get the oil companies to kick some money back in the kitty—an estimated $227 billion in the next ten years)

☞ 10. *plastic-tipped pen* (The first one is from Berol.)

■ ■

OCTOBER

02 ► The House of Representatives expels Representative Michael Myers of Florida for his conviction in connection with the ABSCAM investigation. It is the first expulsion since 1861.

30 ► Senator Harrison Williams is indicted for his role in the ABSCAM affair.

New word for 1980: Gridlock.

November 4, 1980:
Ronald Reagan is swept into office as the fortieth president of the United States.

1980 in buttons & bumper stickers ☞

NOVEMBER

04 ► Ronald Reagan is swept into office as the fortieth president of the United States.

21 ► The "Who Shot J.R.?" episode of *Dallas* is seen by 83 million viewers.

DECEMBER

08 ► Former Beatle John Lennon is shot and killed by a deranged fan outside his New York apartment building.

☞ 1. WHY NOT THE BEST? DUMP CARTER!

☞ 2. QUESTION AUTHORITY

☞ 3. BEAM ME UP SCOTTY—THERE'S NO INTELLIGENT LIFE HERE

☞ 4. SPLIT WOOD, NOT ATOMS

☞ 5. EXXON SUXX

☞ 6. REAL AMERICANS BUY AMERICAN CARS

☞ 7. ANYONE BUT REAGAN

☞ 8. IF THIS VAN IS ROCKIN'—DON'T BOTHER KNOCKIN'

☞ 9. JIMMY CARTER DOES THE WORK OF TWO MEN—LAUREL AND HARDY

☞ 10. Professional bumper stickers come on strong. Some are merely word play (HISTORIANS ARE A THING OF THE PAST, LET YOUR ELECTRICIAN CHECK YOUR SHORTS, CURL UP WITH A HAIRDRESSER, POLICE OFFICERS NEVER COP OUT, RADIOLOGIC TECHNICIANS EXPOSE YOU FOR WHAT YOU ARE), but the vast majority have to do with the professional/sexual nuances of *it* (REPORTERS DO IT ON DEADLINE, HARNESSRACERS DO IT IN 2 MINUTES, DIVERS DO IT DEEPER, BIKERS DO IT IN THE DIRT, NURSES DO IT WITH PATIENCE).

The year that ▶
the AIDS virus ▶
is first diagnosed ▶
1981

JANUARY

20 ▶ Ronald Reagan becomes president on the same day that the Iranian hostage crisis ends with the release of fifty-two hostages who had been seized at the U.S. embassy in Tehran. Members of the Carter administration who had been absorbed by the crisis are disappointed not to see it end on their watch.

24 ▶ Under the leadership of Lech Walesa, several million Polish workers strike for a five-day work week. It is illegal and a great embarrassment to the nation's leadership.

FEBRUARY

08 ▶ An article in the *New England Journal of Medicine* links the consumption of cholesterol to death from coronary occlusion. The role of cholesterol in heart disease remains a subject for debate throughout the decade.

MARCH

23 ▶ The U.S. Supreme Court rules that states can require, with some exceptions, parental notification when teenage girls seek abortions.

30 ▶ President Reagan is shot by John W. Hinckley, Jr., outside

January 20, 1981: Ronald Reagan becomes president.

▶ 275

the Washington Hilton Hotel. Reagan requires two hours of emergency surgery to remove a bullet from his lung. White House press secretary James Brady, a policeman, and a Secret Service agent are also wounded by Hinckley, who apparently hopes that this act of violence will impress actress Jodie Foster.

■ ■

☛ 1. Rubik's Cube is madness in five colors.

☛ 2. Jelly beans show up in every color and flavor—a fad inspired by the commander-in-chief.

☛ 3. The video game Pac-Man shows up in every nook and corner of the country as the nation finds itself in the grips of Pac-Mania.

☛ 4. *Dynasty* is a hit on television.

☛ 5. Indiana Jones and *Raiders of the Lost Ark* bring back the old-fashioned movie adventure.

☛ 6. MTV, an all-music cable channel, comes on like gangbusters.

☛ 7. The freckled and bonneted Strawberry Shortcake is the hot doll for '81.

☛ 8. IBM enters the personal computer field and the race for dominance is on.

☛ 9. Americans find themselves rooting for the Polish Solidarity union and its leader Lech Walesa.

☛ 10. The wedding of Charles and Di is a major event.

■ ■

APRIL

12 ▶ The space shuttle *Columbia* makes its maiden voyage from Cape Canaveral. It will return to Earth on the 14th when it becomes the first manned spacecraft to land as an aircraft with its wheels down rather than to splash down.

Fads and Trends for 1981 ☞

1981

MAY

01 ▶ Senator Harrison Williams of New Jersey is found guilty of ABSCAM-related criminal offenses while in office. He is the first senator to find himself in this position since 1905.

13 ▶ Pope John Paul II is shot and wounded by a Turkish criminal as he rides through the crowds in Rome's St. Peter's Square.

JUNE

12 ▶ For the first time in history, there is a midseason baseball strike. It is not resolved until a third of the season is used up. The issue is free agency and the fans are not amused.

15 ▶ The Centers for Disease Control in Atlanta publishes its first report on the AIDS epidemic, based on recent cases of pneumocystis in Los Angeles. A month later, CDC releases its first report on Kaposi's sarcoma in gay men.

18 ▶ Supreme Court Justice Potter Stewart announces he will be retiring after twenty-three years, creating a vacancy that is filled in July by the first female associate justice.

21 ▶ Wayne B. Williams is arrested in Atlanta and charged with one of the murders of twenty-eight black children and young adults in the city. The arrest ends the city's two-year reign of terror.

25 ▶ The U.S. Supreme Court rules that male-only draft registration is constitutional.

■■■■■■■■■■■■■■■■■■■■■■■■■■■■■■■■

☛ 1. The cost of mailing a first-class letter goes up twice—first to eighteen cents then to twenty cents.

☛ 2. In May milk prices reach a common level of $2.20 a gallon, a high level by any measure (versus $1.95 in May 1989).

☛ 3. In September some mortgage rates are as high as 17.71 percent.

☛ 4. According to the government there are more divorces in 1981 than any year to date, for a total of 1,210,000.

June 15, 1981:
The Centers for Disease Control publishes its first report on the AIDS epidemic, based on recent cases of pneumocystis in Los Angeles.

1981
by the numbers

☞ 5. A dazzling dose of double digits appears on the inflation front—14 percent.

☞ 6. The *Washingtonian* magazine reveals that there are 30,868 practicing attorneys in the capital, of whom 20 percent are women.

☞ 7. To replace 220 place settings at the White House, a private donor antes up $209,508.

☞ 8. Two people bumped from a Delta airlines flight in 1976 are awarded $208,000 by a jury. Actress Carol Burnett is awarded $1.6 million in a libel suit against the *National Enquirer.*

☞ 9. Chrysler announces profits for the second quarter of the year of $11.6 million—a stunning reversal of two years' worth of record losses.

☞ 10. The world's longest suspension bridge opens in England. It is 4,626 feet long and spans the Humber estuary.

☞ 11. By year's end the Census Bureau estimates that the nation's population stands at 230.5 million—an increase of 2.2 million from a year ago.

■ ■

July 29, 1981:
Prince Charles and Lady Diana are married in St. Paul's Cathedral, London.

JULY

07 ► President Ronald Reagan announces he will nominate Arizona judge Sandra Day O'Connor to serve on the U.S. Supreme Court. O'Connor becomes the high court's first female justice.

17 ► Two suspended walkways collapse and plunge to the ground floor of the Hyatt Regency hotel in Kansas City, Missouri, killing 111 people and injuring 200.

29 ► Prince Charles and Lady Diana are married in St. Paul's Cathedral, London.

31 ► The baseball strike ends after seven weeks.

▶ 1981

AUGUST

03 ▶ U.S. air traffic controllers strike.

06 ▶ The air controllers strike is broken when President Reagan announces that he is firing those who did not come to work on the 5th—12,000 in all—and the Federal Aviation Administration announces it will hire replacements.

19 ▶ U.S. Navy fighter jets shoot down two Libyan jets after they open fire on an American plane.

SEPTEMBER

05 ▶ The Soviet Union reports that it has 10,000 troops training near the Polish border—a message to Polish leaders to bring the Solidarity union under control—especially its criticism of the Soviet Union.

■ ■

1981 in ten words (& phrases)

☛ 1. *minority flight* (Census term acknowledging the fact that nonwhites are moving to the suburbs in increasing numbers)

☛ 2. *Libyan hit squad* (real or imagined terrorist team at large)

☛ 3. *Falwellian* (adjective used to describe the rise of the Moral Majority and the Reverend Jerry Falwell)

☛ 4. *significa* (term created by Irving Wallace, his daughter Amy, and his son, David Wallechinsky, for "little-known facts that have too much importance to qualify as mere trivia")

☛ 5. *superfund* (federal till for environmental emergencies first put into use this year)

☛ 6. *context* (one of the nouns that are routinely turned into verbs by Secretary of State Al Haig)

☛ 7. *wall-breaking* (A variation on the old idea of a groundbreaking, a wall-breaking is a common ceremony this year as banks make holes in their walls for automatic tellers.)

8. *gridlock (again)* (last year's term for traffic is now being applied to any kind of congestion, including . . .)

9. *pedlock* (sidewalk crowding)

10. *benevolent capitalists* (term created for former flower children who are now in business)

■■■■■■■■■■■■■■■■■■■■■■■■■■■■■■■■

OCTOBER

06 ► Egyptian President Anwar Sadat, age sixty-two, is assassinated by rebel soldiers in Cairo as he is reviewing troops. He is attacked with automatic weapons and a hand grenade.

NOVEMBER

18 ► In a live speech broadcast throughout Europe, President Reagan proposes an arms control plan that will keep new American missiles out of Europe if the Soviet Union will dismantle comparable missiles aimed at European nations.

DECEMBER

04 ► For the first time, the president authorizes domestic intelligence gathering by the CIA and other agencies.

13 ► Martial law is imposed in Poland, and the United States believes the Soviet Union is behind the order. By the end of the month there will be official reports of deaths and injuries as the new law is imposed and enforced.

■■■■■■■■■■■■■■■■■■■■■■■■■■■■■■■■

1. MAKE SOMEBODY HAPPY: MIND YOUR OWN BUSINESS

2. NATIVE (also SEMI-NATIVE, TRANSPLANT, FOREIGNER, etc.)

3. GOD BLESS AMERICA—AND PLEASE HURRY

4. ANSWER MY PRAYERS, STEAL THIS CAR

December 4, 1981:
For the first time, the president authorizes domestic intelligence gathering by the CIA and other agencies.

1981 in buttons & bumper stickers ☞

▶ 1981

5. GUN CONTROL IS BEING ABLE TO HIT YOUR TARGET

6. LEGALIZE UPDOC

7. SAVE AN ALLIGATOR, EAT A PREPPIE

8. I BRAKE FOR PAC-MAN

9. BETTER ACTIVE TODAY THAN RADIOACTIVE TO-MORROW

10. THE ONLY WAY THEY'LL GET MY GUN IS TO PRY IT FROM MY COLD DEAD HANDS

■■■■■■■■■■■■■■■■■■■■■■■■■■■■■■■■

*The year in which a battle is ▶
fought for the Falkland ▶
Islands and comedian ▶
John Belushi dies from drugs ▶*

1982

JANUARY

08 ▶ AT&T agrees to divest itself of all twenty-two of its Bell Telephone operating systems in concluding an eight-year antitrust suit.

13 ▶ Air Florida flight 90 takes off from Washington National Airport in a snowstorm and slams into the 14th Street Bridge spanning the Potomac. Fatalities total seventy-seven. Dramatic TV footage of rescue and rescue attempts make it one of the most graphic air tragedies of the television era. During the same storm, the new Washington Metro subway suffers its first accident with fatalities.

FEBRUARY

06 ▶ President Reagan's 1982 budget includes a projected deficit of $91.5 billion. The trillion-dollar deficit is now within view.

MARCH

05 ▶ Popular comedian John Belushi is found dead in a rented Hollywood bungalow. Drugs are immediately suspected and later are shown to be the cause of death.

March 26, 1982:
Ground is broken for a memorial to honor the 58,022 Americans killed in the Vietnam War.

26 ▶ Ground is broken for a memorial to honor the 58,022 Americans killed in the Vietnam War.

■ ■

Fads and Trends for 1982 ☞

1. *E.T.*
2. *PCs*
3. *BMX*
4. Smurfs
5. Boy George and Culture Club
6. *Cats* is a runaway Broadway hit.
7. Odd antenna-like thingamabobs that are worn on the head—known as *deely boobbers* (what else?)
8. Michael Jackson's *Thriller* becomes the greatest-selling album of all time.
9. Jane Fonda turns the physical workout into a cash crop.
10. The Ms. Pacman video game comes along to pick up where Pac-Man left off.

■ ■

APRIL

02 ▶ British Prime Minister Margaret Thatcher orders a naval task force to recover the Falkland Islands from Argentina. It is the start of the seventy-four-day Falklands War.

MAY

28 ▶ British forces in the Falklands take Darwin and Goose Green in their move to the capital, and there is little question as to who will win the Falklands War.

JUNE

06 ▶ Twenty thousand Israeli forces invade Lebanon.
12 ▶ To protest nuclear arms 800,000 Americans take to the streets of New York.

► 1982

14 ► Argentina surrenders to the British in the Falklands War. More than 900 have died in the conflict and the British end up with 14,000 POWs.

24 ► President Reagan declares an all-out attack on drugs and creates a new agency, the White House Office of Drug Abuse Policy, to oversee the war on drugs.

■■■■■■■■■■■■■■■■■■■■■■■■■■■■■■■■

1. The largest armed robbery in U.S. history occurs in New York in December. The haul: $9,800,000.

2. Exxon is shown to be the largest U.S. corporation, with sales of $97,172,523,000.

3. By the end of the year, the economy is rebounding from a recession. The consumer price index rises 3.9 percent, which is the smallest increase since 1972.

4. Peak year for postwar unemployment: the rate hits 10.8 percent.

5. After the Tylenol killings in Chicago 264,000 bottles of the drug are recalled.

6. The federal budget deficit for the year is $110 billion—a record.

7. Four—and perhaps as many as six—new moons of Saturn are discovered in photos from *Voyager 2*.

8. A British tanker breaks up off the coast of Lithuania spilling 4.8 million gallons of oil.

9. In July some 4,150 followers of the Reverend Sun Myung Moon are married at Madison Square Garden in a single ceremony.

10. According to the Federal Reserve, the nation's factories are operating at 67.8 percent of capacity, the lowest since figures were first collected in 1948.

11. The Census Bureau says that the poverty rate is now at 14 percent, the highest since 1967.

■■■■■■■■■■■■■■■■■■■■■■■■■■■■■■■■

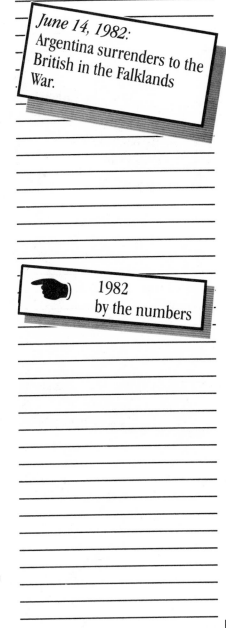

June 14, 1982: Argentina surrenders to the British in the Falklands War.

1982 by the numbers

September 29:
Seven people in the Chicago area die after taking Extra-Strength Tylenol capsules laced with cyanide.

1982 in ten words (& phrases) ☞

JULY

23 ▶ Television star Vic Morrow and two child actors are killed when a helicopter disabled by special effects explosives crashes on the set of *The Twilight Zone* movie.

AUGUST

19 ▶ Congress approves a tax hike as the country slides into recession.

SEPTEMBER

15 ▶ *USA Today* makes its debut in the Washington-Baltimore area. It calls itself "The Nation's Newspaper" and relies on short, punchy articles and the heavy use of color.

29 ▶ Seven people in the Chicago area die after taking Extra-Strength Tylenol capsules laced with cyanide. The unsolved crime perplexes authorities for years to come.

■ ■

☞ 1. *excellent*

☞ 2. *herpes* (A long-established malady works itself into the limelight.)

☞ 3. *Jarvik heart* (The first artificial heart used in a human is named for Dr. Robert Jarvik.)

☞ 4. *McPaper* (immediate nickname for *USA Today* and a reference to the journalistic equivalent of fast food)

☞ 5. *baby bell* (one of the phone companies that are pulled from the apron of Ma Bell in the AT&T antitrust settlement)

☞ 6. *AIDS* (This is the year the American public becomes aware of the disease, although it first shows up in print in 1981.)

☞ 7. *product tampering* (We find a new way to say *murder.*)

☞ 8. *condorminium* (What else do you call the place where the first endangered California condor is born in captivity?)

▶ 1982

☞ 9. *bottomed out* (what happened to the recession in November)

☞ 10. *clone* (This word has a new meaning as Compaq brings out the first clone—semicopy—of the IBM PC.)

■■■■■■■■■■■■■■■■■■■■■■■■■■■■■■■

OCTOBER

05 ▶ The Tylenol deaths in Chicago in late September trigger a nationwide alert and a recall of all Tylenol capsules. There is an eighth death from poisoned Tylenol in California.

NOVEMBER

11 ▶ As the first operational—as opposed to test—space shuttle mission begins, *Columbia* carries two satellites into orbit. The mission ends successfully on the 16th.

14 ▶ Lech Walesa, head of the illegal union Solidarity, is released from prison in Poland after spending almost a year in jail.

DECEMBER

02 ▶ The world's first transplant of an artificial heart into a human is successfully completed at the University of Utah Medical Center. The recipient, Barney C. Clark, sixty-one, lives for 112 days—until March 23, 1983.

■■■■■■■■■■■■■■■■■■■■■■■■■■■■■■■

☞ 1. CARLSBAD CAVERNS: 22 PERCENT MORE CAVITIES

☞ 2. HUNGRY? EAT YOUR FOREIGN CAR

☞ 3. DANGER—I DRIVE LIKE YOU DO

☞ 4. IF YOU THINK THE SYSTEM IS WORKING, ASK SOMEONE WHO ISN'T

☞ 5. I MAY HAVE MY PH.D. BUT I'M NOT STUPID

☞ 6. WARNING! I STOP FOR NO APPARENT REASON

☞ 7. MY TAKE HOME PAY WON'T TAKE ME HOME

> *December 2, 1982:*
> The world's first transplant of an artificial heart into a human is successfully completed at the University of Utah Medical Center.

☞ 1982 in buttons & bumper stickers

1982

8. HAPPINESS IS COMING

9. DON'T HIT ME, MY LAWYER'S IN JAIL

10. SNUGGLE DON'T STRUGGLE (This antifeminist bumper sticker, created by a stripper named Amber Mist, was not well received.)

■ ■

JANUARY

22 ▶ On this the tenth anniversary of legalized abortion there is a major anti-abortion march in Washington.

FEBRUARY

22 ▶ The federal government announces that it will buy the homes and businesses in Times Beach, Missouri, because of the town's lethal levels of the carcinogenic chemical dioxin.

28 ▶ The last episode of *M*A*S*H* is aired on CBS, attracting some 121,624,000 viewers.

MARCH

23 ▶ President Reagan first proposes development of technology to intercept enemy missiles—a proposal officially known as the Strategic Defense Initiative (SDI) but popularly known as Star Wars.

30 ▶ The first California condor born in captivity hatches at the San Diego Zoo. A second arrives in early April.

February 28, 1983:
The last episode of *M*A*S*H* is aired on CBS, attracting some 121,624,000 viewers.

▶ 289

Fads and Trends for 1983 ☞

■■■■■■■■■■■■■■■■■■■■■■■■■■■■■■■■■

☞ 1. Created in 1979 and introduced in the United States from Canada in 1982, this is the year Trivial Pursuit hits with such force that by the end of the year there are back orders for 1 million games.

☞ 2. The synthetic drug PCP—or angel dust—begins to claim a large number of lives.

☞ 3. Old heroes assert themselves as *Return of the Jedi,* starring the *Star Wars* crew, and *Never Say Never Again,* featuring James Bond, are the two most popular movies.

☞ 4. Ripped clothing debuts as a fashion statement (courtesy of the movie *Flashdance*).

☞ 5. Wacky Wallwalkers have their day and begin their creep back into oblivion.

☞ 6. Compact discs and digital players are given wide commercial push.

☞ 7. The Cabbage Patch doll creates pre-Christmas pandemonium.

☞ 8. Great old movies are being released for home viewing on video cassette recorders. *Rear Window* is the first Alfred Hitchcock classic to show up for the home film festival.

☞ 9. Michael Jackson has three number-one hits.

☞ 10. The movie *Flashdance* creates new fashions in dance and dress.

■■■■■■■■■■■■■■■■■■■■■■■■■■■■■■■■■

APRIL

20 ▶ The Supreme Court affirms the right of the states to ban nuclear power plants.

26 ▶ The quality of American education is poor, according to the report of a federal commission that, among other things, has tracked the decline in standardized test scores since 1957.

▶ 1983

MAY

24 ▶ Congress authorizes $625 million in MX missile research and development.

JUNE

13 ▶ Today the *Pioneer 10* spaceprobe—launched in 1972—becomes the first object created by humans to leave this solar system.

18 ▶ Astronaut Sally K. Ride becomes America's first woman in space as she and four colleagues blast off aboard the space shuttle *Challenger.* The vehicle glides to a safe landing at Edwards Air Force Base in California on the 24th.

■■■■■■■■■■■■■■■■■■■■■■■■■■■■■■■■■■■■

☞ 1. Of the babies born in New York City, 33 percent are born out of wedlock.

☞ 2. Jockey Angel Cordera becomes the first jockey to earn $10 million in a year.

☞ 3. William de Kooning's painting "Two Women" sells for $1.2 million at auction.

☞ 4. According to federal calculations as many as 23 million Americans are functionally illiterate.

☞ 5. Television anchorwoman Christine Craft is awarded $500,000 after being fired for her age and appearance.

☞ 6. *A Chorus Line* becomes the longest-running show in Broadway history on September 27 after 3,389 performances.

☞ 7. The International Bureau of Weights and Measures redefines a meter as the distance that light travels in 1/299,792,458 of a second.

☞ 8. The movie *The Right Stuff* costs $27 million to produce and grosses only $11 million in its first year. *The Return of the Jedi,* on the other hand, grosses $6,219,629 the day it opens.

> *June 13, 1983:*
> Today the *Pioneer 10* spaceprobe – launched in 1972 – becomes the first object created by humans to leave this solar system.

☞ 1983 by the numbers

9. In one five-day period 750,000 copies of Michael Jackson's record album *Thriller* sell.

10. In June, for the first time ever, *Billboard*'s hot 100 list of pop records contains more foreign than American artists.

■■■■■■■■■■■■■■■■■■■■■■■■■■■■■■■■■■

JULY

21 ▶ Poland lifts the state of martial law that has been in effect for the last nineteen months.

AUGUST

21 ▶ Philippine opposition leader Benigno S. Aquino, Jr., ending a self-imposed exile in the United States, is shot dead minutes after returning to his native country.

▶ *Also:* A group of young Milwaukeans electronically invade some twenty major computer systems including the one at the Los Alamos National Laboratory. It is the first major attack of the computer hackers and proves that the term "computer security" is an oxymoron.

30 ▶ Lieutenant Colonel Guion S. Bluford rides the shuttle *Challenger* and becomes the first black astronaut to enter space.

SEPTEMBER

01 ▶ A Korean Air 747 is shot down by a Soviet jet fighter after it enters Soviet airspace. It is flight 007 and 269 people are killed in the attack.

06 ▶ The Soviet Union admits to shooting down flight 007 five days after the fact.

■■■■■■■■■■■■■■■■■■■■■■■■■■■■■■■■■

1. *grody to the max...*

2. and *tubular* (both out of the mouths of Valley girls)

August 21, 1983:
A group of young Milwaukeans electronically invade some twenty major computer systems including the one at the Los Alamos National Laboratory.

1983 in ten words (& phrases) ☞

▶ 1983

3. *the day after* (a new image and metaphor for a post-nuclear world. Since half the adults in America watched this special on postatomic society, the term has special relevance.)

4. *rising tide of mediocrity* (widely quoted description of American education by a federal commission)

5. *nuclear winter* (Two studies warn that nuclear weapons could create a soot that will keep the world in perpetual winter.)

6. *evil empire* (This is the term used by President Reagan to describe the Soviet Union.)

7. *mouse* (With the introduction of the Apple Lisa computer this word now describes a cursor mover as well as a rodent.)

8. *Martin Luther King, Jr. Day* (now a legal holiday since the president signed it into law in November)

9. *freedom fighters* (name the administration gives to anti-Communist, anti-Sandinista troops in Nicaragua)

10. *Star Wars* (The name of a movie now is used to describe the White House's invincible missile defense system first proposed in March.)

> *October 23, 1983:* A terrorist attack on the U.S. Marine headquarters in Beirut kills more than 200 marines and effectively causes the United States to drop its attempt at a peacekeeping role in Lebanon.

OCTOBER

09 ▶ Interior Secretary James Watt resigns under pressure after describing the members of a commission as "a black, a woman, two Jews, and a cripple."

14 ▶ A new three-volume collection of Bible readings from the National Council of Churches is released with no allusions to God as a solely male being.

23 ▶ A terrorist attack on the U.S. Marine headquarters in Beirut kills more than 200 marines and effectively causes the U.S. to drop its attempt at a peacekeeping role in Lebanon.

25 ▶ The United States invades the small Caribbean nation of Grenada, which has experienced a bloody, Marxist coup.

November 15, 1983:
Congress refuses to revive the equal rights amendment, which has been unable to attract the required number of ratifying states.

1983 in buttons & bumper stickers

The move is made to restore order and protect the 1,100 Americans on the island.

NOVEMBER

03 ► The Reverend Jesse Jackson announces he will run for the presidency.

15 ► Congress refuses to revive the equal rights amendment, which has been unable to attract the required number of ratifying states.

DECEMBER

10 ► Lech Walesa of Poland is awarded the Nobel peace prize.

22 ► The Federal Trade Commission approves a major joint General Motors–Toyota auto venture that will produce up to a quarter of a million cars a year in Fremont, California.

28 ► The U.S. withdraws from UNESCO, the United Nations Educational, Scientific, and Cultural Organization. The American position is that the group is mismanaged and operates with a political bias that is counter to U.S. policy.

■ ■

☞ 1. WE'RE SPENDING OUR CHILDREN'S INHERITANCE

☞ 2. HAVE YOU HUGGED YOUR ACCOUNTANT TODAY?

☞ 3. WARNING: IN CASE OF RAPTURE THIS CAR WILL BE UNMANNED

☞ 4. 1984: BEDTIME FOR BONZO

☞ 5. GET REVENGE—LIVE LONG ENOUGH TO BE A BURDEN TO YOUR CHILDREN

☞ 6. IF YOU DON'T LIKE THE WAY I DRIVE, GET OFF THE SIDEWALK

☞ 7. IT'S A MAN'S WORLD—UNLESS WOMEN VOTE

☞ 8. BAG YOUR FACE

☞ 9. HONKING IS FOR GEESE

☞ 10. EVERY TIME WE BUY A FOREIGN CAR, WE PUT 10 AMERICANS OUT OF WORK

■ ■

The year of the yuppie ▶
and the eternal question, ▶
'Where's the beef?" ▶ **1984**

JANUARY

03 ▶ His popularity stabilizing at 50 percent, Ronald Reagan says he will seek a second term.

FEBRUARY

03 ▶ A California medical team announces the first successful case of a surrogate conception in which a baby conceived in the womb of one woman is brought to term in the womb of another.

07 ▶ American marines are withdrawn from Lebanon.

13 ▶ Stormie Jones of Texas, age six, is the first person to have a heart and liver transplant.

17 ▶ The Supreme Court decides that individuals can legally videotape television shows for their own use.

28 ▶ Gary Hart is victor in New Hampshire primary.

MARCH

20 ▶ The U.S. Senate rejects a proposed amendment to the Constitution that would allow prayer in the public schools.

February 3, 1984:
A California medical team announces the first successful case of a surrogate conception in which a baby conceived in the womb of one woman is brought to term in the womb of another.

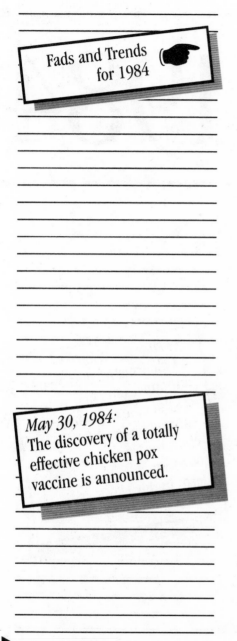

Fads and Trends for 1984 ☞

May 30, 1984:
The discovery of a totally effective chicken pox vaccine is announced.

☞ 1. *Newsweek* declares this the year of the yuppie, or young urban professional or trendy spender.

☞ 2. War toys in the form of action figures make a stunning comeback: 214 million of them are sold.

☞ 3. Holographic 3D credit cards come into being led by Visa.

☞ 4. Introduced in late 1983, the 1984 Chrysler minivan (Plymouth Voyager and Dodge Caravan) reinvents the station wagon and turns many heads.

☞ 5. Singer Madonna makes her presence felt with the help of a hit, "Like a Virgin."

☞ 6. *The Cosby Show* and *Family Ties* bring a new level of quality to the TV family comedy.

☞ 7. Although George Orwell placed his vision of a horrific totalitarian world in this year of 1984, the Western world seems to revel in individualism and free play. It is a notably un-Orwellian year.

☞ 8. The continued success of *Cats* helps stage a Broadway comeback.

☞ 9. Prince achieves superstar status with an assist from his movie *Purple Rain.*

☞ 10. New attention is focused on the aging of the American population—seven states report more than a million residents over the age of sixty-five.

APRIL

25 ▶ David Kennedy, twenty-eight—the son of Robert Kennedy—is found dead in a Florida hotel.

MAY

30 ▶ The discovery of a totally effective chicken pox vaccine is announced.

► 1984

1. The economy has its best year since 1951, expanding 6.8 percent while consumer prices rise only 4 percent.
2. This year McDonald's sold its 50 billionth hamburger.
3. A total of 8,612 medals are awarded for the 1983 invasion of Grenada, although only 7,000 American troops actually take part in the operation.
4. Chevron Corporation acquires the Gulf Corporation for $13.3 billion in cash, the largest takeover to this time.
5. The largest single New York Stock Exchange transaction to date takes place on June 21 as 10 million shares of Superior Oil sell for $423,800,000.
6. There are now 490,000 lawyers in America—about the population of Vermont.
7. Some 685,000 Americans are jailed during the year.
8. Three coffeemakers purchased for the air force's C-5A cargo plane cost more than $7,000 apiece.
9. The government commits itself to $4.5 billion in loan guarantees to Continental Illinois Bank in Chicago.
10. This year, for the first time, the average cost of a new American home tops $100,000.
11. *A GOOD MEAL IN 1984:* Twenty-five dollars will get you a twenty-one-ounce prime-aged steak at Joe and Mo's restaurant in Washington, D.C.
12. One of John Lennon's guitars sells for $19,000 at auction.

July 6, 1984: Michael Jackson's Victory Tour is launched.

JULY

03 ► The U.S. Supreme Court rules that the Jaycees may be forced by state laws to admit women as full members with the same status as men.
06 ► Michael Jackson's Victory Tour is launched.
12 ► Democratic presidential candidate Walter Mondale announces he has chosen Geraldine Ferraro of New York to

_____

July 12, 1984:
Geraldine Ferraro is the first woman to run for vice president of the United States on a major-party ticket.

_____

be his running mate. Ferraro is the first woman to run for vice president of the United States on a major-party ticket. (See July 19.)

16 ► The all-male Junior Chambers of Commerce, or Jaycees, open their membership to women. This follows a July 3 Supreme Court order that tells the organization to obey antidiscrimination laws.

18 ► A gunman opens fire at a McDonald's restaurant in San Ysidro, California, killing twenty-one persons.

19 ► Geraldine Ferraro, congresswoman from Queens, New York, is nominated to run for vice president of the United States on the Democratic Party ticket, the first woman to be so nominated by either of the two major parties. (See July 12.)

23 ► The first black Miss America, Vanessa Williams, relinquishes her crown two months early when nude photographs of her are published in *Penthouse* magazine. She is the first pageant winner to give up her title.

AUGUST

10 ► In the first conviction of a sitting federal judge, Nevada's chief U.S. district judge, Harry Claiborne, is convicted on tax evasion charges.

11 ► During an off-air radio voice check, President Reagan jokes, "My fellow Americans, I'm pleased to tell you today that I've signed legislation that will outlaw Russia forever. We begin bombing in five minutes."

12 ► The twenty-third Olympic games end in Los Angeles with a record attendance of 5.5 million people despite a Soviet-led boycott.

▶ 1984

SEPTEMBER

16 ▶ A baby girl with a failing heart is given the heart of a baboon at the Loma Linda Medical Center in California. She lives until November 15.

20 ▶ The U.S. embassy in Beirut is bombed, killing twelve.

■■■■■■■■■■■■■■■■■■■■■■■■■■■■■■■

1984 in ten words (& phrases)

☞ 1. *Where's the beef?* (The question asked by Clara Peller in a Wendy's hamburger chain ad enters the American lexicon with the help of Walter Mondale, who uses it in his campaign to flush out Gary Hart's "new ideas.")

☞ 2. *yuppification* (one of many derivative terms from the year of the yuppie)

☞ 3. *Baby Fae* (anonymity granted to a California girl who is given a baboon's heart)

☞ 4. *Bhopal* (A new name for toxic disaster, it ranks with Jonestown as a measure of the modern world run amok.)

☞ 5. *legal drinking age* (The Federal government push to raise it to twenty-one includes cutting highway funds going to any state where the age is less than twenty-one.)

☞ 6. *Great American Smokeout* (an institution with growing numbers of converts. More than 5 million use it as an occasion to get off the weed this year.)

☞ 7. *eurosclerosis* (label created to describe the apparent inability of Europe to keep up with the United States and Japan in terms of economic activity and technological achievement)

☞ 8. *megabit memory chip* (Now a reality, this is what you call a chip able to store more than a million bits of data.)

☞ 9. *Ghostbusters* (what one critic termed the name of a new mini-industry replete with logo, videos, music, and— oh, yes—a movie)

☞ 10. *impact* (It is now a verb.)

■■■■■■■■■■■■■■■■■■■■■■■■■■■■■■

▶ 1984

> *October 16, 1984:*
> The Nobel peace prize is awarded to South African Bishop Desmond Tutu.

> *December 3, 1984:*
> Toxic fumes leak from a Union Carbide plant, immediately killing 2,500 people in Bhopal, India.

OCTOBER

03 ▶ Richard W. Miller is charged with espionage. He is the first FBI agent ever faced with spy charges.

12 ▶ British Prime Minister Margaret Thatcher survives an assassination attempt by the Irish Republican Army. Five people are killed and thirty-two injured.

16 ▶ The Nobel peace prize is awarded to South African Bishop Desmond Tutu.

NOVEMBER

01 ▶ Stalin's daughter moves back to the USSR.

02 ▶ For the first time in twenty-two years, a woman is executed for a crime.

06 ▶ In getting reelected Ronald Reagan carries forty-nine states as he posts the greatest Republican landslide in history.

DECEMBER

03 ▶ Toxic fumes leak from a Union Carbide plant, immediately killing 2,500 in Bhopal, India, and the toll mounts in the days ahead. At least 3,329 people eventually die from inhaling the fumes, and 20,000 more are injured in the world's worst industrial disaster. The culprit is a gas called methyl isocyanate.

07 ▶ American lawyers, many of whom rush to Bhopal, India, shortly after the gas leak, file the first of more than $1 billion in claims against Union Carbide in a U.S. court. The suits are later consolidated.

20 ▶ Bell Laboratories announce the development of a chip capable of storing over a million bits of memory.

22 ▶ Shortly after 5 P.M., just north of the World Trade Center on a southbound subway train, Bernhard H. Goetz shoots Troy Canty, James Ramseur, Barry Allen, and Darrell Cabey, all nineteen, and escapes on foot through a subway tunnel. Cabey's spine is severed, leaving him partially paralyzed.

▶ 1984

Goetz's crime and subsequent trial become matters of national attention and controversy as many feel the incident reflects national frustration with and fear of crime and violence. (See June 16, 1987.)

■■■■■■■■■■■■■■■■■■■■■■■■■■■■■■

☞ 1. THE COMPUTER IS DOWN
☞ 2. WANT A TASTE OF RELIGION? BITE A MINISTER
☞ 3. I'M NOT FAT I'M JUST SHORT FOR MY WEIGHT
☞ 4. EL SALVADOR IS SPANISH FOR VIETNAM
☞ 5. ARE WE HAVING FUN YET?
☞ 6. DEMOCRATS CARE
☞ 7. REAGAN '84 / WAR '85
☞ 8. CAJUNS FOR REAGANS
☞ 9. IF YOUR CUP RUNNETH OVER, LET SOMEBODY ELSE RUNNETH THE CAR
☞ 10. I BREAK FOR MUTANTS

■■■■■■■■■■■■■■■■■■■■■■■■■■■■■■

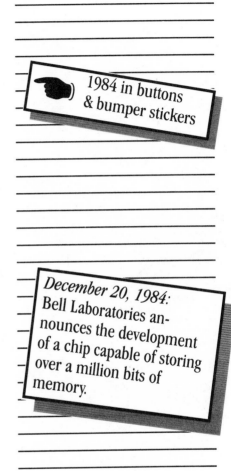

☞) 1984 in buttons & bumper stickers

December 20, 1984: Bell Laboratories announces the development of a chip capable of storing over a million bits of memory.

The year in which there ▶ seem to be too many spies, ▶ terrorists, and mergers ▶ 1985

JANUARY

20 ▶ Ronald Reagan is inaugurated for his second term as a severe cold wave kills forty people and the inaugural parade is cancelled.

FEBRUARY

13 ▶ A federal study targets obesity as a major killer in the same category as smoking and high-blood pressure.

MARCH

13 ▶ Mikhail Gorbachev is the new leader of the Soviet Union.
16 ▶ Terry Anderson, forty, a correspondent for Associated Press, from Batavia, New York, is kidnapped in Lebanon.

■■■■■■■■■■■■■■■■■■■■■■■■■■■■■■■■

☞ 1. Compact discs and disc players are an immediate hit with music lovers.
☞ 2. There is much merchandise created to welcome the return of Halley's comet.
☞ 3. Live Aid and Farm Aid concerts favorably display the consciences of pop musicians.

Fads and Trends for 1985

4. It is the year of Rambo and *Rambo First Blood—Part II.*

5. Bruce Springsteen is especially big in his tenth year of big concerts (hence the album *Bruce Springsteen Live: 1975–1985*).

6. Fascination with every baseball game in which Pete Rose plays leads to the moment when he makes his 4,192nd hit and eclipses Ty Cobb's record for most career hits. The record-breaking game is played on September 11.

7. Manly stubble comes on as male weekday fashion. Mel Gibson, Harrison Ford, Bruce Springsteen, and Don Johnson pioneer the five o'clock shadow. Androgyny takes a step backwards.

8. A song *We Are the World* is sung by an all-star group and nets more than $30 million for African famine relief.

9. Four-wheel drive vehicles assert themselves.

10. Everybody seems to have a warm spot in their hearts for Garrison Keillor's Lake Wobegon.

11. The year is characterized by a large number of spy revelations, including several key cases involving U.S. servicemen and government employees.

■ ■

APRIL

23 ► In a bold move the Coca-Cola Company announces that the company is abandoning its old formula and that the new Coke is now the real thing. By July complaints from cola lovers who do not like the new version convince Coke corporate heads to bring back the old version under the name Coca-Cola Classic.

MAY

05 ► Ronald Reagan lays a wreath at a military cemetery at Bitburg, West Germany, which contains the remains of forty-

April 23, 1985:
The Coca-Cola Company announces that new-formula Coke is the new real thing.

▶ 1985

nine members of the hated Nazi SS. Like the announcement of the visit, the act itself creates a storm of controversy.

JUNE

30 ▶ Thirty-nine American hostages from a hijacked TWA jetliner are freed in Beirut after being held seventeen days.

■ ■

☞ 1. The year sees a strong increase in corporate mergers and takeovers with twenty-four such combinations involving more than a billion dollars.

☞ 2. Officially and for the first time since World War I, the United States becomes a debtor nation.

☞ 3. The highest damage award in history is made and upheld when Texaco is told to pay Pennzoil $11.4 billion as a result of Texaco's interference in Pennzoil's takeover of Getty Oil.

☞ 4. The cost of mailing a first-class letter rises to twenty-two cents.

☞ 5. Willie Shoemaker becomes the first jockey to make $100 million in purse money during his career.

☞ 6. Random House acquires the rights to Ronald Reagan's autobiography for $3 million—said to be the most ever advanced for a single book.

☞ 7. *The New Yorker* is sold for $142 million.

☞ 8. Before the Sergeant York missile program is cancelled because the missile did not work very well, its cost reaches $1.8 billion.

☞ 9. A 17.2-cubic-foot General Electric refrigerator costs $635 (in contrast to a 8.3-cubic-foot GE, which sold for the same price in 1965).

☞ 10. Shel Silverstein's *A Light in the Attic* makes it on the *New York Times* best-seller list for the 112th week in a row, a record.

■ ■

1985 by the numbers

July 19, 1985:
NASA selects schoolteacher Christa McAuliffe from among 11,000 applicants to join the space shuttle.

JULY

13 ▶ Live Aid, an international rock concert in London, Philadelphia, Moscow, and Sydney, raises money for Africa's starving people.

19 ▶ NASA selects schoolteacher Christa McAuliffe from among 11,000 applicants to join the space shuttle.

20 ▶ Treasure hunter Mel Fisher locates a Spanish galleon sunk by a 1622 hurricane off Key West, Florida. It contains $400 million worth of treasure.

25 ▶ A spokeswoman for Rock Hudson confirms that the actor, hospitalized in Paris, is suffering from AIDS. He dies three months later. As the first known celebrity victim of the disease, Hudson brings much needed attention to AIDS and those suffering from it.

AUGUST

02 ▶ The bankrupt Manville Corporation offers $2.5 billion to settle some 16,500 lawsuits seeking compensation for asbestos-related health complaints. It is the largest health-related settlement ever offered by a U.S. company.

08 ▶ On this day President Ronald Reagan either does or does not give permission for arms to be secretly shipped to Iran. "It is possible to forget," the president says to reporters in February 1987: "Everybody who can remember what they were doing on August 8, 1985, raise your hand." What actually takes place on this date becomes an elusive key to the Irangate incident.

12 ▶ In aviation's worst single-plane disaster, 520 people die when a Japan Air Lines Boeing 747 slams into a mountain in central Japan. Four passengers survive.

15 ▶ South African President P. W. Botha, rejecting Western pleas to abolish apartheid, declares, "I am not prepared to lead white South Africans and other minority groups on a road to abdication and suicide."

▶ 1985

SEPTEMBER

01 ▶ A joint French-U.S. team locates the wreck of the *Titanic,* which sunk in 1912 after hitting an iceberg. The seventy-three-year-old wreck is discovered about 560 miles off the coast of Newfoundland.

09 ▶ President Reagan announces sanctions against South Africa that include a ban on sales of American computers.

■■■■■■■■■■■■■■■■■■■■■■■■■■■■■■■■

☞ 1. *crack* (A new form of cocaine first hits the streets late in the year.)

☞ 2. *Titanic* (back in the news after all these years)

☞ 3. *year of the terrorist* (At year's end some think the year should be remembered for its South American death squads and the year-end airport bombings.)

☞ 4. *freeze of the century* (What they are calling the January inaugural freeze takes out 90 percent of Florida's citrus crop.)

☞ 5. *ozone layer* (An established term is given new relevance when a British Antarctic team finds a hole in it.)

☞ 6. *Refrigerator* (nickname for William Perry, the surprise star of the National Football League)

☞ 7. *croissant* (You can now get them everywhere including the freezer cabinet.)

☞ 8. *logorrhea* (word used by the *Washington Post* to describe a Congress that turns out a farm bill with 1,397 pages)

☞ 9. *CD* (Two letters that everyone says will replace LP.)

☞ 10. *Live Aid* (If the 1980s have a Woodstock, this is it.)

■■■■■■■■■■■■■■■■■■■■■■■■■■■■■■■■

OCTOBER

07 ▶ Members of the Palestine Liberation Front hijack the Italian cruise ship *Achille Lauro,* shoot a wheelchair-bound Amer-

> *September 1, 1985:*
> A joint French-U.S. team locates the wreck of the *Titanic,* which sunk in 1912 after hitting an iceberg.

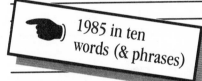
☞ 1985 in ten words (& phrases)

December 27, 1985:
Simultaneous airport
terrorist attacks in Rome
and Vienna kill 18 and
wound 110.

1985 in buttons
& bumper stickers ☞

ican passenger, and dump him overboard. After the hijackers leave the ship in Egypt and are flown out of the country, the United States forces the airliner to the ground in Italy, where the hijackers and other PLF members are arrested.

NOVEMBER

20 ▶ A two-day Reagan-Gorbachev summit in Geneva brings the two nations closer together and establishes a new level of cordiality.

DECEMBER

11 ▶ Congress passes the Gramm-Rudman Budget Reduction Bill, which requires Congress to eliminate the federal deficit by 1991.

27 ▶ Simultaneous airport terrorist attacks in Rome and Vienna kill 18 and wound 110.

■■■■■■■■■■■■■■■■■■■■■■■■■■■■■■■

☞ 1. I OWE. I OWE. SO OFF TO WORK I GO
☞ 2. WHEN TIMES GET TOUGH, THE TOUGH GO SHOPPING
☞ 3. CHILD ON BOARD
☞ 4. YOU'RE RIGHT—I DO OWN THE WHOLE DAMN ROAD
☞ 5. FIGHT ORGANIZED CRIME—ABOLISH THE IRS
☞ 6. SEXISM IS A SOCIAL DISEASE
☞ 7. AQUARIAN CONSPIRATOR
☞ 8. JELLY BEAN IS A LEMON
☞ 9. GOD SAID IT, I BELIEVE IT, THAT SETTLES IT
☞ 10. ELVIS DIDN'T DIE, HE MOVED TO A BETTER PLACE

■■■■■■■■■■■■■■■■■■■■■■■■■■■■■■■

The year in which the shuttle ▶
Challenger *explodes and* ▶
there is a fire in the ▶
Chernobyl *nuclear reactor* ▶

1986

JANUARY

06 ▶ When an overfilled cylinder of nuclear material bursts after being improperly heated at the Kerr-McGee plant in Gore, Oklahoma, one worker dies and 100 are hospitalized. It is the twenty-third recorded nuclear accident since 1952.

26 ▶ NBC attracts 127 million viewers when it airs *Super Bowl XX*—the most watched television show in history.

28 ▶ The space shuttle *Challenger* explodes immediately after an 11:38 A.M. liftoff from Cape Kennedy, killing all seven astronauts, including Christa McAuliffe, a schoolteacher who is the first private citizen picked to go into space. NASA immediately suspends the shuttle program.

FEBRUARY

15 ▶ Oil prices hit their lowest in six years, which helps fuel a stock market rally.

28 ▶ Prime Minister Olof Palme of Sweden is shot dead by an unknown gunman as he walks unguarded in a Stockholm street with his wife Lisbet.

January 28, 1986:
The space shuttle *Challenger* explodes immediately after an 11:38 a.m. liftoff from Cape Kennedy.

MARCH

06 ► A report in the *New England Journal of Medicine* concludes that moderate exercise can significantly diminish the risk of death from all causes.

■■■■■■■■■■■■■■■■■■■■■■■■■■■■■■■■■

Fads and Trends for 1986 ☞

1. The centennial of the Statue of Liberty is the year's prime source for glitz and glitter, and 200 Elvis impersonators help celebrate.
2. Calcium is added to everything from flour to laxatives.
3. Drugs in sports receive unprecedented attention.
4. As oil drops to below $15 a barrel for the first time in years, there is a new fascination with larger cars.
5. Food and drink fads include Mexican beer, flavored seltzer, and turkey as a stand-in for pastrami and ham.
6. Diamond-shaped signs proliferate in car rear windows.
7. Walking shoes (as opposed to running shoes) are marketed.
8. Crack cocaine proliferates as does discussion of its impact (three *Newsweek* cover stories).
9. Max Headroom is the first computer-generated personality of the twentieth century, but he wears thin quickly and many hope he is the last.
10. Folding cardboard sun screens for car windshields are now used in hot, sunny weather. More than 12 million are sold.

■■■■■■■■■■■■■■■■■■■■■■■■■■■■■■■■■

APRIL

02 ► The U.S. Department of Agriculture approves releasing the first genetically altered virus out of the laboratory and into the environment. It is used to attack a form of herpes affecting pigs.

05 ► Based on firm U.S. evidence, Libyan terrorists are blamed

for a disco bombing in West Berlin. Two—an American and a Turk—are killed and 155 people are wounded.

14 ▶ In response to the disco bombing and other acts of terror, the United States launches an air strike against Libya. The Thatcher government allows the U.S. to use British bases in the bombing of Libya.

16 ▶ The first test-tube baby delivered from a surrogate mother is announced by Mount Sinai Hospital in Cleveland.

MAY

13 ▶ The Meese Justice Department commission on pornography urges strong action against the business of pornography, which the commission concludes is a potentially harmful commodity that can lead to violence against women and children.

JUNE

02 ▶ The first gavel-to-gavel television coverage of the U.S. Senate goes into effect on an experimental basis.

09 ▶ A presidential commission determines that the single cause of the January 28 shuttle disaster was a defective seal in the right solid-fuel booster. The space agency is criticized for managerial and technical errors.

19 ▶ Len Bias, a University of Maryland basketball star and the top draft choice of the Boston Celtics, dies of an overdose of cocaine. More than any other incident, this death underscores widespread drug abuse by athletes.

▶ *Also occurring today:* Two Seattle deaths are officially linked to cyanide-laced Excedrin capsules. Although it has been almost four years since the Tylenol killings in Chicago, the threat from product-tampering begins to become a fact of American life.

27 ▶ The International Court of Justice at The Hague rules that

April 16, 1986: The first test-tube baby delivered from a surrogate mother is born at Mount Sinai Hospital in Cleveland.

1986
by the numbers

July 17, 1986:
Dallas-based LTV Corporations, $4 billion in debt, declares the largest bankruptcy in U.S. history.

the United States has broken international law and violated the sovereignty of Nicaragua by aiding the Contras.

■■■■■■■■■■■■■■■■■■■■■■■■■■■■■■■■■■

1. The cost of a Levittown, Long Island, house is $125,000, up from $60,000 in 1980.

2. The national debt exceeds $2 trillion—having doubled in the last five years.

3. For the first time in history, American women professionals outnumber men in professional positions; there are now 29,000 more women professionals.

4. Now in its seventeenth year *60 Minutes* is seen in 22 million American homes each week.

5. A new record is made as $5 million is spent on the hardback and paperback rights to James Clavell's *Whirlwind,* a novel about an Iranian rescue mission.

6. The "fact" is made public that Imelda Marcos has 3,000 pairs of shoes, and this figure remains in people's minds, even though a year later it is discovered that she actually has only 1,060 pairs.

7. A new human-powered land speed record is set by Fred Marckham at 65.48 MPH.

8. The U.S. trade deficit jumps to an unprecedented $18 billion.

9. The penalty for inside trader Ivan Boesky for buying and selling stocks with secret information is a cool $100 million.

10. The nonstop, around the world flight of the extra-light *Voyager* takes nine days, three minutes, and forty-four seconds.

■■■■■■■■■■■■■■■■■■■■■■■■■■■■■■■■■■

JULY

02 ► The Supreme Court endorses numerical hiring goals for minorities, rejecting the Reagan administration view that

▶ 1986

affirmative action be limited to proven victims of race discrimination.

09 ▶ The attorney general's Commission on Pornography releases the final draft of its 2,000-page report, which links hard-core porn to sex crimes.

17 ▶ Dallas-based LTV Corporation, $4 billion in debt, declares the largest bankruptcy in U.S. history.

25 ▶ Former navy radioman Jerry Whitworth is convicted of selling U.S. military secrets to the Soviets through the John Walker spy ring. The government calls it the most damaging espionage case since World War II.

AUGUST

21 ▶ In the Cameroons, a mysterious gas emitted from a volcanic lake kills 1,700 people.

SEPTEMBER

07 ▶ Desmond Tutu is installed as the first black to lead the Anglican Church in South Africa.

14 ▶ President Reagan and first lady Nancy Reagan make a national television speech declaring war on drugs, likening the new effort to World War II. "My generation will remember how Americans swung into action when we were attacked in World War II. Now we're in another war for freedom, and it is time for all of us to pull together again."

27 ▶ A major tax reform bill passes both houses of Congress after two years of proposals and counterproposals.

■ ■

☞ 1. *surimi* (whitefish made to imitate crab, lobster, and other seafood. Americans consume 119 million pounds of it in '86.)

☞ 2. *Hands Across America* (What else do you call a 4,150-human-being linkup?)

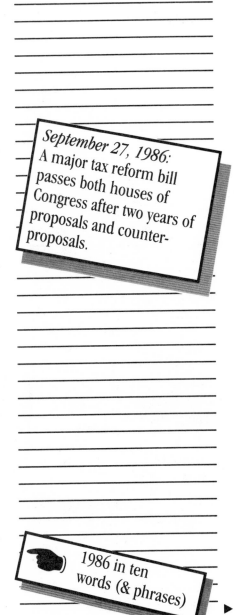

September 27, 1986: A major tax reform bill passes both houses of Congress after two years of proposals and counter-proposals.

☞ 1986 in ten words (& phrases)

3. *surrogate test-tube baby* (The first of these is born in Cleveland on April 16.)

4. *junk bonds* (Whatever happened to plain old bonds? These high-fliers seem to be flying highest at this point.)

5. *three-pointer* (Now college players are shooting for the extra point.)

6. *Helga* (the woman secretly painted by Andrew Wyeth 239 times. Big to-do.)

7. *toxic cloud* (term that takes an ominous meaning after one kills 1,200 in the Cameroons)

8. *classic* (now the name of a soft drink, as in Classic Coke, which is back again)

9. *Chernobyl* (a name that takes over where Three Mile Island left off)

10. *veejay* (what you call a deejay on MTV)

■■■■■■■■■■■■■■■■■■■■■■■■■■■■■■■■

OCTOBER

22 ▶ U.S. Surgeon General C. Edward Koop urges parents and schools to educate children on sexual matters in order to slow the spread of the AIDS virus.

29 ▶ The National Academy of Sciences warns that unless $2 billion a year is spent on AIDS education and research the country is facing a "catastrophe."

NOVEMBER

04 ▶ A report from Tehran insists that administration officials made a secret diplomatic trip to Iran and that the trip involved arms. It is the first of a number of rapid-fire revelations that lead to the conclusion that the Reagan administration sold arms to Iran and used the money to finance the Contra rebels in Nicaragua.

December 23, 1986:
The pilots of the *Voyager* make history by flying around the world in the first non-stop flight without refueling.

▶ 1986

DECEMBER

23 ▶ The pilots of the *Voyager,* Jeana Yeager and Dick Rutan, make history by flying around the world in the first nonstop flight without refueling. The flight begins on December 14.

■■■■■■■■■■■■■■■■■■■■■■■■■■■■■■

☞ 1. PURE BRED MUTT ABOARD

☞ 2. NOBODY ON BOARD

☞ 3. EX-HUSBAND IN TRUNK

☞ 4. THIS CAR STOPS AT ALL GARAGE SALES

☞ 5. YOU'VE OBVIOUSLY MISTAKEN ME FOR SOMEBODY THAT CARES

☞ 6. NO TRILLION DOLLAR NATIONAL DEBT

☞ 7. CRIME WOULDN'T PAY IF THE GOVERNMENT RAN IT

☞ 8. MY WIFE RAN OFF WITH MY PICKUP TRUCK AND I MISS IT

☞ 9. BACK OFF! ANGRY HOUSEWIFE

☞ 10. GO AHEAD HIT ME—I NEED THE MONEY

■■■■■■■■■■■■■■■■■■■■■■■■■■■■■■

☞) 1986 in buttons & bumper stickers

The year in which ▶
there is an October ▶
market crash ▶
1987

JANUARY

05 ▶ President Reagan submits the first trillion-dollar federal budget—$1.024 trillion.

08 ▶ The Dow tops 2,000 for a new high of 2,002.25—fourteen years after it hit 1,000.

FEBRUARY

16 ▶ Paul Ching-Wu Chu, a physics professor at the University of Houston, and the associates at the University of Alabama at Huntsville, announce a stunning breakthrough in superconductivity. Their discovery: that a magical new ceramic becomes superconductive—carries electricity with no loss of energy—when chilled to a relatively balmy minus 283 degrees Fahrenheit.

MARCH

22 ▶ A garbage barge carrying 3,200 tons of refuse leaves Islip, New York, on a six-month journey in search of a place to unload. It eventually is turned away by several states and three foreign countries until space is found back in Islip.

January 5, 1987: President Reagan submits the first trillion-dollar federal budget – $1.024 trillion.

▶ 1987

■ ■

👉 1. A year for scandal with Gary Hart and Jim Bakker in starring roles.

👉 2. There is widespread acknowledgment that the cold war is coming to a close as U.S.–Soviet relations improve and continue to improve.

👉 3. Tie-dyed apparel begins a surprise comeback.

👉 4. Reeboks

👉 5. The Gorbachev-Reagan summit in Washington creates a euphoric time complete with various sideshows and artifacts (Gorby T-shirts, etc.).

👉 6. The Macintosh II and SE from Apple are now the most powerful personal computers available and create an army of converts.

👉 7. It is a career year for a beer-selling dog named Spuds MacKenzie.

👉 8. The bicentennial year for the Constitution underscores its resiliency.

👉 9. The popularity of a horror movie about adultery run amok called *Fatal Attraction* suggests a changing attitude toward casual sex.

👉 10. Once it is realized that the condom is the main line of defense in preventing the spread of AIDS, it becomes an object for discussion. Drug stores bring them out from behind the cabinets.

■ ■

APRIL

22 ▶ The worst violence in South Africa in a year occurs today. In the wake of 16,000 dismissals of striking railway workers, six black railroad workers are killed in clashes with police.

▶ 1987

MAY

04 ▶ This is tax freedom day '87—the day on which all federal, state, and local taxes have been paid and on which the typical worker begins working for himself or herself. In 1980 this day came on May 1.

JUNE

16 ▶ A New York jury acquits Bernhard Goetz of attempted murder in connection with the subway shooting of four black youths he said were going to rob him. Goetz, however, is convicted of illegal weapons possession in the December 22, 1984, shootings.

18 ▶ Charles Glass, a journalist on leave from his job at ABC news, is kidnapped and held hostage in Lebanon. (Glass escapes from his captors the following August.)

■■■■■■■■■■■■■■■■■■■■■■■■■■■■■■■■

☞ 1. The life expectancy of the average American is 73.8 years.

☞ 2. New Mexico has the most highway deaths per 100,000 residents with 40.6, while Connecticut is the safest at 12.1.

☞ 3. An estimated 240,000 people leave the farm this year dropping the farm population to the lowest level since before the Civil War. Only 2 percent of the population now lives on farms.

☞ 4. After expenses and before taxes the average doctor now makes $132,300, but the median is only $108,000. The average radiologist makes $180,700, and the average pediatrician, $85,300.

☞ 5. It is determined that slightly more than 10 percent of all deaths of children over age one are caused by firearms.

☞ 6. The annual cost of a Yale education is $17,020.

☞ 7. Pollster Lou Harris determines that 81 percent of the American public believes that the rich are getting richer and the poor are getting poorer. This is the highest number

May 4, 1987: This is tax freedom day '87.

☞ 1987 by the numbers

agreeing with the statement since Harris first asked the question in 1966 (when 45 percent agreed that it was true).

☞ 8. Vincent van Gogh's "Irises" commands a cool $53.9 million at auction.

☞ 9. The percentage of American adults who have sex once a week is 40 according to a poll—up from 28 percent in 1974 in a similar poll.

☞ 10. The average cost for an executive spending one day in New York City is $270.33.

■■■■■■■■■■■■■■■■■■■■■■■■■■■■■■■■■■

JULY

22 ► Soviet leader Mikhail Gorbachev agrees to a U.S. proposal to ban medium- and short-range nuclear weapons.

23 ► President Reagan names a thirteen-member national commission on AIDS to establish government policy for combating the disease.

AUGUST

13 ► On the fifth anniversary of a bull market, the Dow Jones Industrial Average closes at 2,691.49 after briefly surpassing 2,700.

17 ► Rudolf Hess, ninety-three, Adolf Hitler's former deputy, hangs himself in West Berlin's Spandau War Crimes Prison after forty-six years in custody.

► *Also:* Kidnapped American journalist Charles Glass, held hostage sixty-two days, escapes from a Beirut apartment and is rescued.

25 ► The Dow Jones industrial average closes at a record high of 2,722.42, up more than 800 points for the year.

26 ► West German Chancellor Helmut Kohl says his country will destroy its Pershing 1-A rockets if Washington and Moscow scrap their medium-range nuclear weapons.

July 23, 1987:
President Reagan names a thirteen-member national commission on AIDS to establish government policy for combatting the disease.

▶ 1987

SEPTEMBER

04 ▶ A Soviet court convicts West German pilot Mathias Rust of landing his plane in Red Square. He is sentenced to four years in prison but is released on August 3, 1988.

■ ■

☞ 1. *Black Monday* (October 19)

☞ 2. *meltdown* (a new meaning for this term: October 19)

☞ 3. *dink* (short for dual—or double—income no kids)

☞ 4. *bimbo* (This insulting term makes a comeback thanks to Tammy Bakker and Donna Rice.)

☞ 5. *wimp factor* (a negative invented for George Bush as he begins his run on the White House. He overcomes it.)

☞ 6. *couch potato* (Popularized in a 1983 book—Robert Armstrong's *Official Couch Potato Handbook*—this species comes into its own this year.)

☞ 7. *Iran-Contra* (two names that seemed like an unlikely match until Congress gets the Iran-Contra hearings going)

☞ 8. *pit bull* (a series of horror stories make this breed of dog into a household name and source of fear)

☞ 9. *yuptopia* (the yuppie paradise that turns sour with the October 19 crash)

☞ 10. *genetic fingerprinting* (a suspect in England is convicted of a crime using this new techique)

■ ■

☞ 1987 in ten words (& phrases)

OCTOBER

19 ▶ The stock market crashes. Almost 600 million shares change hands. The Dow plunges 508 points to 1,738. Numerically it is the biggest one-day drop in history. In percentage terms the decline is the largest recorded since 1914. Investors lose more than $500 billion in stock market value.

October 19, 1987: The stock market crashes.

▶ 1987

20 ▶ The Dow rises 107 points. It is the largest one-day advance to this date in history.

23 ▶ The Senate rejects Robert Bork's nomination to the Supreme Court by a vote of fifty-eight to forty-two.

NOVEMBER

07 ▶ Judge Douglas H. Ginsberg withdraws his nomination to the Supreme Court because of the public clamor over his use of marijuana. This is the second nominee to fail in sixteen days.

DECEMBER

11 ▶ A federal judge orders the A. H. Robins Company to set aside $2.475 billion to compensate women injured by the Dalkon shield intrauterine birth control device.

■■■■■■■■■■■■■■■■■■■■■■■■■■■■■■■■

☞ 1. MY OTHER CAR IS UP MY NOSE
☞ 2. THE ONE WHO DIES WITH THE MOST TOYS WINS
☞ 3. NO RADIO—ALREADY STOLEN
☞ 4. IT'S CHIC TO REEK—EAT GARLIC
☞ 5. YOU MAY BE ELIGIBLE FOR A FREE TRIP TO THE NEAREST MOTEL—ASK DRIVER FOR DETAILS
☞ 6. A WOMAN'S PLACE IS IN THE MALL
☞ 7. LIFE'S A BEACH
☞ 8. SAME SHIT, DIFFERENT DAY
☞ 9. PERVERT ON BOARD
☞ 10. MY LAWYER CAN BEAT UP YOUR LAWYER

■■■■■■■■■■■■■■■■■■■■■■■■■■■■■■■■

The year in which ▶
we learn to fear ▶
the greenhouse effect ▶ **1988**

JANUARY

13 ▶ The Supreme Court rules that censorship of student newspapers by school officials is legal and constitutional.

FEBRUARY

05 ▶ The U.S. Justice Department unseals grand jury indictments charging General Manuel Antonio Noriega of Panama with international drug trafficking.

MARCH

16 ▶ Lieutenant Colonel Oliver North, former national security advisor John M. Poindexter, and Iranian-American arms dealer Albert Hakim are indicted on charges that they diverted Iranian arms-sales profits to Nicaraguan Contra rebels.

18 ▶ Colonel North says that he will retire from the Marine Corps and that he may subpoena some of the highest-ranking officials in government for his trial.

■■■■■■■■■■■■■■■■■■■■■■■■■■■■■■■■■■■■■

☞ 1. The California raisins have a career year—our first clay heroes since Gumby.

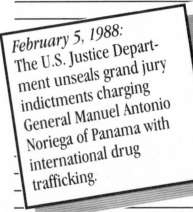

February 5, 1988: The U.S. Justice Department unseals grand jury indictments charging General Manuel Antonio Noriega of Panama with international drug trafficking.

Fads and Trends for 1988

☞ 2. The movie *Rain Man* is a runaway hit and the Best Movie of the Year. It also stirs up a dormant love for old Buicks.

☞ 3. The greenhouse effect is the great topic during a year with an especially hot summer.

☞ 4. This is the year of the fax as prices for an average machine come down to about $2,000 and some sell for less than $1,000. They are now showing up in print shops and small businesses, and some people have them in their homes.

☞ 5. Animation makes a stunning revival thanks to *Who Framed Roger Rabbit?* Cartoon lovers rejoice.

☞ 6. *Phantom of the Opera* is a runaway hit on Broadway. There are no cheap seats for this one.

☞ 7. Televangelism's decline continues as the plight of the Bakkers intensifies and Jimmy Swaggart moves into the realm of the sinner.

☞ 8. The troubles of two whales trapped in the Alaskan ice stir international interest and compassion.

☞ 9. Great hoopla accompanies the installation of lights in Chicago's Wrigley Field.

☞ 10. Cats—Garfield in the lead—suddenly show up stuck to the inside of car windows.

■■■■■■■■■■■■■■■■■■■■■■■■■■■■■■■

APRIL

14 ▶ The USS *Samuel B. Roberts* strikes an Iranian mine in the Persian Gulf, which seriously damages the frigate. Ten American sailors are injured.

15 ▶ After seven years of peace talks led by a United Nations mediator, the Soviet Union agrees to withdraw its forces from Afghanistan by February 15. But the Soviet Union and the United States have continued arming their allies in the civil war, and no political solution is in sight.

18 ▶ American forces attack two Iranian oil platforms in retaliation for the *Roberts* mining on April 14, triggering day-

May 4, 1988:
Margaret Thatcher becomes Britain's longest continuously serving prime minister of the twentieth century.

▶ 1988

long fighting in which Iran loses six naval craft. One U.S. helicopter is missing after the clash.

MAY

04 ▶ After nine years in power Margaret Thatcher becomes Britain's longest continuously serving prime minister of the twentieth century.

15 ▶ Soviet troops begin withdrawing from Afghanistan and complete their withdrawal on February 15, 1989.

JUNE

23 ▶ NASA's James E. Hansen tells a Senate panel that the warming of the earth due to pollution creating the greenhouse effect has already started. Coming at the beginning of a particularly hot summer, his words create alarm in the months ahead.

■■■■■■■■■■■■■■■■■■■■■■■■■■■■■■■■

☞ 1. Budweiser is the top brand of U.S. beer, selling 50.5 million barrels—just over a billion gallons.

☞ 2. There are now 10,513 McDonald's restaurants worldwide, but Pepsi's restaurants (Pizza Hut, Taco Bell, and Kentucky Fried Chicken) total 17,353.

☞ 3. According to the Census Bureau people are marrying later. In 1988 the typical age of a first marriage for men is 25.9 and 23.6 for women. In contrast, in 1955 the ages were 22.6 and 20.2, respectively.

☞ 4. The Bureau also reports that the proportion of one-parent families has grown from 12.9 percent of all families with children in 1970 to 27.3 percent in 1988.

☞ 5. From the same source comes the determination that childbearing among unmarried women age fifteen to forty-four has reached an unprecedented level of 80.9 per 1,000 for black women and 23.2 per 1,000 for white women.

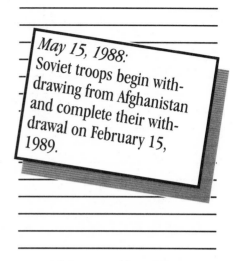

May 15, 1988: Soviet troops begin withdrawing from Afghanistan and complete their withdrawal on February 15, 1989.

1988 by the numbers

6. Kraft Inc. accepts a $13.1 billion takeover bid from Phillip Morris Company.

7. Kohlberg Kravis Roberts & Company wins the largest corporate bidding contest ever and agrees to pay $25 billion to buy RJR Nabicso Inc.

8. A congressional committee estimates that 5 to 7 million latchkey kids in America come home from school while their parents are still at work.

9. A survey conducted by *Good Housekeeping* magazine shows that 84 percent of all Americans believe heaven exists.

10. A Roper poll shows that reading is the most common method of dealing with stress among both men (52 percent) and women (68 percent).

■ ■

JULY

03 ► The USS *Vincennes* shoots down an Iran Air jetliner over the Persian Gulf, killing all 290 passengers and crew, after the crew of the *Vincennes* misidentifies the plane as an Iranian F-14 fighter.

06 ► Needles and vials of blood, some of which test positive for the AIDS virus, begin washing up along Long Island's 120-mile southern shore. This and other incidents like it during the month prompt the Associated Press's Marjorie Anders to write on July 31: "The summer of '88 is already over in the minds of countless Northeastern beach lovers revolted by a tide of dead rats, syringes and sewage that has left miles of shoreline deserted and seaside businesses shuttered even on the hottest days."

31 ► America's last Playboy Club closes, in Lansing, Michigan. A spokesman announces that the demise comes as a result of the company's phasing out of domestic operations. The first Playboy Club opened in Chicago in 1960, and there were once twenty-two throughout the country.

July 6, 1988:
Needles and vials of blood, some of which test positive for the AIDS virus, begin washing up along Long Island's 120-mile southern shore.

► 1988

AUGUST

08 ► Today is 8/8/88, a phenomenon that will not recur until 8/8/[20]88.

16 ► A new wave of strikes breaks out in Poland—the worst since 1981—demanding the relegalization of Solidarity.

SEPTEMBER

08 ► Two nuclear-missile rocket motors are destroyed at an army ammunition plant in Karnack, Texas—the first American arms eliminated under the arms reduction treaty with the USSR.

29 ► The successful launching of the shuttle *Discovery* puts the nation back in space after a long grounding occasioned by the *Challenger* disaster.

■■■■■■■■■■■■■■■■■■■■■■■■■■■■■■■■

☞ 1. *read my lips* (George Bush's introduction to "no new taxes" and other points of emphasis in his presidential campaign)

☞ 2. *global warming* (the premise that promises many hot summers to come)

☞ 3. *trash TV* (A new kind of "news and information" show pushes the limits of taste and judgment.)

☞ 4. *fax* (a verb: to transmit a letter or document electronically over telephone lines)

☞ 5. *AIDS quilt* (a stirring reminder and memorial)

☞ 6. *designer* (This is, after all, the year of the designer trash bag and the designer pizza.)

☞ 7. *NExT* (A new computer is unveiled with unprecedented fanfare.)

☞ 8. *narcoterrorism* (as if we needed a new species of terrorism)

☞ 9. *sleaze factor* (label that the Democratic candidate tries to attach to the campaign of the Republican candidate)

☞ 10. *Senator, you're no Jack Kennedy* (rejoinder from

☞) **1988 in ten words (& phrases)**

Lloyd M. Bentsen to Dan Quayle during a vice presidential debate)

■ ■

OCTOBER

13 ► The bishop of Turin announces that the shroud of Turin, long believed to be Christ's burial sheet, does not withstand scientific testing. It dates back to A.D. 1280 and not to the crucifixion.

NOVEMBER

02 ► Some 6,000 computers malfunction due to a computer virus placed in a major electronic network by Robert Morris, Jr., a Cornell University graduate student.

November 2, 1988: Some 6,000 computers malfunction due to a computer virus.

DECEMBER

01 ► The first world AIDS Day is marked by a concert in Beijing, a march in Harare, Zimbabwe, and a speech by a San Franciscan who has had the deadly disease for six years and says his life is "made richer" because of it. The World Health Organization, which sponsors the event, says 140 nations are holding special activities to focus awareness on the disease that WHO estimates infects 5 to 10 million people worldwide.

21 ► In pleading guilty to fraud in the stock-trading scandal, Drexel Burnham Lambert Inc. agrees to pay $650 million in fines.

■ ■

1988 in buttons & bumper stickers

☞ 1. JUST SAY NO
☞ 2. SHIT HAPPENS
☞ 3. NO FAT CHICKS
☞ 4. LEAVE ME ALONE—I'M HAVING A ROTTEN DAY

▶ 1988

☞ 5. IF YOU'RE RICH, I'M SINGLE
☞ 6. DIE YUPPIE SCUM
☞ 7. I'M IN NO HURRY, I'M ON MY WAY TO WORK
☞ 8. ASK ME ABOUT MY GRANDCHILDREN
☞ 9. HONK IF YOU'RE SMARTER THAN QUAYLE
☞ 10. HANDS OFF OLIVER NORTH—NO MORE KANGA-ROO COURTS

■■■■■■■■■■■■■■■■■■■■■■■■■■■■■■■

The year in which there is ▶
upheaval in China, radical ▶
change in Eastern Europe ▶
and an oilspill in Alaska ▶

1989

JANUARY

20 ▶ George Bush and Dan Quayle take office as president and vice president. In his inaugural speech, Bush says of drugs, "This scourge will stop."

FEBRUARY

14 ▶ Union Carbide agrees to pay the Indian government $470 million to settle the Bhopal case. Earlier, India sought $3 billion from the company.

15 ▶ The withdrawal of Soviet troops from Afghanistan is complete.

20 ▶ The number of AIDS deaths in the United States reaches 49,976—of whom 1,061 have perished since January 1, 1989.

27 ▶ Intel Corporation of California announces that it has created the million-transistor microchip. In other words, they have put a million transistors on a surface half the size of a postage stamp.

January 20, 1989: George Bush and Dan Quayle take office as president and vice-president.

MARCH

09 ▶ Former Senator John Tower's nomination by newly elected George Bush to the post of secretary of defense is defeated

▶ 331

March 24, 1989:
The tanker *Exxon Valdez* runs aground in Prince William Sound, Alaska.

Fads and Trends for 1989 ☞

in the Senate by a vote of fifty-three to forty-seven. It is the first time in history that the Senate denies the president a nomination for his first Cabinet.

▶ ***Also on this date:*** Eastern Airlines files for bankruptcy. Company chairman Frank Lorenzo claims Eastern is $2.5 billion in debt.

24 ▶ The tanker *Exxon Valdez* runs aground in Prince William Sound, Alaska. Before the leaking is stopped, 11 million gallons of crude oil pollute many miles of shoreline and kill wildlife.

■■■■■■■■■■■■■■■■■■■■■■■■■■■■■■■■■

☞ 1. The sports car of yore stages a comeback in the incarnation of the Mazda Miata, a $13,800 two-seat roadster that commands $5,000 above list by year's end. People are willing to pay an extra $10,000 on top of the sticker price of $58,995 to get their hands on a new Corvette ZR-1.

☞ 2. The movie *Batman* is an immense hit, which brings back a fascination for all the trappings of Batmania, including the Joker.

☞ 3. Blue corn is hot for foods ranging from tortilla chips to breakfast flakes.

☞ 4. Oat bran proliferates in many new products from oat bran bagels to oat bran pasta.

☞ 5. Baseball experiences an odd, startling, and yet endearing year—the romantic *Field of Dreams,* the Pete Rose problem, the rise and sudden death of Commissioner Bart Giamatti, and the "shaken" World Series.

☞ 6. Aliens are reported in the Soviet Union and these reports appear in detail in *Tass* (three eyes, elephant-like footprints, pink banana-shaped spaceships).

☞ 7. Much attention is paid to art because of controversies surrounding federally assisted shows, all centering on the homoerotic photography of the late Robert Mapplethorpe. Also . . .

☞ 8. Phenomenal prices are paid at auction for paintings—such as $20.6 million for a de Kooning work from 1955.

1989

☛ 9. Hair styles of young black men include head lines—marks, logos, and initials—and odd slopes, valleys, and tinted patches.

☛ 10. Zsa Zsa Gabor slaps a policeman and the aftermath attracts more media coverage than most small wars. Great fun.

■■■■■■■■■■■■■■■■■■■■■■■■■■■■■■■■

APRIL

05 ▶ In Poland, Solidarity and government leaders agree on a new agreement that legalizes the trade union.

17 ▶ Pro-democracy marches begin in Beijing. Within a few days more than 100,000 protesters will occupy Tiananmen Square.

MAY

07 ▶ Panamanian elections are held and it is immediately apparent that the Noriega victory is based on fraud and rigged ballots. One of the U.S. observers, former president Jimmy Carter, storms out of the main vote tabulation center in disgust.

10 ▶ Thugs loyal to Noriega beat the opposition candidates for president and vice president and kill one of their bodyguards. This occurs as defense forces watch. The beaten and bloodied vice presidential candidate Guillermo Ford is shown to the world on television. He insists his side won the election and vows to continue to fight.

11 ▶ President Bush sends 2,000 American troops to Panama to add to the 10,000 already there.

30 ▶ Chinese students begin erecting a Goddess of Democracy statue in Tiananmen Square, Beijing. It revitalizes antigovernment demonstrations and draws crowds to the square. This event comes at a time when the number of students in the Square has diminished because of fatigue and poor sanitary conditions.

May 30, 1989: Chinese students begin erecting a Goddess of Democracy statue in Tiananmen Square, Beijing.

June 4, 1989:
In China, after a series of bloody attacks on protesting students the government announces that the army has suppressed the rebellion in Tiananmen Square. Estimates of the dead range from 700 to thousands.

1989
by the numbers

JUNE

03 ► In China the army assaults students in Tiananmen Square where some 5,000 students remain. Initially the soldiers are persuaded not to enter but later fire into the crowds.

04 ► In China, after a series of bloody attacks on protesting students the government announces that the army has suppressed the rebellion in Tiananmen Square. Estimates of the dead range from 700 to thousands.

► **Also:** Japan begins the world's first daily broadcasts of high-definition television programs, thereby leaping ahead in a politicized race with the United States and Europe for command of the next generation of television technology.

07 ► There is a moment early in the morning (and later in the afternoon) when the time is 1:23:45/6/7/89.

■ ■

☞ 1. With a circulation of 20,314,462 *Modern Maturity* is by far the nation's best-read magazine.

☞ 2. In August Congress votes $50 billion to bail out failed savings and loan institutions—by October the question is whether this is enough.

☞ 3. Postmaster General Anthony Frank reveals that the number of suggestions received annually for commemorative stamp subjects is 30,000. The number produced: 25.

☞ 4. Japan's Sony Corporation acquires Columbia Pictures Entertainment for a cool $3 billion.

☞ 5. A federal study of hunting accidents conducted in Georgia determines that 36 percent of those injured while hunting fall out of trees.

☞ 6. Despite much fluctuation in housing prices, it is determined that the percentage of a family's monthly paycheck that the average homebuyer has to pay out every month to afford a median price home has not changed in twenty years—about 23 percent.

☞ 7. AIDS victims who have been paying between $7,000 and $8,000 per year for AZT, the only drug approved to fend off the disease, find that the cost of the drug has been cut by 20 percent in September.

☞ 8. On the thirty-fifth anniversary of the TV dinner it is determined that the original turkey dinner, which cost $.99, now, with modifications, costs $1.99.

☞ 9. A 1948 Tucker Torpedo four-door sedan sells for a record price of $275,000 at auction.

☞ 10. The amount of nonindustrial trash—from homes and businesses—has grown from 78 million tons in 1960 to almost 160 million tons.

☞ 11. The Internal Revenue Service determines that it is losing approximately 2 million tax returns and related documents a year.

☞ 12. According to the surgeon general, more than 40 million Americans have quit smoking since the initial 1964 *Surgeon General's Report*.

■ ■

JULY

03 ► In the matter of *Webster v. Reproductive Health Services,* the Supreme Court in a five-to-four decision provides states with new authority to limit a woman's right to an abortion but stops short of reversing the 1973 decision legalizing abortion.

AUGUST

22 ► Nolan Ryan of the Texas Rangers becomes the first pitcher in major league baseball to strike out 5,000 batters. On July 11, 1985, Ryan became the first to fan 4,000 batters.

24 ► After teasing investors for two zig-zag weeks, stock prices leap to all-time highs as the market completes its recovery from the historic crash of October 19, 1987. Propelled by a combination of favorable economic, business, and market

1989 by the numbers: More than 40 million Americans have quit smoking since the initial 1964 *Surgeon General's Report.*

trends, the Dow Jones industrial average shoots up 56.53 points to close at a record 2,734.64.

SEPTEMBER

04 ▶ The last *Titan 3* rocket lifts a secret military satellite into space. Beginning in 1964 more than 200 probes and satellites have been launched with this incredibly successful workhorse of the space age. Among its most famous missions, the two *Viking* spacecraft to Mars in 1976 and the *Voyager 1* and *2* probes to the outer planets.

05 ▶ President Bush announces his new $7.8 billion antidrug program—tougher street-level law enforcement, stiffer penalties for casual users, and attacks on drug traffickers in source countries—which he says is much more than has been deployed by previous administrations.

18 ▶ A major financial realignment is underway, as the *Wall Street Journal* reports, "The heyday of the junk bond . . . seems to be coming to an end."

■■■■■■■■■■■■■■■■■■■■■■■■■■■■■■■■■■

☞ 1. *the big one* (the long-feared California earthquake, which will be much more powerful than the October '89 version)

☞ 2. *Baysball* (what they are calling the San Francisco–Oakland World Series before it is interrupted by the earthquake)

☞ 3. *Lyme disease* (a bona fide new cause for concern)

☞ 4. *wilding* (an act of random violence, from a grotesque attack in New York's Central Park)

☞ 5. *ice* (1989's hottest drug moving from West to East. It is said to be far more addictive than cocaine.)

☞ 6. *pledge* (given a new political meaning as new drug czar William J. Bennett pledges to give up cigarettes and defense secretary nominee John Tower pledges not to "consume beverage alcohol of any type or form")

☞ 7. *Sinatra doctrine* (a puckish term used by Soviet officials

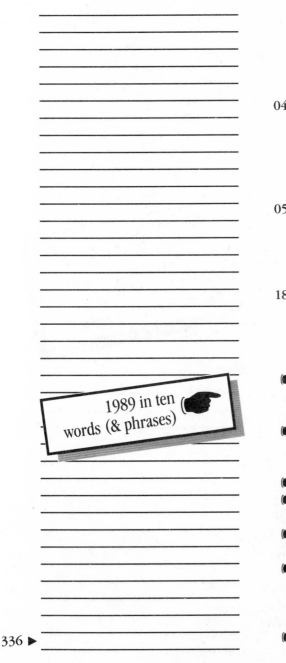

1989 in ten words (& phrases)

to indicate that the Warsaw pact nations are in a position to do things "their way"—an allusion to Frank Sinatra's song "My Way")

8. *dignity battalions* (The misnomer of the decade, this term is used by Noriega to describe bands of goons who beat up candidates in the Panamanian election.)

9. *boarder babies* (infants left in hospitals by drug-dependent mothers)

10. *stand down* (an old military term made public when the navy calls for a forty-eight hour period in November in which all normal activities are stopped for a review of safety procedures after a rash of accidents)

OCTOBER

13 ▶ The stock market takes its steepest plunge since the 1987 crash as the Dow falls 190 points.

18 ▶ A violent earthquake strikes Northern California at 5:04 P.M. PDT. The most devastating effect is the collapse of the upper deck of a highway in Oakland, which traps and kills more than forty people in their cars. It occurs just as the third game of the World Series is about to get underway.

NOVEMBER

05 ▶ The Civil Rights Memorial is dedicated in Montgomery, Alabama. It honors those killed during the struggle.

07 ▶ An off-year election is held today that demonstrates that black Democrats have an ability to win elections in pre-dominantly white jurisdictions. The two most notable winners are L. Douglas Wilder, who becomes governor of Virginia, and David N. Dinkins, who becomes mayor of New York City.

09 ▶ The Berlin Wall is opened and for the next few days hundreds of thousands of East Germans stream into West

November 9, 1989: The Berlin Wall is opened and for the next few days hundreds of thousands of East Germans stream into West Berlin.

▶ 1989

Berlin. This is taken as evidence that the cold war is over.

10. ▶ Bulgarian president Todor Zhivkov of Bulgaria resigns after thirty-five years in power. The resignation of the hard-line Communist leader is seen as a surprising element in the reform movement spreading through Eastern Europe.

■■■■■■■■■■■■■■■■■■■■■■■■■■■■■■

1. TO KNOW ME IS TO LOVE ME
2. I DON'T CARE WHO YOU ARE, WHAT YOU ARE DRIVING, OR WHERE YOU WOULD RATHER BE
3. HOMEWORK CAUSES BRAIN DAMAGE
4. GIVE ME A BREAK, I HAVE TEENAGERS
5. WHO CARES WHO'S ON BOARD?
6. GIRLS JUST WANT TO HAVE FUNDS
7. I SURVIVED CATHOLIC SCHOOL
8. YES, BUT NOT WITH YOU
9. SKATEBOARDING IS NOT A CRIME
10. SO MANY PEDESTRIANS, SO LITTLE TIME

■■■■■■■■■■■■■■■■■■■■■■■■■■■■■■

1989 in buttons & bumper stickers

INDEX

▶ Index

▶ Index

▶ Index

► Index

▶ Index

► Index

▶ Index

▶ Index

▶ Index

► Index

▶ Index

► Index

► Index